Breakaway Planning

Breakaway Planning

8 Big Questions to Guide Organizational Change

PAUL LEVESQUE

AMACOM

American Management Association

New York • Atlanta • Boston • Chicago • Kansas City • San Francisco • Washington, D.C.
Brussels • Mexico City • Tokyo • Toronto

This publication is designed to provide accurate and authoritative information
in regard to the subject matter covered. It is sold with the understanding that
the publisher is not engaged in rendering legal, accounting, or other professional service. If legal advice or other expert assistance is required, the services of a
competent professional person should be sought.

Library of Congress Cataloguing-in-Publication Data

Levesque, Paul, 1947-
  Breakaway planning: 8 big questions for achieving organizational change /
  Paul Levesque.
    p. cm.
    Includes index.
    ISBN 0-8144-0426-X
    1. Organizational change—Planning. 2. Corporate Planning.
  I. Title.
  HD58.8.L477 1988   98-27143
  658.4'012—dc21   CIP

Printing number

10 9 8 7 6 5 4 3 2 1

"*The difficulties and disagreements, of which history is full, are mainly due to a very simple cause: namely to the attempt to answer questions, without first discovering precisely* what *question it is which you desire to answer.*"

George Edward Moore

For my beautiful Sandra,
who brought wondrous transformational
change into my life
by answering my One Big Question with a yes.

Contents

One) • Plan Review and Ratification • Communicating the Plan to the Rank and File

Part II: The 8 Big Questions

Part III: Next Steps

Acknowledgments

To date, more than 350 organizations from around the world have participated in planning workshops at which it was my pleasure to serve as instructor/facilitator. The planning models and exercises outlined in this book are a direct offshoot of these planning "academies," as they were called.

I owe a great deal to all of these organizations for having taught me so much more over the years than I hoped to teach them. Particular thanks go to Simon Wood and Chris Galtress at Beefeater, Helen Chapman at David Lloyd Leisure, Pamela Miller at Blue Cross Blue Shield of New Jersey, Lynda Zavits at Canadian Airlines International, John P. Boes at Quaker Oats, Mimi Andrews at AETS, and Bob Heberling at Triangle Auto Springs for generously sharing candid highlights of their stories for inclusion in this book.

To my friend and business partner Vic Bergman (and Anneth, too!) special thanks for wearing a number of vital support hats while I was globetrotting and toiling away on the book. The same goes for my team of friends and colleagues in the United Kingdom: to Mark Reynolds, Bill Moir, Kéké, Angela, Lynne, Carly, and the whole team at Catalyst, many thanks for making writing and working away from home feel so easy and, well, "homey." Warm thanks to Colin and Paula Mitchell, whose immense talent and creativity serve as a constant source of personal inspiration; and to my three brothers, Ray, Hector, and John, whose loyal support means a great deal to me.

Thanks, too, to my trusty research assistant, the unflappable Maurene Hopp. Last but not at all least, thanks to my perceptive and helpful editor at AMACOM books, Adrienne Hickey, for keeping me on track, and to B. K. Nelson, my literary agent, for helping get me on the track in the first place.

Part

1

Preplanning

Introduction:
Is Planning Really Necessary?

It's a given: Planning is one big pain in the neck. A real drag. Right? A lot of things in life are a drag. For example, having to learn—I mean *really* learn—something new strikes many people as a fairly dreary prospect. Going to the dentist is often literally a pain. In business, investing a huge amount of time and money in an effort to create some sort of change in the organization, and then not succeeding, is a major drag. So is having the business go under because it cannot change, cannot adapt to a changing marketplace. Or losing your job. Megadrag.

But is it "learning" that's a drag, or the way things are taught? Dentists, or dental problems? They're not the same thing. Some people, those lucky enough to stumble upon a good teacher somewhere along the line, find that really learning something new doesn't have to be boring. Some people get so used to looking after their teeth that when they find one little food particle the toothpick can't get at it drives them crazy for the rest of the night. And there are even some, admittedly not many, who have discovered that the whole process of planning for change in their organization can be not only painless but downright satisfying.

In *Winnie-the-Pooh*, among all the denizens of the hundred-acre wood, Tigger appears to be the one most inclined to embrace change in his world. When, for example, he encounters a frozen pond for the first time and sees others skating on it, without hesitation he exuberantly announces to everyone, "Tiggers love skating!" He promptly races onto the ice, falls on his first attempt to skate, hurts his nose, and thereupon flatly proclaims, "Tiggers hate skating!" A CEO learns about "quality," promptly tells everyone in his business how much "we" love it, tries to implement it, fails on the first attempt, and thereupon flatly proclaims, "We tried quality here. Quality doesn't work for us." From other directions come a chorus of echoes: "Employee recognition programs: tried that. Doesn't work for us." "Customer service: tried it. Doesn't work for us." "Planning: tried it. Doesn't work for us." All very tiggerlike.

LESSONS FROM "THE ROAD RUNNER"

"Road Runner" cartoons provide an even more pointed representation-in-miniature of the standard business approach to introducing change. The coyote is hungry—a condition he is of course deeply, personally committed to changing. Acquisition of the road runner (food) represents the coyote's *strategic objective.* (In some versions, the coyote actually shares his *corporate vision* with us: imagining the bird rotating on a spit, or steaming on the coyote's dinner plate.) The coyote also has a *mission,* though this changes frequently. One mission might, for example, require suspending an anvil from a hot air balloon, using an electric fan to propel the rig along, and relying on a stick of dynamite with a long fuse to release the anvil once everything is nicely in position over the bird. In preparation for the launch, the coyote lights the long fuse; to his horror, the fuse burns along its entire length in less than a second, and the dynamite blows up in his face. The coyote's blackened, charred figure walks dejectedly out of the frame. Fade out. Fade in: the coyote has rigged up a whole new approach for a whole new mission, using a large catapult and a massive boulder, etc.

This coyote, already dangerously emaciated, is almost certainly going to starve to death. He has abandoned the whole anvil-and-balloon idea because of one defective dynamite fuse. He will subsequently abandon the whole catapult-and-boulder idea because of a defective spring mechanism in the catapult. The coyote has come up with dozens, if not hundreds, of ingenious schemes by which to catch the road runner—any one of which might still be made to work with a little more careful planning. But this coyote is in far too big a hurry to sit down and plan things out. Like most of the people watching his antics and laughing, he would much rather just get on with it. Like many in the audience, he is a big believer in winging it, in flying by the seat of his pants. Also like many in the audience, he consistently finds himself dealing with failure and disappointment.

My counsel to the coyote: Stick with any one of your basically sound ideas, plan it out, and see it through. In the case of the anvil idea, for example, ask yourself what the optimal fuse burning time would be. Or do you have to use dynamite at all? What about some sort of remote-control anvil-release mechanism you could activate yourself? Create a checklist: What are all the things that could blow up in your face, pound you into the ground, or cause you to fall from a great height, with an accompanying whistling sound that matches in pitch your descent toward the canyon floor? How will you prevent them from happening? Experiment with the various elements separately, under safe, controlled conditions. Anticipate and work out all the bugs. Then, at last, enjoy your dinner of succulent fowl.

Effective planning makes the difference between longing for success and achieving it.

TAKE ME TO YOUR CHANGE AGENT

Remember when, back in the 1950s, aliens from other planets used to be polite? Instead of just showing up and blasting everything in sight to smithereens, they would at least begin by asking to be taken to our leaders. Today's aliens are quite another breed. What the heck are all those other worlds coming to?

My personal hunch is that it was really our *change agents* they were after. They knew that in order to introduce the sweeping changes they had in mind for us earthlings—abolishment of nuclear arms, an end to all international conflicts and hostilities, prosperity and happiness for all—change agents were the ones to talk to. With their highly developed superintelligence, the aliens just naturally assumed that leaders and change would be the same thing. They could not imagine that in our backward, primitive way we had actually divided the two functions.

Nor would it have occurred to them, I suspect, that businesses that created a written plan for change would treat the plan as separate and distinct from their so-called business plan. How could the aliens possibly anticipate that we had clumsily divided up the planning processes?

Though this dualistic approach has clearly been ineffective over the years, most businesses cling to it to this day. If leaders see any value at all in planning for transformational change, they typically delegate the planning process to a dedicated "coordinator" in order to free themselves up to handle the seemingly much more important succession of "real work" crises that require their minute-by-minute attention. This is like the captain of a ship, floundering among the rocks, who abandons the helm to a junior officer so that he can descend to the cabin and help patch up the growing number of leaks down below. Delegating the process of planning for change is, in effect, abdicating the essence of leadership itself.

This book assumes—based on observations I have made in more than a decade of helping several hundred international organizations plan and implement strategic change— that most business leaders delegate the planning process to change agents not to avoid being personally involved, but rather because they do not know *how* to be personally involved. They suspect it's a complex, time-consuming process, fraught with dangers and pitfalls. They assume it takes a lot of time and effort to master all the disciplines and theories involved, and they simply do not have the time to devote to it. Leaders cannot do everything, after all; there are only so many hours in a day. This is why leaders have "experts" and "advisors," to let others do the data gathering and the legwork, condense it into manageable proportions, and present summaries to the leaders. Let the leaders then make well-informed executive decisions.

It all sounds so reassuringly plausible. For many aspects of business, it almost works. But not when it comes to planning for organizational change. Not for setting new directions for the business. This can only be done by those who hold positions of leadership within the organization, if it is to be effective.

Thus, the purpose of this book is to provide leaders with the *how* of planning effectively for change, to permit them to do the planning themselves. The encouraging news, as the following chapters make clear, is that it is not some mysterious, arcane black science requiring a lifetime to master. Rather, it's quite simple, and actually satisfying. We inadvertently make it seem difficult and painful by our perpetual, coyotelike bunglings.

TAKE ME TO YOUR AMBASSADOR

Fundamental to the role of leadership, as understood in these pages, is the concept of leaders as ambassadors of change. Totally apart from the specifics and particulars of any given change effort, business leaders must help their organizations learn to embrace change itself. Consider two big ifs:

1 If a change effort is seen as coming directly from the organization's top leaders . . .

2 If a change effort is successfully implemented and is seen to clearly make things better . . .

. . . Then the next time a change effort is announced, the fear and resistance factors are likely to be reduced. If the two big ifs are met a second time, a third endeavor is likely to be easier yet.

We all know that change is not going to go away. Society progresses. Science advances. Technology improves. Capabilities expand. Needs evolve. Expectations rise. And organizations adapt, or they perish. As ambassadors of change, we must teach our organizations not to fear and resist change, but to embrace it and use it for competitive advantage.

This book intends to equip the reader to meet the two big ifs. Doing so may involve redefining (changing) roles slightly. For leaders, part of the new role is to become an ambassador of change. For anyone in a coordinator's (or change agent) function, the new role becomes something more akin to implementation stage manager. (More about these roles in chapters to come.)

PLAN TO SUCCEED

At the heart of this book's planning approach is a fundamental article of faith: The greater the leaders' anticipation of success, the greater the likelihood of achieving it. In my experience, this is often the make-or-break issue. Ultimately it plays the largest role in determining whether a given business is to prosper or perish. In order be successful, leaders must learn to cultivate—in themselves and in those around them—a fiercely optimistic view of their organization's future. They must burn brightly with an all-consuming sense of mission. They must be able to develop, and share with the whole organization, a compelling vision of triumphant success. The elaborate plan building to follow is all predicated on this initial vision; it feeds every branch of activity within the organization, the way a trunk nourishes every branch of a tree. In a reciprocal way, the organization draws renewed energy from these activities, the way the tree trunk collects energy from every leaf on every branch. Without this energizing, reciprocating vision, this "trunk," there is no living, growing tree at all; there is only a pile of lumber.

As part of your organization's leadership team, you must take up part-time residence in the future. You must learn to stand with one foot squarely in the here and now, while the other is perfectly at home in the yet to come. Of course, there are many potential futures; you must determine—and favor— the particular future in which your business achieves real success. (Not success in a general sense, but the particular success that, of all the cherished dreams, is the one most cherished of all today.) Then you must teach others to dream the same dream, to share and become enthusiastic about the vision. Finally, the entire leadership team must ask the big questions that, when answered, spell out how to make the vision a reality, how to proceed step-by-step from the here and now to the cherished yet to come.

This is the essence of this book: developing a glorious, triumphant view of future success, and then getting down to determining all the mundane, tactical, day-to-day details to be undertaken so as to achieve the triumph. The chapters that follow outline a planning method for introducing transformational change, a method that hundreds of client organizations over the past decade and more have found eminently practical, clear, and easy to apply.

The cartoon coyote, hungry though he may be, seems unwilling to change his approach. No ambassador of change has led the way for him, to help him overcome his great reluctance to embrace new ways of doing things. He cannot, or will not, apply the discipline of planning to his endeavors. Like many organizations that similarly resist taking a more thoughtful approach to achieving their objectives, in the final analysis he will almost certainly go hungry.

For our part, let's begin to work out precisely where we hope to take our organization, and all that needs to be done to get us there as quickly and easily as possible. The plan we create serves as a master checklist, ensuring that nothing is left to chance, that nothing critical falls between the cracks, that nothing important is overlooked in our forward movement toward success. It assumes that we plan to succeed, and it shows us the way.

Learning to See the Future

In 1997, the leadership team at England's Beefeater restaurant chain was attempting to redefine its corporate vision. Pondering what *compelling* meant in terms of a vision statement, they knew it had something to do with creating excitement and inspiration, and that an effective vision was supposed to be dynamic, memorable, "sexy"; and they knew what they'd come up with so far was lacking on all counts.

Beefeater was (and remains today with 294 stores and 12,500 employees) the largest full-service restaurant chain in Europe. But the gap from their nearest competitor was narrowing every day. They knew their basic mission involved widening the gap.

After extensive discussion and debate, this was the best mission statement they'd come up with: *To achieve the highest growth rate in our market by developing and expanding the Beefeater restaurant experience as an affordable and more distinctive offering in terms of food and hospitality which delights every guest.* As mission statements go, this was better than average. It said it all: They were going to improve all aspects of the customer's experience. They were going to keep prices competitive ("affordable") while differentiating themselves by improving basic product quality ("[a] more distinctive offering in terms of food") as well as customer service ("hospitality which delights every guest"). By doing all of this, they hoped ultimately to outgrow the competition. A valid and worthy strategy. But how were they to transform this rambling mouthful into a sexy corporate vision that would resonate within the bosoms of people throughout the organization?

SELECTING THE RIGHT FUTURE

The structure of Beefeater's mission statement was basically "To do A by doing B; to achieve this result by these means." For their vision, they needed to focus on A, the intended result: their desired destination, their future of choice. Of all their possible futures, the best seemed to be to experience "the highest growth rate in [their] market"—that is to say, to leave the competition far behind.

Now began the process of raising the "compellingness" factor. This word *growth* needed to be defined; did it mean more stores? Larger stores? More customers? More meals sold? All of the above? Some of the above? None of the above?

After further, animated debate they eventually agreed that growth would mean enjoying a greater increase in the number of meals sold than any of their competitors would.

Now the question became, "How will we know?" Was there some way to accurately and continuously find out the extent to which competitors' sales were increasing, to be able to compare rates of growth? Dispiritedly, they acknowledged there was not.

Many leadership teams experience this dejection when attempting to distill their complex multifaceted mission into some kind of short, snappy vision statement. They're frustrated at going around in circles, like a dog chasing its own tail: *If we say this, then that won't make sense; if we change that part, then this part doesn't work.* But the solution is often very close; all that is required is to ask the right question in the right way.

In this instance, the question was, " We have a pretty good general idea of what our competitors' current sales volume is, and how it compares to our own; so can we come up with a number they could not possibly match? In other words, during the next twelve months, how many more meals would we need to sell above our current volume to know with absolute certainty that we have achieved a level of growth well in excess of anything they could conceivably accomplish in the same period?" (Wordy, yes, but this was the level of detail and discipline in their thinking.)

The reply came from several mouths at once: "One million!"

"To sell a million more meals across the whole chain of stores in a year, how many additional meals would each store need to sell per day, on average?"

Out came the pocket calculators. The arithmetic was completed, checked, and rechecked. The answer was three to four additional meals per day per restaurant.

"Is this doable?"

"Hell, yes!" came the unanimous reply.

The resulting Beefeater corporate vision is one of the shortest, sexiest, most compelling, most memorable in my experience, since it manages to convey the essence of an elaborate corporate mission *using only two characters:*

$$\boxed{1M}$$

According to managing director Simon Wood and several other members of the executive team, those two little characters have generated a greater level of energy and shared sense of purpose within the company than many can ever remember having experienced in the past. Now everyone sees the relationship of all of the customer focus workshops, all the food preparation training, all the menu revisions—in short, all the change being introduced into the business— to the goal of achieving "1M." Individual jobs and activities become visibly part of a larger whole. The vision has "galvanized" the whole organization, to use Simon Wood's word.

A compelling vision establishes a meaningful context for change.

Understand, please, that none of the planning activities outlined in this book are likely to produce profound, lasting change in the absence of a compelling mission and vision. If these two items do not already exist—or if they are not sufficiently compelling—then creating them is the first piece of strategic planning the leadership team must engage in. The success of all that follows rests on the results of this preliminary effort.

I can already hear groans of protest: "But just last year (or last month) we spent hours (or days) hammering out a mission and vision statement. It was a painful process. None of us were entirely happy with the result of our efforts, but at least we finally put the issue to bed. We've had the results printed up on posters and banners and these cute little cards; we unveiled everything at our big national meeting with a lot of fanfare. Are you saying now we have to scrap all that and start the whole rigmarole all over again?"

No. Starting from scratch is probably not necessary. I wasn't there with you, so I don't know how effective your visioning exercise was or wasn't. I don't know how compelling your final vision statement was. But this I do know: if it isn't sufficiently compelling, it isn't able to do its job properly. It isn't likely to stick in people's minds, supplying a context and a rationale for all the day-to-day change and confusion around them. It means all of your subsequent strategic planning is built upon a weak and shaky foundation. Very risky.

The prudent thing is to subject your existing mission and vision to a quick "compellingness test" by assessing how well they meet the criteria outlined below. You may discover that a mere tweak is all that's required to transform a hazy view of future success into a clear and dazzling one. For those with no defined mission or vision at all, what follows should help you get your strategic planning off to a solid start.

THERE'S NO MOVIE WITHOUT A SCRIPT

The role of mission and vision in business can be compared to the function of the written script in filmmaking. There's little to be gained in carefully scouting locations, hiring and scheduling actors and crew, renting production equipment and facilities, designing costumes and sets, and planning out all the other elements that go into movie production if, in the first place, we do not have a compelling story to tell. Similarly, navigating a business through times of change without a compelling mission and vision is little more than going through the motions. It can generate a lot of busywork, but it's not likely to yield an audience-pleasing end result.

THE MISSION COMES FIRST

The first step in developing an inspiring, compelling vision for your business involves putting *vision* out of your mind altogether and concentrating on your *mission* instead.

The corporate mission answers the question, "What is this organization, at this point in time, striving hardest to accomplish?" It articulates—sometimes in considerable detail—what the business considers its top objective(s).

In the absence of a well-defined mission, the members of the leadership team frequently find themselves pulling in different, sometimes opposing, directions. The head of financial services is struggling to control costs; the head of marketing wants to launch a splashy but costly promotional campaign to attract new customers. These two perfectly legitimate objectives happen to be completely at odds; throw in a few more from human resources and product development, and watch the fur fly.

Without a shared view of strategic priorities, who's to say which personal agenda is the better one, the more deserving one, the right one? In such a climate, leadership meetings are forever doomed to degenerate into elaborate and time-consuming political contests in which each player takes turns attempting to sway as many votes in his or her direction as time, persuasiveness, and sheer force of character permit. It's an exhausting and unproductive way to do business.

How to sort out this mess? Put your entire senior leadership team through the following exercise, designed to help you identify and agree upon the strategic priorities for your business. Because the exercise typically takes only about an hour and can greatly help the whole team focus on a common set of high-priority corporate objectives, it is very much worth including as an ice-breaker or a reenergizer in your next leadership strategy meeting, even if you feel your current mission and vision are absolutely impeccable. If you sense that your mission and vision need some work, consider using it as a kickoff exercise for day one of your formal plan-building workshop, or "academy" (see the next chapter for more information about the academy plan-building workshop).

THE STRATEGIC-PRIORITIES EXERCISE

This relatively straightforward group exercise quickly brings to light the elements necessary to create an effective corporate mission statement. It does so by asking the team to isolate those aspects of the overall operation which, if mismanaged during the next year or so, would have a catastrophic effect on the organization. The word *catastrophic* is emotionally loaded, but I use it deliberately. Managers are notorious for their inability to prioritize; they insist on maintaining that everything is of equally high priority. Of course, this is a contradiction in terms; if everything is of equal importance, then there are no priorities whatsoever. Yet to be effective, an organization's mission must revolve around the top priorities. The exercise therefore seeks to help participants distinguish between the catastrophic and the deplorable—or the merely inconvenient.

The intended participants are the members of the senior leadership team. If the exercise is taking place as part of an academy workshop and the organization already has in its ranks a person assigned to the role of corporate change agent, and if this individual is also attending the academy (as recommended in the next chapter), then he or she is the ideal person to act as facilitator. (This is the default scenario in the description of this and other facilitated exercises in these pages. If in your case the exercises are not to be part of a planning workshop, or if no such change-agent function exists in your organization, then any member of the team can take on the facilitator role—but in this case the facilitator must do double duty and actively participate in each step just as the other team members do.) A whiteboard or flipchart is required, along with markers.

THE STRATEGIC-PRIORITIES EXERCISE

▶ The facilitator asks each member of the team to write down an answer to this question: "What are the things which, if [name of your organization] does not manage them well over the next twelve months, could have a catastrophic effect on our business?" (Allow approximately five minutes for writing answers; no discussion is permitted at this point.)

▶ The facilitator instructs the members of the team to review their written answers, assigning an "importance rating" to each item. For example, if there are seven items on one member's sheet, he or she must assign a different number to each; number 1 designates the most important, and number 7 the least. (Approximately two minutes.)

▶ The facilitator invites the members of the group to approach a whiteboard or flipchart at the head of the room and write down, in large and legible script, their three items (no more than three!) that were given the highest importance ratings. Take as much time as necessary to get everyone's three items recorded. Using tandem whiteboards or flipcharts, if available, speeds up this step.

▶ The facilitator invites team members to search the big list for common themes, and for items that might logically be combined, for example, "Improve customer satisfaction" and "Better customer relations." The objective is to eliminate duplication and shorten the list by grouping thematically wherever possible. This may require rewriting, for legibility. If there is confusion around the meaning of an item, its author is invited to clarify. Open discussion is permitted at this point, but it should not be allowed to digress into pointless executive babble (PEB).

▶ The facilitator now asks the members of the team to come forward and, using a marker, cast three checkmark votes beside those items from the big list that they feel need to be incorporated into the final mission statement. Members can assign two or even all three of their votes to a single item if they wish to give it extra weight.

▶ The votes are tallied. The three items (no more than three!) that garner the most votes are prime candidates for inclusion in the mission statement.

The value of this exercise is that it allows the group to reach a form of democratic consensus relatively quickly. Even if an individual team member's pet priority doesn't make it to the final short list, there is a feeling that at least he or she is given a voice and is ultimately outvoted fairly and democratically. The team now shares a sense of which issues among many important ones qualify as *most* important for the future success of the organization.

••

RAISING THE COMPELLINGNESS FACTOR

Let's say the members of the leadership team at Finster Bridal Supply & Chain Saw Repair have created their big list, cast their votes, and come up with three items for inclusion in their mission:

1 Dramatically improve safety standards for chain saw repair technicians

2 Expand range of veils and trains to attract younger brides

3 Reduce operating costs

How do they then turn this into a meaningful mission statement? And how do they make such a mission compelling to the rest of the organization? Indeed, what are the qualities that make a mission statement compelling in the first place?

A COMPELLING MISSION:

1 Articulates a change being introduced into the organization

2 Strikes a balance between challenge and achievability

3 Provides a context for strategic decision making

First, in order to be compelling the mission must describe a specific departure from the status quo. Mission statements that say "Continue to . . . " or "Maintain our . . . " or "Preserve the . . . " are utterly *un*compelling. The only things they inspire are yawns. They're simply saying, "More of the same old stuff comin' your way." The essence of leadership is to lead to a *new place*; there must be a sense of movement, progress, change.

What are the top strategic priorities in your business? What would qualify as significant success milestones for these particular priorities? What must change for you to reach these milestones? Once again, this is really the key: Plan to succeed. Your leadership team needs to agree on what "success" means precisely in your case, and what kind of change is required to achieve it. We discuss how to communicate the mission to the rest of the organization later; for now the objective is merely for the leadership team to agree upon the key elements of the mission.

For the folks at Finster Bridal & Chain Saw, their first item (improving safety) represents a clear top priority; their corporate history is strewn with ghastly accident reports. Indeed, their third item, reducing costs, is a natural offshoot of the first, in terms of reduced liability claims and legal costs. Their second item—expanding their product line—really intensifies current activity rather than departing radically from the status quo. Thus, they might first take a crack at a mission statement such as *We will dramatically improve technician safety standards, in order to reduce accidents and associated costs. We will also expand our entire veil-and-train product line to attract younger customers.* Although this isn't very compelling yet, it's a start.

As for the second quality (balancing challenge with achievability), consider two ambitious young men sharing a drink in a bar. One says, "I intend to be very rich some day." The other says, "I'll have made my first million before I turn thirty." Which declaration is more compelling? As a rule, the more specific and measurable the mission is, the more compelling it becomes. Once the mission's particulars are defined, they need to be quantified in some way. If the mission involves growth, for example, it should spell out *how much growth*, and *by when*. Increase profitability—by how much, and by when? Improve customer satisfaction, reduce costs, expand the product line, enlarge the manufacturing facility, decrease the staff, reduce employee turnover, etc., etc. Yes, but by how much, and by when?

Once some by-how-much and by-when values (or their equivalent) are proposed, the team must subject them to a rigorous feasibility check: Do they transform the mission into a clear-cut case of "Mission Impossible"? Or—just as bad— are they perhaps too easy to achieve? To be compelling, they must strike a delicate balance. When the rest of the organization hears them for the first time, the majority of the reactions should fall between, "Oh, wow, that's going to be quite a stretch for us . . . " and ". . . but you know, I really think if we all pulled together on this thing, we could do it!" From a nonverbal standpoint, a mission that is truly compelling first causes eyebrows to go up and then almost immediately provokes big smiles. Any time you're outlining your mission or vision to one or more listeners, or even a large audience, if you observe that particular facial one-two punch of eyebrows shooting up and then wide grins, you'll know you've passed the compellingness test with flying colors.

For the team at Finster Bridal & Chain Saw, the key element of the mission involves improving safety standards to reduce accidents and associated costs. But by how much and by when? They hammer it out and emerge with a revised mission statement: *By improving our safety standards, we will within a year reduce the number of chain saw-related technician-dismemberment accidents to no more than one per month, with a further reduction to no more than one every six months by the end of the following year.*

By year three, our ultimate goal is zero. This will produce a reduction in legal and operating costs of at least 70 percent within a year. In addition, we will use an expanded line of bridal veils and trains to increase our under-twenty-five customer base by 30 percent within twelve months.

This rambling mouthful is not easy to recite from memory, but then memorableness and brevity are by no means as important for the mission as they are for the vision. Indeed, some mission statements occupy pages of text, but because they stick to the organization's two or three key objectives and merely elaborate upon them in some detail, they still qualify to be termed effective. The employees at Finster know how dismal the previous accident rates were, and know their public image in the bridal market has traditionally been characterized as stodgy and old-fashioned; for them, the fact that senior management is committing to ambitious targets within ambitious time frames on both these fronts is enough to raise eyebrows and prompt grins.

The third quality of a compelling mission statement is a great and often unexpected benefit: the ability to focus and facilitate executive decision making. At every strategic fork in the road, whenever competing priorities clash, the question becomes, "Which course of action is most in support of our mission objectives?" If, for example, the mission stresses the importance of attracting new customers, the favored course of action is surely different than if the mission emphasizes cutting costs. Raising customer satisfaction prompts different choices than does developing innovative new products.

A clearly articulated, clearly understood mission statement affects decision making and alters executive and organizational behavior—and results.

ENVISIONING THE MISSION

Once a compelling mission is defined, creating a compelling vision to accompany it becomes much easier.

The vision statement is the snappy, highly memorable catchphrase that captures the spirit of the mission and symbolizes it in shorthand. It creates in the mind's eye an image that perfectly represents success achieved. Though everyone in the organization may learn about the mission in detail, no one is expected to commit the actual text of the mission statement to memory and recite it verbatim at the drop of a hat. The vision, on the other hand, should crop up in every second conversation at every level of the business every day. For that to happen, it needs to be compelling. But what makes a vision statement compelling?

A COMPELLING VISION:

1 Defines the means for confirming that the mission has been successfully accomplished

2 Depicts a defining moment of triumph that can be seen drawing ever nearer

3 Creates an opportunity for organizationwide celebration

First, the vision answers the question, "What do we need to see to indicate unequivocally that we've done it, that the mission has been achieved?" It defines how the organization is going to know, beyond a doubt, that it is a case of mission accomplished. What is the measure, the indicator, the event that clearly, unmistakably signifies success? The vision needs to spell it out, preferably in a catchy, easy-to-remember phrase that strikes a chord within the organization. The mission may be complex and convoluted, requiring many paragraphs or even pages to adequately summarize; even so, the accompanying vision should trip off the tongue in a single breath. For Raytheon Corporate Jets, the mission incorporated three separate objectives: "guaranteed delivery performance" (the aircraft is *always* ready when promised), "customer friendly facility," and "the highest technical capability." Raytheon developed a customer feedback questionnaire that assigned a 1–10 rating scale to each critical element. Their vision statement: *10/10/10 by the year 2000*. At David Lloyd Leisure (DLL), a British chain of fitness clubs, the vision statement is *Heartbeat 135*. "One hundred thirty-five represents a healthy heart rate for most people," explains DLL change agent Helen Chapman. "Our corporate mission involves increasing our membership numbers to 135,000 by the year 2000. And the 'heartbeat' theme also reflects the fact that the British Heart Foundation is our recognized charity partner. The phrase *Heartbeat 135* thus means a great deal to everyone throughout the business."

At Finster, the thoughts of the leadership team turn to the American Chain Saw Safety Review Board. For years, Finster has been blacklisted as a "worst offender" in the annual year-end edition of the ACSSRB's national newsletter. Perhaps, if the improvement in Finster's safety record were judged sufficiently dramatic, the company might find itself eligible for inclusion on the ACSSRB newsletter's Honor Roll for a change.

Second, in order to be compelling, the particular measure (or indicator, or event) reflected in the vision must be reached (or be observed, or occur) at a specific future point in time, a particular moment in which the organization visibly and dramatically moves from "almost there, not quite there . . ." to "There!" An electric tote board needs to keep changing from a number ending in 999 to the next thousand. Or the winner of some highly prestigious award needs to be announced amid much nail-biting suspense: "And the winner is . . . us!"

When much of the civilized world paused to observe the live televised image of an astronaut taking "one small step" onto the lunar surface for the first time, it was a defining moment of triumph marking the realization of a mission declared nearly a decade earlier. Cutting a ribbon, lighting a torch, unveiling a plaque, ringing a bell, laying a first brick, hammering a last spike, cutting a cake, breaking new ground, raising a flag—achieving a difficult and challenging objective is a defining moment that people vividly remember years after the fact. The greater the suspense as the target moment draws closer and closer, the greater the sense of triumph when it finally arrives.

Perhaps, a member of the Finster leadership team suggests, the ACSSRB might even consider the improvement in Finster's safety standards significant enough to warrant bestowing a Gold Star Award for "most impressive turnaround." Think how that would make everybody feel!

Third, ambassadors of change ensure that any time a mission is achieved, there is jubilation and celebration galore. Everyone involved in helping achieve the moment of triumph needs to feel that his or her involvement has been fully acknowledged and recognized. The celebration should be lavish and memorable. Thus, when a new compelling mission is unveiled, accompanied by its own snappy new vision, everyone begins anticipating the profound sense of accomplishment that will ensue if it is successfully achieved—a far more favorable response than the mixture of cynicism and resistance that is the more typical greeting of announcements of impending change.

At Finster the ideas begin to fly furiously. "Doesn't the ACSSRB year-end newsletter come out just before Christmas? Don't they notify Gold Star Award winners prior to publication? If we won, and if we also succeeded in attracting a 30 percent increase in younger customers, couldn't we organize a huge Christmas party for the whole staff, with spouses and all, to celebrate our achievement in style? Since the award in is the shape of a star, couldn't we call the event the 'Christmas Star'?" Suddenly the words *Christmas Star* become the nucleus of a vision of success, shorthand for "we're going to improve safety around here to such an extent that the federal safety board is going to bestow upon us their special award, and we're going to make all our people feel like stars for achieving it (and for helping expand our under-twenty-five customer base) at a big celebratory Christmas party—if not this year, then one year soon." Suddenly, all the various changes being introduced at Finster Bridal & Chain Saw are seen to be contributing to the effort to move the organization closer to Christmas Star. Suddenly it all seems to make sense.

ARE VALUES OF ANY VALUE?

Beyond attempting to clarify their mission and vision, many leadership teams also grapple with an attempt to define their core values: the fundamental beliefs or ideologies that govern how they do business. Does such an exercise serve a useful purpose?

As with mission and vision, clearly articulated corporate values facilitate decision making. Any time two mutually exclusive courses of action seem to support different aspects of the mission's objectives to roughly the same extent, the question becomes, "Does either course of action violate any of our core values?" If not, then ask, "Which course of action more clearly supports one or more of our core values?" The values thus become a final, overarching set of guidelines to help in decision making. Suppose, for example, one of the core values at Finster is *We provide our employees with a safe work environment*. Then suppose a director focuses on the cost-cutting element of their mission in saying, "If we're so determined to lower our legal costs, rather than going through all the hassle of beefing up our safety standards, why don't we just automatically start offering quick, out-of-court settlements instead? Probably cost us a whole lot less in the long run." The inappropriateness of the suggestion now becomes immediately apparent. Values don't only help you make the right decisions; they help you make the right decisions for the right reasons.

How does a leadership team go about defining its organization's core values? Here is a relatively simple exercise that usually does the trick, in addition to providing a pleasant hour or two of diversion for the team. It is not essential for this exercise to be paired with the strategic-priorities exercise described above, although the two are particularly effective when undertaken in succession and combine to create a half-day experience with a profound and long-lasting effect.

THE CORE-VALUES EXERCISE

This exercise divides the leadership team into two groups. The exercise has the greatest impact if one group of participants remains unaware of what the other group is doing until the end, even if everyone knows at the outset that the ultimate objective has something to do with defining core values. Therefore, it's advisable to use two separate rooms (main room and breakout room) such that neither group can see nor hear each other working. Equip each with flipchart and markers, and masking tape or some other means by which to post for display in the main room the flipcharts created in the breakout room.

THE CORE-VALUES EXERCISE

The exercise begins by having the entire leadership team stand and form a line in descending order of seniority. That is, the person with the longest tenure is at the head of the line, followed by the person with the second-longest, and so on, to the newest member of the team. The line is then broken in half at the midpoint, thus creating two separate groups, designated "the old timers" and "the new kids on the block." (If the team comprises an odd number of members, assign the extra person in the middle to the new-kids group.) The new kids now move to the breakout room, to await instructions from the facilitator.

▶ In the main room, the facilitator invites the old timers to list all the aspects of their organization's culture that made the so-called good old days so good—what they feel they may be in danger of losing or have already lost outright over the years. One of the old timers is to act as a scribe and record everyone's ideas on the flipchart. (15–20 minutes)

The facilitator moves to the breakout room and asks the new kids on the block to list all the things they feel are missing in the organizational culture and that they would like to see improved or added to make the organization a better place to work in the years to come. One of the new kids is to act as a scribe and record everyone's ideas on the flipchart. (15–20 minutes)

▶ In the old timers' camp, the facilitator instructs the group to identify, for each item listed, the fundamental value or principle it represents. Responses can be single words (*trust,* or *honesty*) or phrases (*The customer always came first, or Pride in our technical expertise*). (10–15 minutes)

In the new kids' corner, the facilitator similarly instructs the group to identify, for each item listed, the fundamental value or principle it represents, using single words or phrases as appropriate. (10–15 minutes)

▶ The facilitator next invites both of the (still separated) groups to assign an importance rating to the values or principles that were identified and create a new, clean list that presents only the top three. (10–15 minutes)

▶ The new kids in the breakout room are instructed to carefully remove all of their flipcharts for transport and return to the main room to join the old timers. They post their flipcharts for display, although both groups conceal their Top Three Values flipcharts for the time being.

▶ Each group makes a presentation to the other, explaining what they were asked to do and displaying the results. Each presentation concludes with an unveiling of that group's final Top Three Values flipchart. Surprise: they're (typically, at least!) very much alike. What the organization "valued" in the past, it seems, is not too different from what it values for the future.

▶ The reunited leadership team now endeavors to meld the best from both Top Three Values lists into a single unified list of three fundamental values for the organization. These become the guiding principles they will strive to live by daily, the nonnegotiable standards of behavior they will attempt to adhere to in all their dealings, the ultimate guidelines for decision making.

This last step can be quite challenging, especially in cases where the overlap between the two source lists is not particularly obvious. But the team must be allowed to struggle with the issue; it is in the process of struggle that each value statement is most deeply considered. For this reason, I do not normally apply a rigid time limit to this part of the exercise; rather, I let the team pace itself and point to the clock only if the debate appears to be stalling. As a general guideline, however, most teams are able to get through this final step in less than thirty minutes.

• •

One particular time-wasting trap to avoid is the you-can't-have-that-before-you-have-this argument. To illustrate, if both *trust* and *honesty* are vying for the third spot on the final list and the group is favoring *honesty,* the individual acting as a champion for *trust* may argue, "Yes, but you cannot be truly honest with people unless you first trust them not to betray your honesty. Trust must come first!" (If it were the other way around, with *trust* shaping up as the favorite, the champion for *honesty* might similarly argue, "Ah, but you'll never learn to trust people unless you first risk being honest with them, in order to satisfy yourself that they won't betray you. Honesty must come first!") This may be an intriguing chicken-and-egg exercise for armchair philosophers to wrestle with, but the most desirable value for an organization to adopt is not "the one that comes first"—chronological sequence is not pertinent—but rather "the one that is most useful in helping us make the right decisions for the right reasons, to guide us along to our vision of success." It's a simple case of selecting from a menu. When I'm choosing between chicken salad and egg salad for lunch, I really don't tend to base my selection on whether one choice could exist if the other did not come first.

By the way, you may be wondering what is so magical about the number three. Why only three values? The answer is that two would be even better. When it comes to strategic priorities, and to ideological principles, fewer is always better. It's axiomatic: the more things we try to do at once, the less effectively we tend to get any of them done. Three is a compromise. It gives us some scope and flexibility, but it still keeps us narrowly focused on the big issues that really matter.

This is what makes values valuable. Like a well-prioritized mission, like a compelling vision, they keep us on the straight and narrow. They protect us from distractions and detours that might otherwise get us moving in the wrong direction.

ANTICIPATE SUCCESS

You know your mission and vision are sufficiently compelling when you yourself feel the excitement every time you think about them. If they don't make you tingle, if they don't resonate deep inside you, they probably fail to do so for others as well. The primary feeling that the mission and vision convey should be optimism: *This is our ambitious objective, but by jiminy, we are going to make it.* The more you treat your mission and vision as if you believe them to be potentially self-fulfilling prophecies, the more likely they will become so.

You know when your core values are doing their job because every time there is heated debate about alternate courses of action, conflicting priorities, opposing options, your trusty values help settle the dispute and simplify the choice.

Armed with a solid mission, vision, and set of values, you're ready to get down to the nitty-gritty of figuring out everything that needs to be addressed to make the dream a reality. You're ready to start asking the big questions. You're ready to build a formal, disciplined, comprehensive plan.

Asking Big Questions

T his chapter outlines the mechanism and the process that are used to create a formal, written plan for organizational change. If you want the rest of the book to function as a useful tool, think of this chapter as the accompanying instruction manual. Of course, for many readers in our highly instruction-manual-averse society, this disclosure automatically inspires a response of, "Oh good, it means I can skip this chapter." I address the next paragraph to those readers in particular.

PLANNING TO PLAN EFFECTIVELY

The planning approach outlined in this book differs most dramatically from conventional planning practice in its emphasis on structure and discipline. The traditional impulse is to hurry up and get on with it (which results in a high incidence of failure); I replace this with admonitions to take the time to do it right. Whereas failure to learn how to program a VCR may lead at worst to occasional inconvenience or disappointment, failure to plan effectively for organizational change usually has far more profound and unpleasant consequences. The discipline of effective planning begins now, as we take the time in this section to do it right—that is, to master the mechanics of the planning process itself.

A CHECKLIST FOR EFFECTIVE PLANNING

If you've ever tried it, you know that attempting to introduce change into an organization can feel like trying to keep a number of plates spinning on the ends of sticks. You keep adding new plates and setting them spinning, while frantically scrambling to keep the already-spinning plates—some of which are beginning to develop a dangerous wobble—safely aloft as well.

For the professional plate-spinner, more is better. A plate spinner who specializes in keeping only a single plate spinning, no matter how skillfully, may find it difficult to get good bookings in the top plate-spinning venues. For the rest of us, faced with what feels like a similar challenge, fewer would be better. But what's the minimum number we can get away with? How many separate elements, or factors, or issues need to be addressed to effectively plan for organizational change?

There can never be a single right answer to this question, of course, since every organization possesses a unique combination of inter-related variables. As a starting point, we can safely conclude that there are a minimum of eight "big questions" that need to be considered as part of effectively planning for the introduction of any strategic-change initiative.

Think of the 8 Big Questions simply as an eight-point planning template. Answers to the 8 Big Questions ultimately become the contents of the plan. The eight-point checklist prevents any key planning element from being overlooked. More elements can be added, of course—but in more than a decade of experience I have found that these 8 Big Questions identify all of the basic and critical issues that need to be incorporated into an effective plan for organizational change.

The 8 Big Questions

1 How will we become ambassadors of change?

2 How will we spread the word internally?

3 How will we acquire and use customer data?

4 How will we bring new employees up to speed?

5 How will we make things better for our employees?

6 How will we make things better for our customers?

7 How will we measure our successes?

8 How will we celebrate our successes?

In each question, the pronouns *we* and *our* refer to "we the members of the leadership team," or "we who are collectively responsible for setting the strategic direction for the organization (or for the division, department, or functional team)."

These are the eight major issues that need to be carefully considered if any sort of transformational change is to be successfully implemented within an organization.

1 First, and most important, the leaders must be seen to be leading the change effort personally. By their actions, decisions, and day-to-day behavior, they must unfailingly demonstrate their determination to make their compelling vision of organizational success a reality. Moreover, they must strive to reduce the fear and uncertainty associated with change, and they must impart to others throughout the organization their own high level of optimism that the shared vision of success will be realized.

2 A leadership strategy must be developed to ensure that the entire organization feels it is consistently being informed about what is changing, why, and how. Progress must be reported, successes highlighted, and solutions shared, all continuously. If new elements of change give rise to new fears and anxieties, these must be addressed and lain to rest quickly, before destructive rumors spread and fuel resistance.

3 As changes are introduced, it is important to verify with customers that the organization continues to move in the right direction. Mechanisms must be defined that make acquiring and using customer feedback simpler and easier. Increasingly, the leadership team should strive to base key strategic decisions on real data, as opposed to best guesses.

4 The processes of recruiting, hiring, and orienting new employees must clearly and visibly support the organization's values, mission, and vision. No longer are technical skills and academic qualifications sufficient to ensure selection as an employee; ideological "fit" also becomes a critical prerequisite for hiring. Orientation of new employees must emphasize their key role in supporting the change initiative and helping to make the corporate vision a reality.

5 Management must demonstrate its own willingness to adopt change by identifying, and then removing, the main organizational obstacles to employees' doing what is expected of them to make the vision a reality. Those particular policies or procedures that tie their hands, and the systems and technologies that get in the way, must be streamlined or replaced.

6 In tandem with the organizational change effort, there must be a collective focus on improving the total customer experience; otherwise, the attention paid to achieving internal objectives easily diverts the organization's attention from external aspects of the business, including relationships and interactions with customers. Here are the greatest opportunities to create direct employee involvement, which is a powerful neutralizer of resistance to change.

7 Is the change initiative actually bearing fruit? Are the various strategic objectives being satisfactorily met? How is the organization to tell? Consideration must be given to the measurement of results. Progress must be carefully tracked, to ensure that no wrong turns are taken, no costly mistakes unknowingly perpetuated.

8 Last, provision must be made to recognize good work and celebrate achievements. Employees must feel that their efforts to support the change and realize the vision are being acknowledged and appreciated.

Although seemingly simple and straightforward, each of the 8 Big Questions actually represents a fairly broad canvas. I devote a separate chapter to each, to clarify terms of reference, share relevant real-world examples and best practices, and highlight potential hazards and pitfalls.

It will become clearer in later chapters that there is a considerable amount of redundancy, and overlap, built into the 8 Big Questions. That is, a particular activity undertaken in response to one of the questions often satisfactorily addresses one or more of the others as well. In this way, the overall workload that derives from the completed plan is often considerably lighter and more manageable than is anticipated at the outset.

USING SUBQUESTIONS TO BE MORE SPECIFIC

Because the 8 Big Questions are so broad in nature, some means is required to narrow their scope, in order to arrive at highly focused, highly specific answers. We achieve this narrowing effect through applying three successive sets of secondary, related subquestions, each of which derives from, and serves to further narrow, the ones before. The sequence and wording of the subquestions is the same for each of the 8 Big Questions, as is the three-phase process for applying them. This is where the template aspect comes into play; once the flow of the three phases of subquestions is comfortable and familiar, it becomes increasingly simple and easy to apply them to each of the 8 Big Questions—indeed, to any other big strategic question or issue. In planning for change, as in all things, practice makes (closer to) perfect.

APPLYING THE SUBQUESTIONS

To understand how these standardized subquestions work, let's go through the entire three-phase progression in a simulated example.

By way of illustration, let's say that the members of the leadership team at Smedley Peanuts & Ball Bearings have reached that part of their planning exercise where they are considering big question number three, "How will we acquire and use customer data?" The description here of the retrolinked subquestions thus revolves entirely around the Smedley team's efforts to find some detailed, specific answers to the third big question.

In phase one, the subquestions are called "status-quo questions." They are intended to capture something of how "customer data" (the subject of the third big question) is or is not currently being acquired and used at Smedley.

. . . .

STATUS-QUO QUESTIONS (10 MINUTES)

▶ Strengths: What do we currently do well to address the third big question?

▶ Weaknesses: What prevents us from doing a better job of addressing it?

On a flipchart, under the heading "Strengths," in five minutes or less the Smedley team lists all the methods, activities, mechanisms, etc., by which they currently acquire and use customer data in their business. It's important, when introducing change, that we not accidentally discontinue doing useful, effective things. Part of our subsequent plan building may involve formally ensuring that we continue to do some of the things already being done.

Under "Weaknesses," the team spends another five minutes or less identifying all of the internal and external obstacles, impediments, factors, etc., that prevent them from acquiring more and better customer data, and using the data more effectively. The object, here, is not to analyze, speculate, or resolve any of these weaknesses, but merely to list as many of them as possible in five minutes or less.

In five minutes, the members of the Smedley team make nearly a dozen entries of strengths, among which are:

▶ Annual customer survey questionnaire

▶ Interviews of key customers by sales reps in focus groups

▶ Well-maintained complaint file

Five minutes later, under "Weaknesses," they've identified such items as:

▶ Everyone too pressed for time

▶ Questionnaire results never properly collated and analyzed

▶ Some managers may "fear" what data will reveal about them

The subquestions of phase two are brainstorming questions. These direct the team to review the list of strengths and weaknesses created in phase one and use the list as the basis for some creative thinking around potential activities at Smedley to answer the third big question.

BRAINSTORMING QUESTIONS (15 MINUTES)

▶ What can be done to amplify our strengths?

▶ What can be done to overcome our weaknesses?

On a fresh flipchart, the Smedley team considers their first strength: the annual customer survey questionnaire. They ask themselves how the questionnaire can be made more effective, more customer-friendly. They record their answers on the flipchart, without evaluation or discussion. When they run out of ideas, they turn to their second strength, interviews of key customers by sales reps in focus groups. Once again they ask themselves how the effectiveness of these interviews might be improved, and they list their answers.

After about seven or eight minutes of brainstorming on their strengths, they turn their attention to the first of their weaknesses: everyone too pressed for time. They ask themselves what can be done to rearrange schedules, reevaluate priorities, free up more time for collecting and using customer data. As before, they list their answers without evaluating or discussing them. They turn to their second weakness, questionnaire results that are never collated and analyzed. Again, they brainstorm ideas for correcting this situation. All ideas are listed.

In fifteen minutes of brainstorming, they generate quite a lengthy list of ideas. These include:

▶ Create streamlined, simplified, airline-specific questionnaire (airlines are a major customer category for both of Smedley's key product lines)

▶ Videotape customer focus-group interviews, and play back to entire staff

▶ Each manager to schedule one hour per week to meet with customers

▶ Appoint a survey analysis task force

▶ Educate managers that they have nothing to fear from customer data

....

The subquestions in the final phase are activity-planning questions. To apply these, the team begins by selecting one (to begin, only one!) of the brainstormed ideas generated in phase two. They select one that clearly helps them accomplish one or more of the objectives in their mission statement, that makes a significant stride toward achieving the vision, or for any other valid reason seems a logical candidate for consideration. For the one selected idea, they then answer all of the activity-planning questions.

··

ACTIVITY-PLANNING QUESTIONS (20 MINUTES)

▶ What exactly will be done?

▶ How will it be done?

▶ Who will do it?

▶ Who will ensure that it gets done?

▶ When will it begin (or be completed)?

▶ How will success be measured?

From among all of their phase two ideas, the Smedlians selected *Videotape customer focus-group interviews, and play back to entire staff* as the first idea they wish to translate into a planned activity. After twenty minutes of discussion and debate, they come up with the following:

▶ What: Customers participating in focus group sessions will be asked for permission to allow their interviews to be videotaped. These tapes will be regularly screened for the entire Smedley staff. Objective will be to help staff at all levels make key decisions based on current customer data.

▶ How: Special once-monthly two-hour customer feedback screenings will be held in the main cafeteria. Key pieces of video feedback content will be highlighted and discussed immediately after the screening. Written transcripts of key portions will also be prepared and distributed.

▶ Who: Customer reps will supply and operate the video equipment during the focus group interviews. Technical training available from _____ in A/V Department, if necessary. Screening sessions will be organized by _____ of Marketing Services.

▶ When: Screenings will be held on third Friday afternoon of each month. First screening in April.

▶ Measure: Employee survey (after sixth screening session) will ask, "Have the video screenings provided any useful data? Have they helped you in your job in any way?" Decision to continue or modify format will be based on survey results.

....

This activity represents one item to be included in the Smedley strategic improvement plan, as an answer to the third big question. It is up to the team to determine whether, in their particular case, it is appropriate to tackle more than one customer data activity; if so, they then select another of their phase-two brainstormed ideas and for twenty minutes or less subject it, too, to the phase-three activity-planning questions. The answers to these questions provide an additional item for their improvement plan. Once they feel the issue has been dealt with in sufficient depth, they turn to big question four ("How will we bring new employees up to speed?") and begin the entire three-phase progression again, applying the phase-three subquestions to as many of the phase-two brainstormed ideas as seems appropriate. Thus, piece by piece, the Smedley strategic plan comes into being.

STRATEGIC PLANNING: ART OR SCIENCE?

Most of this book concerns the science of building a plan: the methods, techniques, and how-to. But applying this know-how well can be something of an art.

I don't pretend to know a great deal about art. From what I gather as a casual observer, in most conventional art forms (literature, theater, dance, painting, sculpture, and so on) the artist is attempting to suggest—within the limitations of the chosen medium—some recognizable aspect or element of human experience. In many cases, the greater the limitations imposed upon the artist by the form and structure of a given medium, the greater the triumph when some familiar and believable aspect of life emerges from rhyming-and-metered lines of text, or blotches of paint on canvas, or whatever other medium the artist has chosen for self-expression.

Similarly, I have discovered over the years that imposing limitations of form and structure upon the planning process greatly enhances and enrichens the output. These imposed disciplines are not meaningless and arbitrary; they are the product of careful and extensive field testing and refinement.

First among these disciplines is the *time constraint*. No doubt you have observed in reviewing the three phases of retrolinked subquestions above that specific numbers of minutes were allocated to each. The time limits indicated for each phase of subquestion application need to be very strictly enforced. Nature abhors a vacuum, but it is even truer that all (management) tasks expand to fill the time allotted to them. The nature of this task is to think fast and loose, to capture lightning in a bottle. Managers need to be dissuaded from engaging in unproductive analysis and discussion; one way is to convince them, and keep reminding them, that there's no time for pointless executive babble. (When I preside over strategic planning workshops, during the subquestion exercises I play a videotape whose screen-filling numerals count down the minutes and seconds toward 00:00. It's fascinating to watch senior teams glancing anxiously and repeatedly at the timer and using it to keep things moving briskly. Some team members exhibit the unmistakable discomfort of PEB withdrawal symptoms.) By trial and error, I have found that the indicated time limits are just about right: long enough to get the job properly done, while maintaining the sense that "we have to keep moving." If you allow the time to expand even once, the message becomes, "Relax, there's no need to sweat it; we can take as long as we want." Focus and creativity are then replaced with more typical, drawn-out blah-blah-blah, which usually leads nowhere.

In addition to time constraints, these exercises also benefit handsomely from imposing specific "disciplines of form." It's sometimes helpful to appoint a "process cop" within the team, who ensures that throughout the exercise the disciplines described next are being adhered to.

Status-Quo Questions (Phase One)

In listing strengths and weaknesses, the team must resist all temptation to exchange "historical anecdotes" and "analytical overviews." Members have only ten minutes in which to list as many items as possible; there's no time for discussion or extrapolation.

Brainstorming Questions (Phase Two)

The discipline required here applies to all classic brainstorming: Ideas for ways to amplify strengths and overcome weaknesses must not be evaluated or elaborated upon. They are to be merely listed; no discussions of feasibility, desirability, or how to solve foreseeable implementation problems are permitted at this stage. Such discussion is relevant in phase three, but only in relation to those ideas being considered for phase-three activity planning.

In the occasionally furious pace of brainstorming, it's also useful for whoever is acting as flipchart scribe to ensure that entries are not abbreviated to such an extent that they become meaningless. If, for example, while brainstorming ideas to recognize employee achievements (the eighth big question) someone calls out, "personalized employee parking spaces," it is unwise to record this idea with the single word "parking." Later, when the complete list of ideas is being reviewed to select a candidate for phase-three activity planning, no one is likely to recall what *parking* specifically referred to, and the idea is lost. If the team consistently generates a flurry of brainstormed ideas at a frantic pace, it makes sense to use two flipchart scribes, alternating entries.

Activity-Planning Questions (Phase Three)

To properly answer the question of what will be done requires the discipline of clearly distinguishing between objectives and activities, and favoring the latter. *Improve internal communication,* for example, is a noble and worthy objective, but it does not qualify as an activity. Communication of what information? Between what parties? Communicated by what means? *Create customer service newsletter for employees* is more like it. One admittedly simplistic way of thinking about activities is to ask if one can take a photo of someone doing it at 10:15 on a Tuesday morning, and whether a third party seeing the photo gets some sense of what is going on: "In this photo, Ralph is holding a mockup for the design of the newsletter's front page, and the other members of the editorial team are looking it over—they are creating a customer service newsletter for employees."

If the answer to the question "How will it be done?" is not self-explanatory, the team needs to spell out some particulars. Does an editorial team for the newsletter need to be created from scratch? How will the newsletter be designed, printed, distributed, etc.? There may not be time to resolve all of the *how* questions within the actual academy, but if not, then the plan should highlight those issues that need to be resolved later, by whom, and by when.

Who will do it? Who will ensure that it gets done? Here the team needs to distinguish between who is to be directly engaged in the activity in question and who is to be held accountable for its completion. These are frequently not the same persons. Who is to actually "own" the activity? Who gets called on the carpet if it isn't carried out? It's better to specify who with actual names (they would fill the blanks we saw earlier in the Smedley example) rather than functional titles; no one can then plead, "Well, yes, that is my job title, strictly speaking, but in actual fact Sylvia's been looking after that aspect of things since last November. I was sure you meant Sylvia." People expected to implement a part of the organization's plan for improvement need to be unmistakably aware of the fact. At all costs, resist the temptation to use the word *everyone* when assigning ownership. Show me an activity that "everyone" is going to responsible for, and I'll show you one that almost certainly *no one* is going to be responsible for.

When will it begin (or be completed)? As with the *who* question, answering *when* with such clever responses as "right now" or "yesterday" (or the all-time favorite, "ASAP") simply means that the real answer is "probably never." This question calls for a specific, and realistic, calendar date.

The final activity-planning question, how to measure success, calls for a great deal of discipline, but it also frequently spells the difference between long-term success and failure of a given improvement activity. There is no point in undertaking any new activity unless it's sure to bring us closer to success in some way; this final question forces us to devise some method for confirming that it does so. It allows us to validate our assumptions about the usefulness of a given activity, or else provide an opportunity to discontinue any activities that turn out to be less effective than anticipated.

The objective here is to confirm that the activity is *useful*, not that it merely takes place. For example, suppose in response to the third big question each member of the leadership team agrees to demonstrate personal support for becoming a more customer data-driven organization by personally spending one-half day a week with customers. In terms of measuring success, the question is not, "How will we ensure that each member of the leadership team spends one-half day a week with customers?" Rather, the question should be, "How will we ensure that, by spending one-half day a week with customers, we are effectively demonstrating our support for becoming more data-driven?" This is a very different question.

Discipline Rewarded

Applying these disciplines of form during the actual plan-building exercise serves to keep everyone's thinking highly focused and generally produces a dramatically superior result. It can transform the completed strategic plan into something so pure and effective that it almost qualifies as a work of art. Be advised: Organizational leaders who elect to disregard this disciplined approach in their planning exercises do so at their own peril.

THE ACADEMY

In more than ten years with the consulting arm of the California-based Achieve/Zenger-Miller organization, I became the lead instructor for five-day executive planning workshops in which individuals and teams from more than 350 international corporate clients created written plans for transformational change in their own organizations. The original site for these workshops was a stately campuslike facility near Niagara Falls, which, with its ivy-covered atmosphere of higher learning, we dubbed "the academy." As demand for the workshop increased, we established a second site at Jekyll Island, in Georgia. This, too, became known as "the academy." We soon discovered, however, that although we were using the word *academy* to describe a place, our clients were using the same word to describe an event, as in, "When's the best time for us to schedule our academy?" or "Should we consider running an academy internally for all our regional directors?" It didn't take long for this meaning to creep into our own usage as well. So, beggging your indulgence, I will hereafter use the word *academy* to refer to an event.

The chapters that follow provide a step-by-step guide for creating a written strategy for success in your organization within a structured planning workshop—an academy. As a rule, success in business does not happen by accident; it must be carefully planned. The academy thus becomes an extremely important milestone in the history of the organization. Decisions made here, directions taken, courses set, priorities assigned, and commitments made may determine the nature of day-to-day activity for the whole organization for years to come. An exercise of this magnitude is not to be taken lightly.

Determining Who Should Participate

Ultimately, responsibility for defining the strategic direction in any organization rests at the top. Thus the ideal plan-building team is made up of the CEO (or equivalent) and all of his or her direct reports. No member of the senior team must be allowed to abdicate participation in this critical event. Even so, it never fails: The very executive who is too busy with "real work" to attend a key strategic planning session is the same one who later spends the most time openly resisting the plan and tearing it apart, line by line, detail by detail.

If the organization has already appointed a dedicated change agent or coordinator, he or she should also attend and participate—not as a plan builder but as a facilitator of certain key exercises as well as an involved observer. This individual is in a position to oversee creation of the plan document, and even to take a key role in coordinating the actual implementation of the plan, as discussed in Part Three of this book; being present during the rounds of brainstorming that give rise to the plan's content makes it significantly easier later on to ensure that the final plan document reflects the plan builders' intentions accurately and completely.

In certain sensitive situations, where high levels of mistrust or cynicism prevail, it may be advisable to include other stakeholders as well, such as members of the board, union reps, etc. As the old adage reminds us, those who at the outset help plan the battle are less likely later to battle the plan.

Determining the Length of the Academy

Historically, the academy has been a five-day event. In most cases, the attendees are from a variety of different organizations, which adds considerable richness—but also complexity—to the group exercises. So, if the participants are all part of the same organization, what is the right length?

Unless your total employee population numbers ten or fewer, and unless you do business with an equally small number of customers, it's impossible to adequately cover the 8 Big Questions in anything less than two full days. In most cases, it is advantageous to preface the plan building with the strategic-priorities and core-values exercises outlined in the chapter "Learning to See the Future," along with a mission-and-vision-clarification exercise based on the guidelines presented in that same chapter. This requires a three-day session at a minimum, and it also permits the stump-speech exercise to be used as an effective kickoff on all three days. (The exercise is described in the first of the big question chapters and included in the sample three-day academy agenda in the appendix of this book.) In the many "internal" academy sessions I have personally facilitated for clients over the years, this minimum-three-day design has consistently produced the best results.

Creating a Sense of Occasion

In an ideal situation, the academy is held off site, away from phones, faxes, e-mail, and other pesky real-world distractions. (A snazzy hotel in the tropics is nice, if the budget allows it.) If off site is impractical, then a firm no-interruptions policy must be communicated to all secretaries, assistants, receptionists, etc., and rigidly enforced.

The rest of the organization—middle management in particular—is obviously going to sit up and take notice when everyone on the senior leadership team suddenly goes marching off together into closed chambers to do something out of the ordinary. On this occasion, it's highly *desirable* for the academy to attract attention. In fact, it should not seem sudden at all; everyone should have some sense of what's going on even before the event. Middle management especially should be briefed not only regarding the academy objectives but also in regard to the role they are expected to play in ratifying the final plan; more on this below.

If the academy is to be held on site, lunches and refreshments should be brought in; participants must understand that "quick" visits to their desks to see "what's up" are forbidden, as are cell phones in the meeting room. One way or another, everyone involved needs to perceive these three days as a conspicuous departure from the everyday norm: three very special, very important days that take priority over all other workaday concerns.

Maintaining Energy Levels

Sitting at a table and thinking about answers to tough questions for three solid days can be hard work. If physical energy starts to fade, creativity quickly suffers in turn. Aerobics breaks, guided walking tours, or any other opportunities to get up and move around should be built into the academy agenda. Games, contests, physical challenges, team-building activities, whatever fits your team's style is a good investment in terms of reenergizing and maintaining momentum in an intense three-day strategic planning session.

THE WRITTEN PLAN: CREATING THE DOCUMENT (PART ONE)

At the end of their grueling but exhilarating three-day academy, the team ends up with a cluttered collection of papers containing a well-thought-out strategy for success. Who should be responsible for turning this messy assemblage of great ideas into an orderly document fit for internal distribution and future reference?

An obvious candidate is the dedicated coordinator/change agent (if you have one). This individual is ultimately destined to become the keeper of the plan, the "conscience" of the organization, who personally verifies that everyone on the leadership team is doing the plan-approved things at the plan-approved times and in the plan-approved ways. (For more on the role of the keeper of the plan, see the chapter "Finishing Touches.")

If no one holds such a function in your organization, then someone has to assume responsibility for producing the finished planning document. You save time within the academy proper if a candidate for such a role can be agreed to beforehand. If the designated individual is not part of the senior leadership team, it is extremely beneficial to invite him or her to attend and participate in the academy. (If for whatever reason it is not possible to assign such a role prior to the academy, see "Finishing Touches" for recommendations on how to do so within the academy proper.)

How elaborate should the actual plan document be? What does a written strategic plan actually look like? A useful rule of thumb is the concept that less is more, simpler is better. At its heart, the document devotes clearly separated pages or sections to each of the 8 Big Questions, spelling out in clear language the answers to the phase-three activity-planning questions for each of the brainstormed ideas selected for inclusion. This does not mean that what emerged from the academy as *bullet points* now need to be expanded into *essay-length treatises*; rather, it means that in some cases it may be necessary to elaborate on the original bullet points to make them understandable for those who were not a part of the original academy. Plenty of empty space should be incorporated into the plan, to permit each person who owns a copy to add notes and record details alongside each activity entry.

It may be appropriate to preface the heart of the plan with some introductory material clarifying the corporate mission and vision and summarizing the organization's core values, or other ideological or philosophical underpinnings to the plan. Readers may also appreciate a reminder about the kinds of competitive and marketplace pressures forcing the leadership team to conclude change is necessary in the first place, a description of the techniques used to create the plan, and so on. Such material, while clearly valuable, remains essentially optional; if you have the resources to produce it, by all means do so. But the essence of the plan remains the collection of answers to the 8 Big Questions.

PLAN REVIEW AND RATIFICATION

Once the document itself has been put into shape, the plan is ready to be scrutinized by the rest of the organization's management team. Every individual who has employees reporting directly to him or her should be expecting to receive a personal copy of the first draft of the completed plan, along with clear instructions outlining the procedures for subjecting the plan to detailed review and submitting any proposed corrections or amendments. Above all, it should be completely clear to the recipients of these preliminary copies of the plan that they are expected to formally sign the document on an introductory page provided for the purpose, alongside the signatures of the senior team responsible for creating the plan. Signatures from frontline and middle managers serve as an indication that they are aware of the plan's contents and have had an opportunity to propose revisions, and that they fully support the plan in its final form. (If there are members of the senior leadership team who for whatever reason were unable to take part in the academy, they too must review and sign the completed plan; indeed, their endorsement is particularly important. As suggested earlier, these are the very leaders who will most easily shrug their shoulders and say to employees, "Hey, don't look at me, I had nothing to do with putting this plan together!") All copies of the plan that are to be distributed throughout the organization must prominently bear the signed endorsement of every member of the leadership and management team.

COMMUNICATING THE PLAN TO THE RANK AND FILE

The mission defines what the organization is attempting to accomplish. The plan outlines, in detail, all that needs to be done to accomplish the mission. The vision describes what successful accomplishment of the mission will look like. The values articulate the guiding principles to be adhered to throughout the process of realizing the vision. Chapter 2 in Part II explores options for communicating the mission, vision, and values to the rest of the organization.

But what about the plan? Obviously, it is necessary for all management-level staff to become intimately acquainted with the plan in its entirety, before they can be expected to sign their names to it in a gesture of personal endorsement and become directly involved in implementing it. As for the rest of the employees, is it important, or even advisable, to share the specific details of the plan with the rank and file?

The answer is a firm, unequivocal "it all depends."

The security issue is sometimes raised as possible justification for keeping the details of the plan close to the corporate vest. If, for example, the specific strategies outlined in our plan were to fall into competitors' hands, it is argued, would we not forfeit the very competitive advantage the plan is intended to create? Perhaps so, particularly if the plan discloses any highly proprietary, innovative, or time-sensitive ideas. But one can also argue that such ideas should not be spelled out within the plan in sufficient detail to make the organization vulnerable.

Think of competitors in an Olympic foot race. They may have elaborate strategies in mind concerning, say, at what specific point in the race they intend to begin running flat out. Yet even if they succeed in keeping the fine details of their personal strategies to themselves, they surely recognize that all their fellow racers already have a pretty good idea what the basic drift of their overall strategy entails—something like "run faster than everybody else and be the first to get to the finish line." If that much of their plan slips out and is overhead by a competing racer, the originator's competitive advantage is not unduly compromised. It's hard to imagine other racers anxiously whispering just before the starting gun, *"Pssst—apparently number 11, Jorgensen, intends to run faster than the rest of us and be first across the finish line. Pass it on."* Indeed, without wanting to open up a whole psychological-warfare hornet's nest, one might even argue that a corporate plan that falls into a competitor's hands and delineates an aggressive strategy for market domination, with all the details confidently and optimistically spelled out, could conceivably so unnerve and intimidate a competitor as to enhance the originator's competitive advantage. (I said one *might* argue it, which does not mean I am arguing it myself. Please do not do anything foolish and then tell the world you got the idea here!)

More relevant, perhaps, than the question of security is the question of usefulness. Does hearing about all the activities that the various players are undertaking in response to the 8 Big Questions help employees better appreciate the *how* and the *why* of the change effort around them? In most cases, the answer is yes.

The approach that has worked best in many organizations is one in which the pages of the plan are individually reproduced as overhead transparencies and are projected onto a screen as part of a general staff meeting. One or more members of the senior team (or the designated change agent) walk through some of the "highlights" from each page. Employees are not given individual copies of the plan but are advised that a copy has been assigned to their department, and that the department head will happily make it available to them for perusal at any time. (For the security-conscious, this approach affords a certain measure of control over the document's movements.) Questions are invited from the floor. Later, in smaller departmental-level meetings, the department head or functional leader (with at least one member of the senior team in attendance) elaborates upon those elements of the plan that have a direct bearing on the department or team in question; once again, questions are fielded.

The ultimate purpose of sharing the contents of the plan with the whole organization in this way is obviously not so that the audience absorbs, digests, and retains every piece of it; rather, the purpose is to draw attention to the striking fact that a detailed plan exists, pure and simple. It helps the employee population conclude that there may be some method, after all, in what they might forgivably perceive as the madness of change swirling all about them. It suggests that the members of the leadership team are doing their homework and have mapped out a viable strategy for the organization's future success.

A particularly vital message to emerge from any general overview of the plan is that the plan does not invalidate the good work everyone has done up until now. Whatever new strategies are being pursued, new tactics deployed, new training provided, new structure imposed . . . whatever changes are being introduced all intend to build upon what has come before, and not negate it. The organization continues to strive to improve, but it does so by evolution, not revolution. The more frequently presenters of the plan make direct links to what has come before, the better: "Of course, this whole new customer focus strategy is really just taking the great work you've all done on our old familiar 'Customer Service Comes First' program and expanding it to make it even more powerful and effective. . . . "

Sharing of the plan provides an ideal opportunity to create a sense of excitement and movement throughout the whole organization. But before this, of course, the plan has to be created in the first place. The process of doing so occupies Part Two of the book.

Part

II

The 8 Big Questions

How Will We Become
Ambassadors of Change?

To be successful, an organizational change initiative must be led. That is, not only must the leaders of the organization set the course; they must visibly lead the way.

The role of the leader-as-ambassador-of-change is multifaceted. The leader must constantly emphasize the corporate vision of success and reinforce how everything else relates to turning the vision into a reality. The leader must demonstrate unwavering determination to achieve success, especially when there are downturns or setbacks. The leader must help the organization overcome its fear of change and see in change the opportunity to make the organization a better place to work.

Planning for change thus begins with members of the leadership team defining what they can begin doing differently in order to help the change effort succeed.

IMPOSING CALM IN THE MIDST OF UPHEAVAL

When the going gets tough, why do so many leaders seem to suddenly disappear? When the organization most needs up-to-the-minute information, why is the flow of information often at its lowest ebb? Many people attach a sinister interpretation to this common manifestation: weakness, cowardice, arrogant indifference, and so on. Others argue that it's simply a matter of having one's hands full dealing with the crisis in question: no time to take one's eye off the ball and start spewing platitudes of reassurance. But to disappear for days? For weeks? Perhaps there are less obvious interpretations.

On a recent trans-Atlantic flight, the plane I was on encountered heavy turbulence. The captain wasted no time advising the passengers via the public address system that all was well, and that he was looking for a different, calmer air zone to take us to. He apologized for the inconvenience and concluded his announcement. Less than a minute later, a particularly severe jolt rocked the plane. The captain was back on the PA system *immediately*, reassuring us that we had merely passed through the "wake" of another airliner crossing our flight path a moment earlier, no cause for alarm, we should be in a smoother area in about ten minutes, etc.

The nature of my work requires that I travel a great deal. I have experienced turbulence and wind-shear effects even more pronounced and unsettling than in this instance, but on those occasions the silence from the flight deck was deafening. We had to make do with an occasional "Please ensure that your seat belts are fastened" announcement from one of the flight attendants. It's not difficult to feel the anxiety levels rising in the passenger cabin as the turbulence continues to shake, rattle, and roll the aircraft; headphones are removed as movie viewers lose interest, books and magazines are put down as reading ceases to be engrossing. Sleepers sit up, wide awake; all conversation is suspended. Everyone is quietly thinking about . . . things. Everyone is *waiting*. Surely, soon, somebody up front is going to tell us that we're all right, that we have nothing to worry about. Surely they're not going to keep us wondering for much longer, are they?

The turbulence on the flight in question was heavier than usual; yet the level of anxiety among passengers was clearly low. The in-flight movie happened to be a comedy, and people were laughing out loud at the jokes, even while being briskly buffeted around. This captain seemed to genuinely understand what was required to produce "something special in the air"; he was concerned with safety, of course, but also with the passengers' *perception* of safety. All it took to transform a potentially harrowing experience into a reasonably calm and pleasant one, for customers and crew alike, was a few key words spoken at just the right moment.

Why is this not standard airline practice? Why the more typical silence from the flight deck as the plane encounters turbulence—and from the boardroom as organizations do so as well?

Could it be as simple as not fully appreciating how important such timely communication really is? Is it less a matter of not interested and more a matter of not sure just how to proceed? "Just what exactly am I supposed to say? Do I leave out all the bad stuff, or do I truly tell it like it is? What if I don't fully know what's happening myself: shouldn't I wait until I have all the facts straight before I start shooting off my mouth?"

If I proclaim to a group of executives, "In times of change it's critical that you communicate frequently to your organization, to keep everyone updated and reassured," their heavily-lidded eyes glaze over. Boring; tell us something we don't know. If I tell them, "Here's precisely what you need to say to your employees, and how, and when," the same group scrambles for sheets of paper and pens.

Here is what you need to say to your employees, and how, and when.

SPEECHES THAT DO NOT STUMP

The effective ambassador of change consciously says things and does things to reduce the anxiety and fear associated with organizational change. Much of this book deals with determining what needs to be done; here we concentrate on some of what has to be said. And since all of the next chapter focuses on the various *formal* means by which *we* will spread the word internally, in this section we limit ourselves to informal communication.

They're sometimes referred to as "stump speeches": not speeches intended to stump the listener, but rather speeches delivered from atop imaginary tree stumps (that is, from an informal platform rather than a stage or podium). Sometimes they're called "soapbox speeches" or "elevator speeches." They're the short, chatty discourses leaders often find themselves delivering without prior knowledge that they would be asked to do so. Unlike the formal, prepared speeches scheduled in advance and typically delivered to larger audiences—often with the visual support of flipcharts or overhead transparencies—these are the little "exchanges" that develop when a single employee or a small group of employees spontaneously approaches the leader in a corridor or en route to a meeting, and with big, trusting eyes asks for a clarification "off the record, just between you and me, on the level." Ironically, these little impromptu communiqués often have a deeper, longer-lasting effect on the listeners than even the slickest, most polished formal speech. It's worth ensuring that we have something ready in the back of our minds for situations of this sort, to be sure we do not inadvertently omit key elements or further confuse matters.

Whenever any sort of organizational change is introduced, the most common questions concern what precisely is being changed, and why it's necessary. Ambassadors of change need to be able to address both topics effectively and consistently—that is, a single member of the leadership team must deliver a consistent message from speech to speech, while other members of the team deliver messages consistent with those of their peers. Is there a quick way to raise the effectiveness and consistency of stump speeches among the members of your leadership team to the required level? There is. Put the team through this powerful exercise.

THE STUMP SPEECH EXERCISE

This exercise takes an hour or two to complete. Its purpose is to provide ambassadors of change with two potent, prestructured communication "modules" that can be delivered on a moment's notice, alone or in combination as the situation warrants. It defines the *key content points* that form the basis of two informal speeches, focusing on what the organization is attempting to change and why. (Naturally, we also need to expound on how the change is to be introduced, but the *how* element is addressed when the detailed contents of the plan itself are communicated; it is not something that lends itself quite as easily to an off-the-cuff stump-speech format.)

This exercise has proven to be a major confidence builder in leaders who might otherwise not be inclined to communicate informally—that is, without elaborate preparation—to smaller groups of employees casually and spontaneously. As outlined on the printed page, the exercise may seem a little dry and repetitious, but in actual battle conditions it crackles.

For the purposes of this exercise, a stump speech is a self-contained speech that can be delivered in its entirety in three minutes or less. The exercise is divided into two parts, reflecting the two speeches (*what* and *why*).

A stopwatch or countdown timer is required, as are a number of easels stocked with blank flipcharts and markers. Two prepared visual aids (flipcharts or overhead transparencies) are to be created beforehand; these are described within the part of the exercise to which each applies.

PART ONE: MISSION AND VISION

In the next chapter, we determine the best ways of formally communicating the mission and vision to the organization as a whole. But ambassadors of change frequently encounter opportunities to reinforce this communication informally; it is here that their personal enthusiasm and commitment can really shine and have an impact. Every member of the leadership team, when discussing the vision of future success, needs to make crystal clear his or her absolute determination to make this vision a reality. The mission-and-vision stump speech must leave no doubt: We definitely plan to succeed.

▶ The facilitator advises members of the team that they are to work alone, as individuals, for fifteen minutes. They are each to prepare for themselves a written crib sheet that contains, as bulleted points only, (1) the key elements they feel need to be covered to summarize the organization's mission priorities, (2) the meaning behind its vision statement, and (3) the rationale for using this particular vision as an indicator of success—all in an informal speech of three minutes or less. Display the first prepared visual aid ("Mission and Vision") as a helpful outline for the content of their speech.

MISSION AND VISION

▶ Mission Priorities

▶ Vision Statement

✦ Meaning

✦ Rationale

▶ At the conclusion of the fifteen minutes of preparation, the facilitator instructs team members to select a partner and form pairs. (If the total number of team members happens to be an odd number, the facilitator can even things out by including himself or herself in this pair-partner activity.) In each pair, the partners take turns being speech deliverer and listener—but only after the facilitator has given the go-ahead to begin. Listeners are told to give highly specific feedback to their partners after hearing a speech. They are thus encouraged to keep paper and pen at hand and make notes during the speech, recording key words that will help them recall elements that worked well and opportunities for improvement, to feed these back to their partners. Listeners are to be especially watchful for evidence of *enthusiasm* and *optimism* and must be prepared, as part of their feedback, to cite specific instances where these come through, and to make recommendations about how they might be strengthened, if necessary.

Speakers are advised that a stopwatch or timer is set in motion when the various speeches get underway, and that once three minutes have elapsed all speeches are to be concluded—even if not all of the speakers' intended points have been covered. To improve their "enthusiasm and optimism score," speakers are encouraged to replace hedging phrases such as "We hope to . . . " and "By then we should be able to . . . " with unequivocal substitutes: "We will . . . " and "At that point we can. . . . " Speakers are allowed to refer to their crib sheets during their speeches. They are to imagine that they are responding to a question from an individual employee, a question along the lines of, "Can you just clarify for me precisely why all these changes are going on around here?"

▶ The clock is set in motion, and the first round of speeches begins.

▶ After three minutes, the speeches are brought to an end. (One simple but effective way is to tap the rim of an empty drinking glass to serve as a bell, as is often done at weddings to encourage a kiss from the bride and groom.) Listeners are advised that they have two minutes to provide feedback about what worked well and where there are opportunities for improvement, both in terms of content and personal enthusiasm and optimism. The clock is set in motion, and the feedback begins in pairs.

▶ After two minutes, the feedback process ends. Now listeners and speakers exchange roles. The new listeners are reminded of the elements they must listen for, and advised to take notes to permit highly specific feedback. The new speakers are encouraged to "steal shamelessly" from their partners any phrases, examples, or ideas that they particularly liked, and to incorporate them into their own speeches without hesitation. What better way to promote teamwide stump-speech consistency? They're encouraged not to feel self-conscious about repeating much of what they've just heard; in their imagination, they are responding to an employee who's hearing it from their lips for the first time.

▶ The clock is set in motion, and the second round of speeches begins.

▶ After three minutes, the facilitator brings the speeches to an end. Once again, listeners have two minutes to provide feedback about what worked well and where there is room for improvement, in terms of content as well as enthusiasm and optimism. The clock is started, and the feedback begins.

▶ After two minutes, feedback ends. The facilitator asks for a show of hands: "How many of you were unable to cover all the points on your crib sheets within the three-minute limit?" Those who raise their hands are advised that their "homework assignment" is to determine where they might tighten up their speech to get it all in within the time limit.

▶ The facilitator asks whether any listeners were sufficiently impressed with their partners' speeches that they would like to nominate their partner to come to the head of the room and provide an instant replay of the speech for the whole team; doing so permits everyone to steal shamelessly from an effective model. If nominations are made and time permits, the group hears one or more model mission-and-vision stump speeches. Afterwards, the facilitator asks whether any listeners recall particular highlights from their partners' speeches that they would like to offer to the team as candidates for shameless theft. If so, these are heard.

. . . .

PART TWO: INDICATORS FOR CHANGE

The members of the leadership team all know the good reasons behind their strategic change effort. But how often, and how well, are these reasons communicated to the rest of the organization? Are employees generally convinced that the change effort is unavoidable, that their organization truly has no alternative but to struggle through it? Or—as is more commonly the case—do they suspect that many of the changes complicating their lives are arbitrary whims trickling down piecemeal from a disorganized, unfocused leadership team?

Ambassadors of change recognize that those who are expected to support the change initiative and help implement it frequently need to have their "conviction batteries" recharged. Each time the level of disruption and uncertainty begins to rise, those affected require regular reminders about why all of it is necessary in the first place. Leaders need a stump speech that distills all of the various factors which together add up to the *why* behind the whole change strategy.

For the initial preparatory step in part two, the leadership team divide into separate workgroups of two or three members each. It is not necessary in this case to work in different rooms, although each workgroup does require its own blank flipcharts and markers.

▶ Referring to the second prepared visual aid ("Indicators for Change"), the facilitator asks the workgroups to identify, for each of the four C-words, what the indicators are to the organization that change is necessary.

INDICATORS FOR CHANGE

- ▶ Customers
- ▶ Competitors
- ▶ Changes
- ▶ Costs

In other words, they are to discuss and list on their flipcharts answers to these questions:

What sort of things are our customers telling us, or doing, that indicate we must change?

What sort of things are our competitors doing that indicate we must change?

What types of change inside and outside our organization (regulatory, social, political, economic, etc.) are forcing us to change in response?

What indicators are there, if any, that we must find better ways of doing things to control or lower our current operating costs?

▶ The groups have a total of twenty minutes to answer these questions, or roughly five minutes per C-category. The facilitator monitors the clock and advises the groups of the elapsed time at five-minute intervals.

▶ Once the first step is completed, the facilitator instructs the members of the team to work individually for five minutes. Their assignment is to extract, from their own flipcharts (and, if they like, from those of the other work groups as well) what they consider the most persuasive indicators for change under each of the four Cs, and to list these as bullet points on a personal crib sheet to serve as an outline for a stump speech.

▶ The facilitator instructs team members to select a partner—a different person from part one—and again form pairs. Listeners are reminded to keep paper and pen at hand for note taking. This time, in addition to evaluating for general content, they are encouraged to look for qualities of *urgency* and *persuasiveness* in their partners' speeches; as part of their feedback they should be prepared to cite specific instances where these qualities came through, as well as make recommendations about how they can be strengthened if necessary. Once again, speakers are allowed to refer to their crib sheets during their speeches. They are to imagine that they are responding to a question such as, "Who says all these changes are really necessary?"

▶ The clock is set in motion, and the speeches begin.

▶ After three minutes, the facilitator brings the speeches to an end. Listeners are given two minutes to provide feedback, both in terms of content and level of urgency and persuasiveness.

▶ Two minutes later, feedback concludes. Listeners and

speakers exchange roles. Speakers are again encouraged to steal shamelessly from their partners' ideas.

▶ The clock is set in motion, and another round of speeches begins.

▶ After three minutes, the speeches end. Once again, listeners have two minutes to provide feedback.

▶ As before, after the feedback the facilitator asks, "Were any of you unable to cover all the points on your crib sheets within the three-minute limit?" Those who raise their hands are encouraged to determine how they might best shorten their speech as homework.

▶ The facilitator invites nominations for instant replays for the benefit of the whole team. Afterwards, the facilitator invites listeners to share highlights from their partners' speeches.

Of course, as with virtuosity of any sort, real stump-speech mastery comes only with frequent practice and application.

As suggested in the previous chapter, if this stump-speech exercise is to be part of a three-day academy it should take place on day one. Then, as an invigorating way to kick-start days two and three, team members can pair up in new combinations and further hone their stump-speech skills, gaining fresh feedback from different partners. Note that because the preparatory steps that led to creating personalized crib sheets do not need to be repeated in subsequent iterations of the exercise, the entire three-speech format can be completed in less than an hour; the instant-replays element is optional. Many of my client organizations like to reward those who, through nomination or volunteerism, come to the front of the room to deliver an instant replay. At the conclusion of the day three exercise, they are presented with an unexpected token of recognition of some kind, such as a gift certificate for the hotel gift shop where the academy is being held. It makes the whole exercise that much more fun for all involved.

To keep things lively, team members should be advised at the close of the exercise on day two that crib sheets aren't permitted on day three; thus, as homework, they should commit crib-sheet content to memory. Back in the workplace, it's difficult for these messages to be perceived as truly heartfelt when they are simply being read to their audience. The members of the audience might be tempted to suggest, "If it's all written out, why not just fax the darn thing to me? I'll read it later—if and when I get a chance."

Proficient communicators also resist the temptation to continually reinvent their message to keep it from becoming stale to themselves. Like successful pop musicians, who are expected to keep performing their big hit of 1975 exactly the same way for a quarter of a century, once ambassadors of change have settled on the basic content of their stump speeches they should lock it in and stick with it. An occasional refinement here, the odd tweak there, is fine; but by and large it should be the same core message every time. The old maxim still holds true: When you have delivered the same basic message so often that you're convinced your listeners are rolling their eyes and moaning, "Oh no, not this one again," they're probably really only hearing it for the first time.

Even if the stump-speech exercise is not part of an academy, opportunities for members of the leadership team to practice their delivery on one another should be engineered into the agendas of regular senior-level meetings of any sort. This basic skill is simply too vital to overlook; it is virtually impossible to be an effective leader without it.

As an ambassador of change, once you've got the skill, use it! Don't patiently wait for those big trusting eyes to approach you; go find them yourself. Don't wait for stump-speech opportunities to arise; create them. Every time discussion turns to any element of change, bingo: "Customers this, competition that, hate these new procedures, can't find my supplies since things got moved around, are there going to be layoffs, why is this form so complicated, nobody ever tells anybody anything around here, would somebody please get that phone, are the rumors true," and so on and so on, day in and day out. There is no shortage of opportunities for the ambassador to flex those stumping muscles.

RESISTERS AND CONDUCTORS

What are ambassadors of change to do when confronted with open resistance? What if cynicism and bitterness have reached the point where some employees openly cross their arms, dig in their heels, and proclaim, "Hell no, we won't go!"?

Several rules of thumb apply to dealing with resistance. First, recognize that resisters usually constitute a minority. It's a mistake to direct 80 percent of your ambassadorship efforts toward 20 percent of the population. Focus on helping the receptive critical mass within the organization to accept and support the initiative, and to keep it moving forward. Give vocal resisters a generous second and even third opportunity to get on board, and then make it clear that you're prepared to move on. Sooner or later, they'll have to decide to join you or let the organization pursue its destiny without them.

Second, resistance is almost always a plea for reassurance. Employees who express emphatic resistance usually do not pose a grave threat to the success of a change initiative. Rather, in voicing their resistance aloud—even if in anger—these people are usually telling their leaders, "I don't believe, as you do, that this is the right course of action for us. I would like to believe it, but you haven't yet convinced me. Try again." In expressing resistance aloud, the resister is inviting dialogue. It may be noisy, challenging, even at times offensive, but at least the communication channels remain open; the potential for conversion remains alive. The louder the resistance, the greater the fear of change the resister is expressing. A skillful ambassador of change knows how to give the required reassurance.

The third rule of thumb is that not those howling in protest but rather those who are *apathetic* place the organization's vision of success in greatest jeopardy. I mean those who publicly nod in bland, disinterested agreement but privately have no intention of supporting the change in any way. Their public posture is bored: "Yes, yes, no big deal, we've seen this sort of thing before, we'll see it again, nothing to get too worked up about (yawn) . . . " In private, though, they attempt to discredit, or even sabotage, the whole initiative. Their comparative silence discourages dialogue. They have no wish to be persuaded into adopting a different view; they desire only to sit things out until this latest change effort fizzles and is forgotten—and perhaps even to help it fizzle. .

It is up to the ambassador of change to draw these people into the very dialogue they hope to avoid: "How about you, Bernie? Haven't heard too much from you about all this. What do you think about the whole thing?" More importantly, the ambassador of change must coax commitment and support out of those who hide behind a mask of apathy—preferably before peer-level witnesses: "I'm glad you don't foresee any problems with any of this, Bernie. Does this mean I can count on you to be completely behind this whole thing along with the rest of us? We really can't do it without your full support. Can we count on you as one of our champions for this thing?" If Bernie allows himself to be labeled a champion or equivalent, it's much more difficult later for his apathy to go unnoticed. If he resists commitment, then the skillful ambassador of change has upgraded Bernie to resister status, and communication remains open. Sabotage becomes foolhardy for Bernie, since his acknowledgment of resistance would make him a prime suspect. Soon enough, Bernie finds himself confronting a shape-up-or-ship-out dilemma.

The final, encouraging rule of thumb is that converted resisters often make excellent advocates. Although it can be wasteful to expend a great deal of effort in converting resisters, those you do convert will often bring the same noisy intensity they used in resisting to their support of you. Every smoker knows there's no one quite as tiresome as a reformed ex-smoker. The same assertiveness that produces strident resistance can also generate boundless enthusiasm for the very cause that originally inspired the resistance.

A corporate trainer at Amdahl in Toronto encountered hostility and vocal resistance during a quality improvement course. As the "everyone has an equally important role to play" issue was raised, a feisty superintendent named Hugh objected. "Now hold on! We build high-tech digital data communications equipment in this factory. But all I do is push a broom around and replace burned-out lights and so on. Please, do not insult me by trying to suggest that what I do is as important as what the head of engineering does around here, or I'm going to throw up."

The trainer smiled and announced coffee break. During the break, he visited the CEO in his office and requested permission to make an announcement in the training room. Mr. Peabody granted the permission.

When the training session resumed, the trainer made his announcement. "As you know, some months ago this company, along with a number of our competitors, was invited to submit proposals for a huge contract, in the millions, with the North American Air Defense Command. Some of you may have heard that we made it to the short list; it was down to a choice between ourselves and two competitors. What you may not know is that the NORAD officials simply could not make up their minds. To help them make their selection, they decided to pay surprise visits to all three sites. Some of you may have seen them touring the place last week. Mr. Peabody is going to make the formal announce-ment to the whole company tomorrow, but he has given me permission to announce to you, now, that we won the contract."

Cheering and applause erupted in the training room.

"According to NORAD," the trainer went on, "the engineering excellence of our products was a big factor in their decision. But not the biggest factor. Our competitors' products were in fact judged to be essen-tially as good, if not in some respects marginally better. They said the main reason we got the contract was because our factory was the cleanest of the three. They said the floor was spotless, clean enough to eat off of. They said a company that keeps its factory that clean is clearly a company that looks after the details, like keeping dust and static electricity away from the components, which could affect their reliability. Hugh, I'd hate to be responsible for making you throw up, but I'm afraid what you do *is* as important as what engineering, or anybody else, does around here. It's your broom-pushing, as much as anything else, that got us that contract."

The others in the training room stood and gave Hugh an ova-tion. From that day forward, Hugh became Amdahl's drum-beating, flag-carrying quality-improvement champion, and he remained so until he left the organization.

(Epilogue: several years later, the trainer was surprised to receive a call from an executive at Motorola, offering him a plum position in their training organization. How, the trainer asked, did the executive even know of his existence? It seems a relatively new Motorola employee named Hugh had frequently sung the trainer's praises. The trainer accepted the offer. His tour of duty at Motorola paved the way for work with a major consulting firm and an international career as a consultant, speaker, and author—writing this book, among other projects. Will the person giving you the most flak in your communication sessions turn out to be one of *your* biggest allies?)

ALL ROADS LEAD TO THE VISION

An ant walking across a huge billboard photo of a popular celebrity doesn't recognize the image. The billboard is just too big, and the ant is just too close. An ambassador of change, too, must recognize that employees are usually too close to the action to be able to see the big picture on their own. To them, the daily landscape of the workplace is just a confused jumble of tasks and hectic activities.

Now someone lifts the ant off the billboard, carries it some distance away, and says, "Look, see whose face you were walking across? See the left eye? You were right there, just a little southwest of the eyebrow." The ant has a whole different appreciation of its whereabouts and the nature of its journey. Put back in the same spot on the billboard and allowed to continue along its way, the ant might even, on its own, conclude that this darker jumble of dots must be the hairline at the left temple, because there's a vast lighter-colored area to the south that would correspond to the ear. . . . Suddenly the journey becomes much more interesting.

Before long, the dots once again become a confusing and meaningless jumble. For the journey to remain interesting, the ant needs regular you-are-here updates. It needs frequent views of the whole billboard, with its present location clearly indicated.

This is one of the basic roles of the leader as ambassador of change: to provide frequent views of the big picture (the vision) and indicate to employees their progress towards it. Whether through formal communication efforts, informal stump speeches, or casual dialogue; whether through highly publicized strategic-level decisions or through the thousands of choices made and behaviors exhibited every day, the effective leader ties everything to the vision. Not just in his or her own mind; the link is spelled out, every time:

- "Absolutely everything going on in this place, in some way, helps bring us closer to the vision, and here's how. And if there is something that's not connected, then perhaps we'd better question whether we should be doing it at all."

- "Here's how the change in office layout helps us achieve our vision."

- "Here's how that new policy, the new training course, even the recent layoffs are going to help bring the vision closer."

The chaotic jumble of seemingly unrelated daily problems and pressures must be transformed into meaningful parts of a larger, worthwhile whole.

In a modern retelling of an ancient story, a VIP visiting the NASA complex during the Apollo program asks a custodial worker in dirty coveralls, "What do you do here?" The worker answers, "I'm helping to put a man on the moon, Sir." This particular ant knows precisely where he is on the big billboard.

In building a formal plan for achieving a vision of success, it's appropriate for members of the leadership team to begin by considering what they can do to help the rest of the organization better understand and embrace the whole effort. What shall we do to demonstrate our personal determination to succeed? How do we create opportunities to deliver our stump speeches? How do we help employees see the big picture, and where they fit in? How do we convey our personal enthusiasm and optimism? How do we make our support for the effort dramatically visible? In short, how do we become ambassadors of change? Questions like these should be in the back of leaders' minds as they work through finding their answer(s) to the first of the 8 Big Questions.

BIG QUESTION 1 PLANNING EXERCISE

For larger leadership teams (fifteen or more members), plan building can be somewhat cumbersome if the team works as a single, large workgroup. Breaking the team into smaller subgroups assures greater personal involvement for each member of the team and usually leads to higher levels of creativity. As a general guideline, if there are more than fifteen members on the leadership team, it should be broken into two separate subgroups; if more than twenty-five, three groups. Teams of fifteen members or fewer can usually work effectively as a single group, though splitting into two subgroups remains an option. Membership in the subgroups is entirely arbitrary; it can be determined by seniority, alphabetical order, the luck of the draw, or personal choice. It's useful for each workgroup to have a designated facilitator, who, while participating, also keeps an eye on the clock and helps get derailed explorations back on track.

With two or more groups engaged in concurrent plan building, provisions need to be made for consolidating the output from all groups into the final plan. Therefore at the conclusion of each round of phase-three activity planning, each group makes a presentation to the other(s), summarizing and clarifying its planned activities; the entire team then determines whether all the planned activities should go into the plan as they are, or whether there is sufficient similarity and overlap to warrant consolidating elements of two activities into a single item for the plan. The tradeoff: multiple groups produce richer output, but concluding each round of brainstorming takes considerably more time. The proposed agenda for a three-day academy, outlined in the Appendix, is predicated on a single group brainstorming together; multiple groups would almost certainly expand the agenda to four full days.

· ·

PHASE ONE: STATUS-QUO QUESTIONS

For no more than ten minutes and without any discussion or analysis, list on a flipchart as many answers as you can think of to these two questions (approximately five minutes per question):

1 Strengths: What do we currently do well as ambassadors of change?

2 Weaknesses: What prevents us from being more effective as ambassadors of change?

The first question really asks: How do we presently communicate our strategic objective(s)? How do we demonstrate our determination to make the organization more successful? How do we help reduce resistance to change? What do we currently do to visibly support our mission, vision, and values?

The second question asks: What impediments make it difficult for us to help the organization accept a specific change (or change in general)? What factors get in the way? What obstacles complicate our efforts?

PHASE TWO: BRAINSTORMING QUESTIONS

For no more than fifteen minutes, review the list of strengths and weaknesses created in phase one, and for each, without evaluation or discussion, list on a flipchart as many ideas as you can think of to answer these two questions (approximately seven minutes per question):

1 What can be done to amplify our strengths?

2 What can be done to overcome our weaknesses?

For each strength listed, the question becomes, If we had unlimited resources, time, and authority, what could we do to derive even more benefit from this? How could we make this even more effective? What would it take to give this even more impact?

For each weakness: If we had no constraints whatsoever, how could we eliminate this problem? What could we do to get around this obstacle? How might we turn this weakness into a strength?

PHASE THREE: ACTIVITY-PLANNING QUESTIONS

Spend no more than a minute or two selecting one idea that seems a suitable candidate for inclusion in the plan from the list generated in phase two. For this one idea, take no more than twenty minutes to answer all of the following questions on a flipchart. (It's prudent to allow five full minutes at the end for the final question.)

▶ What exactly will be done? (Distinguish between objectives and activities, and concentrate on the latter. The response to this question should begin with a verb, such as *create, establish, communicate*, etc.)

▶ How will it be done? (If it is not immediately obvious, describe in broad terms how this activity will be implemented. Make note here of any implementation details or issues that remain to be resolved.)

▶ Who will do it? (Use actual names where possible.)

▶ Who will ensure that it gets done? (In most cases, the person who will be held accountable should be a member of the leadership team.)

▶ When will it begin, or be completed? (Specify an actual date.)

▶ How will success be measured? (By what means will we confirm that this particular activity has truly helped make us better ambassadors of change? Has helped reduce anxiety levels within the organization? Has improved the general understanding of our mission, vision, and values, or of the reasons behind the changes being introduced?)

The three phases of the planning exercise typically generate a considerable number of flipcharts bearing a lot of similar-looking entries. It's important at the conclusion of each three-phase round that those flipcharts bearing content destined for inclusion in the final plan be separated from the rest and put safely aside for preservation. Even if the team ultimately decides to preserve all of the flipcharts for future reference (as some organizations like to do), it is still vital to separate *content* charts from the others.

Before proceeding to any more plan building, collect the flipcharts bearing the responses to the phase-three activity-planning questions. Using a marker of a different color than already appears on the charts, "brand" them by inscribing *Big Question Number 1 (BQ1)* prominently on each sheet, wherever space permits; this indicates to the creator(s) of the final planning document the section to which this activity should be assigned. The answer to the what question thus becomes the descriptive heading for this particular activity, the first entry in the section of the plan devoted to the first big question, "How will we become ambassadors of change?"

A second category of flipchart that needs to be separated from the rest and preserved is that from phase one which bears the list of strengths. This chart, too, needs to have *BQ1* inscribed upon it. During the creation of the planning document, it may be appropriate to include in the section on the first big question certain items from this list of strengths, under the heading "Things We Will Continue to Do."

Once the content flipcharts have been separated from the rest, branded, and put safely aside for preservation, the team can elect to do one of the following:

▶ Take a break.

or

▶ Select another item from the existing brainstormed list of ideas for the first big question generated in phase two, and subject it to the phase-three activity-planning questions, for no more than twenty minutes.

or

▶ Proceed to the second big question, and begin by answering the phase-one status-quo questions, for ten minutes or less.

••

There is no hard-and-fast rule for determining when a given team has planned enough activity under one big question and is ready to proceed to the next. Each team must assess its own current performance relative to each of the big questions and decide how urgently they need to take action. In most cases, the team can tell when the proposed level of new activity feels about right. When in doubt, however, it's wise to err on the side of plenty; it's easier to omit a fully planned-out activity from the final plan than it is to reconvene the entire team after the fact for a remedial planning session.

Once the first big question has been addressed to the team's satisfaction, it's time to begin thinking about ways to formally spread the word internally.

How Will We Spread the Word Internally?

T he word *culture* crops up from time to time in our discussion around organizational change. Most people seem to understand what the basic concept of "corporate culture" means, even if they may have some difficulty explaining it to someone who does not.

A CULTURAL GREEN THUMB

There can be certain distinct cultural elements associated with various nations of the world (England versus America, for example). Some would argue the same with various cities within each nation (San Francisco versus New York), even—some might insist—with various sections within each city (Manhattan versus the Bronx), and maybe even with various neighborhoods within each section (and, if we really wanted to push it, with various houses within each neighborhood). And so does every organization possess its own unique cultural flavor.

For the ambassador of change, an organization's culture can be thought of as resembling a garden. It is not some intangible entity that simply exists by happenstance, an unchanging state of affairs that those within the organization are pretty much stuck with forever. Rather, an organization can by conscious design be cultivated, transplanted, trimmed, expanded, controlled, and generally groomed in any number of ways. Of course, as with a garden, it can also be neglected and allowed to grow wild on its own. In its wild state, it may produce flowers, but more often it develops into an inhospitable tangle of scrub, thorns, and poisonous weeds.

71

Resistance to change is fundamentally a cultural manifestation (as is its opposite, receptivity to change). Which would you expect to encounter in businesses that consistently neglect the cultural aspects of their organizational life?

A set of shared core values goes a long way toward shaping and defining a corporate culture. By emphasizing what the organization collectively believes in and considers important, values help spell out what is and isn't acceptable in terms of behavior; this gives the culture some clear boundaries. Beyond core values, many other elements bear on the process of grooming an organization's culture. In effect, all of the issues reflected in the 8 Big Questions have a part to play.

Examples of elements that play a particularly significant role in shaping corporate culture are:

- Rewards, recognition, and celebration that are (or aren't) used to acknowledge employees' contributions; we explore this in our discussion of the eighth big question

- The degree to which employees are empowered and encouraged to participate in making decisions that affect customers (the sixth big question) or their own work (the fifth big question)

- How information is shared—the kinds of efforts the organization makes to help employees feel they're being kept in the know, rather than in the dark; this is the central issue of big question number two, on which this chapter focuses

As mentioned earlier, the ambassador of change needs to develop the ability to operate with one foot in the present and one in the future. A similar and parallel faculty worth developing is the ability to think tactically and strategically at the same time. The skilled gardener can devote a great deal of attention to the unique needs of a specific plant in one corner of the garden, while at the same time never losing sight of the garden's overall structure and requirements. While focusing on tactical issues related to one of the 8 Big Questions in particular, so too the ambassador of change must not lose sight of the strategic objectives behind the whole of the change effort. The issue in the second big question, at ground level, is dissemination of information; simultaneously, at fifty thousand feet, the issue is cultivation of a more supportive, less cynical cultural climate within the organization. If the two

purposes are pursued in tandem, each can contribute to the success of
the other.

SHOWCASING MISSION, VISION, AND VALUES

For organizations undertaking any sort of transformational change initiative, the first big selling job the leadership team faces, from an internal communications standpoint, involves sharing with the entire
employee population the specific nature of the change effort they are
being asked to help implement. The previous chapter prepares members
of the leadership team to address some general aspects of this question in
an informal stump-speech format; but of course it is also necessary to present to the organization as a whole, in a more formal presentation setting, a detailed overview of the strategy for success.

No single forum or agenda is the only right one for such a presentation. Considerations such as visual material (whether to use slides,
transparencies, or video), room layout, choosing one huge all-hands event
versus a traveling "road show"—these and many more factors need to be
addressed and resolved by the leadership team well in advance, based on
a host of variables unique to each organization. There are, however, some
useful general guidelines and recommendations.

The fundamental objective should be to ensure that at the end of
the event(s) the whole organization understands:

- The meaning of the core values and their implications in
  terms of influencing behavior and decision making at all levels

- The key strategic objectives that form the basis of the organization's mission, and why these objectives are so important

- How the vision represents in shorthand the successful realization of the mission

A great deal of creativity can be (should be!) brought to bear on
this event to make it fun, exciting, and dramatic for all present. At its
conclusion, there should be no doubt in the minds of those in attendance
that they have just witnessed an important milestone in the history of
their organization. Some businesses add weight to such an event by
bringing in a prominent guest speaker to validate that the change effort
being introduced is appropriate. Companies invest in banners, mugs,

tote bags, or other articles upon which the corporate vision is inscribed, distributing them with much fanfare before, during, or at the conclusion of the event.

A particularly successful occasion of this sort was staged by the Beefeater restaurant chain for its senior management team. The two-day event was billed as a strategic workshop, and the facilitators were none other than the five members of the board of directors, who took turns personally delivering virtually all of the workshop content. (Getting them to agree to this was a tough sell, according to change agent Chris Galtress; but the impact was tremendous.)

However it is done, a sense of electricity should be generated. The event is a howling success if a critical mass of the employee population comes away feeling that the members of the leadership team have been doing their job, that they've come up with something attractive in terms of a direction for the organization, and that everyone has a role to play in making it happen—and in celebrating the triumph when it is achieved.

Of course, in the real world not every worthwhile endeavor turns out to be a howling success. In many organizations, a significant level of cynicism has built up over the years. The fact that cynicism exists should not dissuade the leadership team from enthusiastically outlining their strategy for success (though perhaps downplaying the fanfare element slightly). But as part of the ongoing effort to transform the organization, some conscious effort must be made to bring cynicism down to manageable levels. This is where the second big question comes in.

ROOTING OUT CYNICISM

What mysterious process transforms idealistic new employees, who initially believe in the organization and what it stands for, into bitter cynics who seem always to suspect the worst? Why do so many work so hard to keep the rumor mill so active with so much pessimistic nonsense? Why must every attempt to improve things be greeted with the same old sneers and snorts of derision from the back of the room?

At the root of most organizational cynicism is the perception among employees that every day vital information is deliberately (and perhaps even maliciously) being withheld from them. Weighty decisions are being made behind closed doors, their fate is being decided, and none of it reaches them until a bombshell explodes in their faces. But even when employees are deluged with memos and reports and documents of every kind, there is often a sense that this is only the sanitized stuff; the real low-down is known by only the select few, and everyone else can only guess . . . and fear the worst.

This perception becomes especially prevalent when the scent of change is in the air. As with predators in the wild whose appetite is awakened by the smell of blood carried on the wind, employees' appetite for information becomes ravenous when the winds of change begin to swirl around them.

Ambassadors of change know that when it comes to cynicism and resistance, information is the best cure. Hand-in-hand with any organizational change effort, serious thought must be given to how the relevant information can best be communicated to the whole organization, day in and day out. In this regard, there is much to be learned from those who move information every day for a living.

FOREGROUND NEWS VERSUS BACKGROUND OVERVIEWS

Highlights from this week's TV listings:

Tuesday

7 **8:00—MOUNT PUSHKAVELL: THE AFTERMATH**
Coverage of the continuing cleanup and rescue efforts from the deadly volcano that erupted last week in Uruguay. (Live and recorded, via satellite)

7 **9:00—SCIENCE WORLD: WHEN MOTHER NATURE BLOWS HER TOP**
How volcanoes are formed, and efforts scientists are making to develop better ways of predicting eruptions. (60 min.)

Wednesday

2 **9:00—REMEMBERING JORGENSEN**
Friends, family members, and fellow athletes retrace the Olympic runner's career and speculate on the motives behind his recent murder at the hands of Scabbay Bayosch terrorists. "His only crime," says his

older brother, "was that he wanted to run faster than everybody else and be the first to cross the finish line. Is that so wrong?" (60 min.)

4 **8:30—REIGN OF TERROR: THE SCABBAY BAYOSCH**
Until recently, few had heard of the violent coterie of international terrorists. This documentary traces the group's origins and growth and chronicles its attempts in recent years to thwart the "personal success movement" in Western society by targeting for elimination anyone in the public eye who discloses a "vision of success." New evidence suggests that one of the group's early victims was Lennie Stempkie, founder of Buster Burgers, who went on record as "wanting to sell more hamburgers than any other burger chain." (60 min.)

Thursday

5 **3:00—TBN NEWS SPECIAL: THE END OF INCOME TAX**
Live coverage of the president's federal budget review, in which the abolishment of personal income tax will be formalized. (Live, 90 min.)

9 **10:30—THE "TEMPORARY" TAX**
Animation and still photos trace the troubled eighty-five-year history of what humorist Alphonse Bishop calls "the most despised institution in America, after those hot-air hand-drying machines": income tax. (30 min.)

Most information-based television broadcasts (as well as magazine articles, newspaper stories, etc.) typically fall into two broad categories: (1) those that report on breaking news, hot topics of the day, issues of the here and now; and (2) those that supply a documentary perspective, or historical background, or an analytical overview—that is, a more general type of educational information that heightens the audience's appreciation of a specific issue or topic in the headlines.

This two-pronged approach to disseminating information serves as a useful model for ambassadors of change. Once the winds of change begin kicking up some dust, people throughout the organization find themselves hungering for both types of information: "Tell me right now as much as you know about what's going on and how it's going to affect me (and continue to update me right away as soon as you know more)" and "Help me understand where all this is coming from, and why it's happening, and how it may or may not be similar to what's happening elsewhere, and what effect it had on others who have been through it, and what we can reasonably hope the final outcome will be; in short, help me become more sophisticated in my grasp of this whole complex issue."

Thus, if your organization engages in a total quality management initiative, the most effective strategy to spread the word internally is to apprise employees of progress, achievements, obstacles, solutions, and so on (that is, *news*), along with exposure to videos about the power of TQM to create competitive advantage, access to articles or books that identify TQM trends in the marketplace, guest speakers who share case studies in TQM improvement, and so on (that is, *overviews*). Each half of this communication equation behaves like constituent metals making up an alloy: the tensile strength of the combination is significantly greater than the purely numerical sum of the strength of the two individual metals.

In planning for spreading the word internally, therefore, it is advisable to keep the news-overviews distinction in mind, and to consider activities that address both.

EXORCISING DEMONS

A rumor is nature's way of filling the void created by the (real or perceived) absence of information. The rumor mill creates in employees' imaginations a parallel world in which dark fears take on form and substance, like evil specters flitting menacingly in the shadows.

The ambassador of change knows how to exorcise these demons. Professor Van Helsing makes a cross from two candlesticks and holds it at arm's length to ward off Dracula or other vampires. A wooden stake through the heart usually finishes off the vampire for good. What is the ambassador of change to use to similarly dispose of organizational fear-demons (again, usually for good)? The answer: Give the demons a name, and *speak their name out loud*.

> " . . . I'm sure many of you are concerned about whether the zmove to a team-based structure will jeopardize your jobs; I want to begin by stating categorically that there is no. . . . "

" . . . Some of you may be wondering whether the new pay
system might lead to possible cuts in pay; allow me to reassure you right now that there will be absolutely no. . . . "

" . . . You may be thinking, 'Yes, but does changing our
business hours mean we're now going to be expected to
work more weekends?' The answer is definitely not. In fact,
some of you may even. . . . "

" . . . For those of you worried about this, let me just say. . . . "

" . . . In case anyone is concerned about that, allow me
to. . . . "

As with vampires, when the fear-demons are brought out into
the sunlight of open discussion, they (usually) wither into dust and perish for good. It is inherently reassuring when those who hold some measure of control over our destinies articulate the precise concern we have
and waste no time putting that particular concern to rest. Conversely, it
is especially unsettling to be waiting on the edge of our seats for the "big
one" to be addressed, and to have the discussion come to an end without
any mention or acknowledgment whatsoever of what for us constitutes
the biggest, most obvious concern.

Now, allow me to speak aloud the name of a possible fear-demon
of yours. "Yes," you may be thinking, "but what if the employees' fears
are justified? What if some jobs *will* be made redundant? What if there
will be a need to work more weekends, or take a cut in pay? What if
employees are anticipating the very hardship that is actually about to
befall them?"

There are two separate issues at play here, and they are easier to
deal with if kept separate. The first involves employees' anticipating bad
news before it is officially disclosed to them. The second acknowledges
that it is occasionally necessary to disclose bad news to employees. Let's
consider these one at a time.

WHEN BAD NEWS IS NO SURPRISE

The fear-of-change demons travel to and fro within the organization
along a conduit known as the grapevine, and they do so at great speed.
At tremendous speed.

For employees to anticipate and dread a particular piece of bad
news before it has been announced, something must happen beforehand to

inspire that particular fear. It is during this interval between the something that allows them to anticipate the bad news and the official word confirming it that the demons roam the grapevine and do all their damage.

"The problem with corporate newsletters," points out Pamela Miller, vice-president of strategic planning at Blue Cross Blue Shield of New Jersey, "is that usually by the time they come out, the so-called news is old." Lynda Zavitz, manager of in-flight strategic planning for Canadian Airlines International, agrees. "When the airline was in crisis," she says, "employees were getting more and better information about what was going on from the daily newspaper than they were from the management in their own company." It meant, of course, that management then had no opportunity to soften the blow when the news was bad.

To help accelerate the flow of news internally, Newark-based Blue Cross Blue Shield introduced "BTV": ceiling-mounted television monitors positioned near elevators on all floors. "People stand at the elevators for between five and seven seconds," Miller explains, "so we time key messages which appear on the screen so that they can be read completely in five seconds." Canadian Airlines established an 800 line on which anxious workers from around the world could record questions or comments. Recorded responses to important questions were accessible at the same number the next day. Frequently asked questions were reproduced in print in a daily news brief distributed via computer systems and e-mail to the entire management population. Significant news was attached to the weather information or passenger lists that flight crews are required to pull up prior to departures. In addition, a cascading phone call system was instituted in which the senior group received a news briefing from the president; they then briefed the directors at the level below them, who briefed the managers below them, who briefed their frontline employees. The entire cascade cycle was designed to take place within a single day.

Through these and other means, many organizations have put their rumor mills virtually out of business. "Employees actually began asking us directly for information," says Zavitz. "It indicated how well we had regained their sense of trust." In effect, when conditions are right, workers collaborate with leaders to help stamp out rumors and misinformation.

The ambassador of change looks for ways to eliminate altogether the interval between any event likely to precipitate fearful speculation and the official announcement that confirms it. That is, with every element of change, good or bad, an effort is made to anticipate every conceivable concern to which it might give rise, justified or not, and to address them by name. Even though rumors may travel along the grapevine at warp speed, they cannot outrace simultaneity.

Dispose of all the groundless fears you can think of at the front end; then, if it later becomes necessary to disclose some bad news, it really is news to your audience. Delivering a shocking blow is never very gratifying, but at least if the shock comes from you it means you retain some ability to control and minimize its effects. If the grapevine beats you to it, all you can do is mop up the mess left by the full destructive force of confirmation.

BEING THE BEARER OF BAD TIDINGS

A second and separate internal communication issue appears in times of crisis. How best to spread the word internally in announcing unpopular decisions or disheartening developments? This is a topic worthy of an entire book itself. Let's touch on it briefly here, with some general guidelines:

■ *Acknowledge how bad the news truly is.* Do not attempt to downplay or sugarcoat the situation; this merely alienates the "victims" and erodes credibility with everyone else. ("Yeah, I know he said everything is fine, but that's what he said last time too, and heads rolled, remember?") To the contrary, indicate your appreciation of the full magnitude of the blow this represents for those directly affected.

■ *Clarify the lack of alternative options.* Enumerate in detail all the other courses of action that have been considered, and spell out the compelling reasons for which each ultimately was rejected. The audience needs reassurance that this step is not taken lightly but rather is a measure of last resort once all other alternatives have been fully explored and exhausted.

■ *Avoid searching for a scapegoat.* Among those who see themselves as victims, some may be eager to know who deserves to be "blamed" for this sorry state of affairs. Avoid having a mob take to the parking lot with torches and snarling dogs. Resist attempts to assign blame for the situation, and instead simply acknowledge that the situation exists and must be dealt with.

■ *Outline what is being done to help.* The more elaborate the organization's plans to ease the discomfort of those directly affected, the greater the level of trust engendered in everyone else. Spend the bulk of your presentation time outlining in detail what the organization is prepared to do to make things easier for everyone involved.

When obliged to be the bearer of bad news, the ambassador of change endeavors to strike a delicate balance. On the one hand, a setback must not be allowed to seriously damage the general confidence and optimism of the organization as a whole. At the same time, it is equally inappropriate to allow those most affected to conclude that recovery is to be achieved at their expense, that the subsequent triumphant march to glory for the rest of the organization will be over a road paved with their broken bones. In other words, the announcement of bleak news is not an ideal forum for a huge, splashy demonstration of enthusiastic commitment to the vision of future success. Rather, the announcement must strive to instill in all listeners a calm, sober sense that things are under control, and that despite the setback the danger is now past and overall the organization remains sound and in good hands.

BEING THE BEARER OF GOOD TIDINGS

A far more pleasant challenge for ambassadors of change is to find ways to spread information of a cheerier sort throughout the organization.

Interestingly, many leaders make the costly mistake of failing to treat good news with the same level of urgency afforded to bad. When employees feel they're being kept in the dark, this should not be taken to mean that they sense only grim information is being withheld; it means they feel deprived of information, period. If the grapevine carries a rumor that an influential customer wrote a very laudatory letter to the head of the division, for example, yet no official acknowledgment of the fact is forthcoming, the fear-demons set to work without delay: "Why weren't we told about the complimentary letter? What's the head of the division trying to hide? Are they afraid we'll all ask for raises or something? Is it because they're planning to cut our wages? Will everybody get an equal pay cut, or are some of us going to be singled out for more? What can we do now, to protect ourselves?"

The same leadership team that sees without question the need to disrupt normal operations and quickly pull everyone together to disclose a significant piece of bad news before it gets into the grapevine seldom feels an equal need to quickly call the troops together to disclose a big piece of *good* news. Why is this?

When my friend Art McNeil was head of his own consulting firm, he mounted a large nautical-style bell on the wall near the reception area. Any time he, or an account manager, or the receptionist, or anyone closed a sale or received a positive letter or phone call—or had good news of any kind to report—they were encouraged to ring the bell loudly and without delay. At the sound of the bell everyone throughout the office stopped whatever they were doing and approached to hear and applaud the news. That bell did a far better job of warding off fear-demons than all of Van Helsing's candlesticks and garlic cloves and mirrors put together.

The function of good news is to foster optimism. A single success story, an isolated achievement, cannot alone be expected to engender a lasting sense of positive anticipation. But a steady diet of encouraging news tends to have a cumulative effect. Each successive triumph contributes to making the final triumph (that is, realization of the vision) seem all the more attainable, if not downright inevitable. If for the ambassador of change the objective is to help the rest of the organization anticipate success, good news is the most powerful tool in the entire bag of tricks. It should be doled out whenever possible, with appropriate hoopla.

Observe how, on the front page of the daily newspaper, merely enlarging the size of the headline typography makes the story itself seem more important. The tendency within organizations is always to downplay good news and thus make it seem much less important than bad; counteract this by delivering good news with even more urgency and fanfare than bad news typically receives.

What if there's no news at all to report? The old adage that no news is good news simply does not hold true in the information age. So great is the appetite for information that even the absence of news must be reported. A headline disclosing "Peace Talks Deadlocked for Third Consecutive Day," or a doctor's announcement to concerned relatives that an accident victim's condition "remains stable," is imparting crucial new information. "The situation is being carefully monitored on your behalf, and there has been no change since the previous report": Communications of this sort produce a vastly different result than that generated by dead silence. If there truly were no news to report, this in itself would qualify as big news: "First Eventless Day in History—Scientists Baffled."

There's really no such thing as no news. In our information-hungry organizations, "no news" almost always translates into bad news, grapevine-wise. "Keep me advised of what's happening," the organization cries out, "including especially the good things; and if nothing at all is happening, I need to be advised of that, too!"

CREATING CORPORATE FOLKLORE

As we've already seen, there is a certain amount of automatic redundancy and overlap built into the 8 Big Questions. An example is the opportunity to tie spreading the word internally (big question number two) to the notion of celebrating successes (the eighth big question).

Once again borrowing from the journalistic tradition, what many organizations are learning to do effectively is to publicize not only achievements but also *achievers*. Beyond reporting news, they allow the newsmakers to tell their story in their own words. Through profiles or interviews with employees involved in the success story, they minimize rumors by spreading information, and they cultivate optimism by reinforcing a sense of continuous progress. These organizations also reward those involved in the achievement by publicly acknowledging the significance of their contribution. They make the heroes famous and make them feel like champions.

The histories of great corporations are full of tall tales, the inspiring or heroic or touching or daunting exploits of the founder or some other notable, told and retold, and often embellished in the retelling, so that they pass into near-mythology. These stories become the folklore of the organization, a unifying cultural force that creates a proud feeling of shared history and a sense of belonging. The ambassador of change is ever watchful for opportunities to turn internal heroes into celebrities, thereby to add to the richness of the organization's folklore.

I know of at least one organization that routinely mails copies of its internal newsletter to the *children* of any employee featured in a newsletter story; a personalized note is attached, alerting the children: "Your daddy's picture appears on page 2. . . . " In this particular organization, the folklore is rife with stories of employees who, to their surprise, were met with a hero's welcome when they arrived home, because their picture was "in the paper." One custodial worker recounted how his children brought the "paper" to school for show-and-tell, and it was posted on the school bulletin board for a week. His achievement at work (a safety innovation) made his kids celebrities among their schoolmates! (A colleague confided that this particular worker had always assumed his children were somewhat ashamed of the janitorial work their father did; for months afterwards he cited this experience as the most personally rewarding in his career of thirty-plus years.)

Tie your success stories into your recognition efforts, and double the blow to the cynics and rumormongers.

BIG QUESTION 2 PLANNING EXERCISE

In planning to spread the word internally, ambassadors of change seek to improve (or establish) the mechanisms by which they provide regular news updates in hot-off-the-press fashion, while at the same time making useful background information available on a more relaxed, ongoing basis. It is this search for appropriate internal communication mechanisms that is at the heart of planning to spread the word internally.

•••

PHASE ONE: STATUS-QUO QUESTIONS

For no more than ten minutes and without any discussion or analysis, list on a flipchart as many answers as you can think of to these two questions (approximately five minutes per question):

1 Strengths: What do we currently do well to spread the word internally?

2 Weaknesses: What prevents us from more effectively spreading the word internally?

The first question really asks: What existing mechanisms do we presently have at our disposal for internal communication? What are examples of types of information that we presently do a pretty good job of communicating regularly? What have we done in special circumstances in the past to effectively get the word out in a hurry?

The second question asks: What impediments make it

difficult for us to keep everyone apprised of all that's going on? What factors get in the way? What obstacles complicate our efforts?

••

PHASE TWO: BRAINSTORMING QUESTIONS

For no more than fifteen minutes, review the list of strengths and weaknesses created in phase one, and for each, without evaluation or discussion, list on a flipchart as many ideas as you can think of to answer these two questions (approximately seven minutes per question):

1 What can be done to amplify our strengths?

2 What can be done to overcome our weaknesses?

For each strength listed, the question becomes, If we had unlimited resources, time, and authority, what could we do to derive even more benefit from this? How could we make this even more effective? What would it take to give this even more impact?

For each weakness: If we had no constraints whatsoever, how could we eliminate this problem? What could we do to get around this obstacle? How might we turn this weakness into a strength?

••

PHASE THREE: ACTIVITY-PLANNING QUESTIONS

Spend no more than a minute or two selecting one idea that seems a suitable candidate for inclusion in the plan from the list generated in phase two. For this one idea, take no more than twenty minutes to answer all of the following questions on a flipchart. (It's prudent to allow five full minutes at the end for the final question.)

▶What exactly will be done? (Distinguish between objectives and activities, and concentrate on the latter. The response to this question should begin with a verb, such as *create, establish, communicate*, etc.)

▶ How will it be done? (If it is not immediately obvious, describe in broad terms how this activity will be implemented. Make note here of any implementation details or issues that remain to be resolved.)

▶ Who will do it? (Use actual names where possible.)

▶ Who will ensure that it gets done? (In most cases, the person who will be held accountable should be a member of the leadership team.)

▶ When will it begin, or be completed? (Specify an actual date.)

▶ How will success be measured? (By what means will we confirm that this particular activity has truly helped us reduce or eliminate cynicism and anxiety? Has raised levels of optimism? Has helped dispel the impression that people are being kept in the dark?)

At the conclusion of each three-phase round of the planning exercise, those flipcharts bearing content destined for inclusion in the final plan must be separated from the rest and put safely aside for preservation.

Begin by collecting the flipcharts bearing the responses to the phase-three activity-planning questions. Using a marker of a different color than already appears on the charts, "brand" them by inscribing *Big Question Number 2 (BQ2)* prominently on each sheet, wherever space permits; this indicates to the creator(s) of the final planning document the section to which this activity should be assigned. The answer to the *what* question thus becomes the descriptive heading for this particular activity, the first entry in the section of the plan devoted to the second big question, "How will we spread the word internally?"

Next, isolate the flipchart from phase one that bears the list of strengths. This chart, too, needs to have *BQ2* inscribed upon it. During the creation of the planning document, it may be appropriate to include in the section on the second big question certain items from this list of strengths, under the heading "Things We Will Continue to Do."

Once the content flipcharts have been separated from the rest, branded, and put safely aside for preservation, the team can elect to do one of the following:

▶ Take a break.

or

▶ Select another item from the existing brainstormed list of ideas for the second big question generated in phase two, and subject it to the phase-three activity-planning questions, for no more than twenty minutes. Beyond establishing the means for ongoing, effective internal communication, the team may also want to devote some time to brainstorming ideas for how to specifically publicize their mission, vision, and values, or how (if at all) they might communicate highlights of the plan to the employee population at large.

or

▶ Proceed to the third big question, and begin by answering the phase-one status-quo questions, for ten minutes or less.

••

As before, there is no hard-and-fast rule for determining when a given team has planned enough activity under one big question and is ready to proceed to the next. The organization's performance relative to each of the big questions must be assessed case by case, and there may be considerable variation in terms of the level of attention appropriate to each. (As before, however, it's wise to err on the side of plenty; it's always easier to omit a fully planned-out activity from the final plan than to reconvene the entire team after the fact for a remedial planning session.)

Once the second big question has been addressed to the team's satisfaction, it's time to begin thinking about how to acquire and use customer data.

3

How Will We Acquire and Use Customer Data?

Define the word *real* in this sentence: "Real men don't ask for directions." If this sentiment had any "real" merit, then "real" airline pilots would avoid making radio contact with anyone to confirm their position. "Real" marine navigators would never ask questions to validate their bearing.

MIDCOURSE CORRECTIONS

In business, real ambassadors of change *constantly* ask for directions. They verify with their customers that they remain headed in the right direction, and they check with their employees to ensure that everything's under control. Particularly when their voyage of change leads them into unfamiliar territory, they confirm their position and validate their bearing at every opportunity.

It is almost frightening to find a leader at the wheel of an organization who not only doesn't solicit directions, but actually ignores them when they are volunteered. On a recent trip to the French West Indies, I spoke to the general manager of the resort hotel where I was staying. He complained it was difficult to attract significant numbers of American tourists to his resort. "I notice," I said to him, "you do not offer diet cola at your poolside bar. For American families, I would think that would be pretty important." "Oh, yes," he sighed with a smile, rolling his eyes, "we get asked for that all the time." He gets asked for it all the time? Hello . . . ? Anybody home?

Clearly, not everyone in a leadership position fully appreciates the power of customer feedback as a corporate navigational aid. It obviously helps the organization track its present course, but it also helps plot a new course.

Asking for directions while traveling along unfamiliar roadways allows us to confirm that we are still on such-and-such a road, and that the so-and-so turnoff is indeed just a few miles ahead. But we may also learn that taking the so-and-so turnoff would now be futile, since yesterday's flooding washed out one of the low bridges about sixty miles down the road, and repairs are not yet completed. The provider of this information might be able to recommend a detailed alternative route that means only a slight overall delay. On the other hand, if we do not happen upon this information, we might waste hours driving to the washed-out bridge and then all the way back. We can only learn of this situation by creating, for those in the know, an opportunity to tell us about it.

Acquiring and using customer data often works the same way. In many cases, the organization doesn't know what it doesn't know; it can't always anticipate the best possible questions to ask customers. But if opportunities for customers to provide feedback are frequent and varied, it's much more likely that valuable unanticipated information will come to light.

This was the case at Canadian Airlines International when a peculiar instance of customer feedback prompted a response that backfired badly. In a series of customer surveys, business-class passengers indicated a preference for healthier meal options on the longer flights. At great expense—incurred at a time when the company could not afford great expense—the airline proceeded to revise its catering processes, modify its galleys, and offer customers the healthier meals they had requested. To the horror of the in-flight services staff, the next wave of customer feedback was dismal. The customer satisfaction ratings for the new menu offerings plummeted to their lowest level in the airline's history. How was this possible?

The skeptics and cynics had a field day: "We told you it was folly to try and please customers! We told you they don't know what they want!" But the true believers clung to their convictions. Something had surely been overlooked. It was a clear-cut case of not knowing what they didn't know and therefore not knowing what to ask.

Fortunately, because this was an airline that constantly solicited customer feedback in a wide variety of ways (including sending reps right to passengers' homes to accompany them from their door to their destination, to observe the customer's entire travel experience firsthand), the answer to their question soon emerged, even if no one was too sure just what the question was. Something had been overlooked, after all.

It seems that because the printed menus made no mention of any change in the meal offerings, passengers observed that the traditional beef tenderloins had been unceremoniously replaced by alfalfa sprouts and assorted lawn mower shavings, and they were left to conclude that they were victims of some sort of cost-cutting exercise. Learning that the cost of their meal had been reduced, but not the cost of their ticket, led to resentment and the low satisfaction ratings.

The airline made no further revisions to the catering processes or to the galleys; everything was left exactly as it was. They simply had new menus printed up that bore a message such as "By popular request, we are now happy to offer the following healthier meal options. . . . " This simple change produced a startling result in the next influx of customer data. The very meals that had earned the airline its lowest-ever satisfaction ratings now brought in the highest food-related customer satisfaction ratings in the company's history, even though they had not been changed in any way! Only an organization that creates constant opportunities for customers to make themselves heard can learn that the presence of a seemingly insignificant little tag line on its printed menus makes all the difference in the world. The airline might otherwise have remained in the customer-satisfaction cellar and never known why. The airline might not even exist today.

It's really quite simple: Drivers who frequently ask for directions seldom get lost, and they waste less time going in the wrong direction.

A HIERARCHY OF HUNCHES

The next time you witness an effort by the leadership team to reach some sort of agreement on a strategic issue, disengage your attention from the content of the discussion for a moment or two, and consider the process by which the decision is (or is not) being made.

Note, for example, how frequently the phrase *I think* is used to preface an argument or recommendation. Various petitioners passionately extol this or that position on the issue because they *think* it's the best position to take. "Oh no, I don't agree with that," one says. "In fact, I think it's more a case of. . . . " Another listens for a while and then interrupts with, "Ah, I think you're wrong there. I think what we need to do instead is. . . . "

He thinks, she thinks, we think, they think. Discussions of this sort basically amount to a boardroom game entitled Let's Compare Hunches. The object of the game: Come up with the hunch that sounds most plausible. If your hunch is selected to serve as the basis for the final team decision, you win. (To increase the apparent plausibility of your hunch, try using phrases that are more emphatic than *I think*: "I'm absolutely convinced that. . . . " or "I truly believe there's no doubt whatsoever that. . . . ") Your prize if your hunch wins is status and prestige. ("There goes Richardson. He's the one who believes so strongly that two-piece frammels are going to be the wave of the future. It's because of him that we're gearing up to manufacture a two-piece version, while the rest of the industry moves toward a one-piece design.")

Of course, winning at Let's Compare Hunches is not simply a matter of most emphatically proclaiming righteous conviction. As a rule, hunches automatically assume greater plausibility the higher their point of origin within the organizational hierarchy. Almost inevitably, the CEO's hunches strike everyone as the most plausible-sounding of all. It can sometimes be a career-limiting move to challenge the CEO's pet hunch with a counterhunch, however emphatically presented. (Indeed, the best way to consistently win at Let's Compare Hunches is simply to become the CEO.)

I don't suggest that hunches don't have their place. Henry Ford clung steadfastly to his hunch that there would be a ready market for his horseless carriage. Walt Disney gambled his fortune and reputation on the hunch that filmgoers would buy tickets to see a feature-length cartoon movie; he gambled both again on his hunch that families would buy tickets to visit a new kind of clean, themed amusement park. Some of the greatest triumphs in the history of business enterprise were fueled by hunches that proved to be correct.

Alas, a great many business tragedies have also been the result of hunches that subsequently proved wrong. To act on a hunch is, plain and simple, to willingly take a gamble. ("There goes Richardson. He's the yo-yo that thought people were going to want a two-piece frammel. What a turkey.") The hunch-driven organization does not ask for directions; it plunges ahead on blind faith. It assumes it is moving in the right direction and can do no more than hope that this assumption ultimately turns out to be true.

A certain well-known international package-delivery firm began to lose market share some years ago. This was a company that had built its reputation on providing next-day delivery virtually anywhere in the world. As competitors began to siphon away more and more customers, the leaders of the organization compared hunches about possible causes and remedies. A key hunch that emerged was that perhaps customers no longer considered next-day delivery fast enough; perhaps same-day delivery was going to be the big differentiator that would put them back on top. This hunch had a beautiful aura of plausibility about it.

A great deal of time, manpower, and expense was invested in developing systems to permit same-day delivery to most destinations. But even after the systems were up and running, the company's customer base continued to shrink. It was not until the problem was nearing calamitous proportions that someone suggested asking the droves of defecting customers just what was driving them into the arms of the competition.

To the amazement of the company's leadership team, it turned out that "speedy delivery" was not the most important consideration in customers' minds. "Undamaged delivery" was deemed far more important. In their zeal to deliver packages the next day, it seems, workers were subjecting packages to a lot of rough handling; goods were being delivered on time but broken. Efforts to further speed up handling were worsening the problem! If it had occurred to this company to consult with its customers sooner, a great deal of cost, lost revenue, customer disappointment could have been avoided.

This is the real benefit of working with customer data: It provides another powerful means of simplifying and speeding up decision making at the executive level. (Indeed, show me an organization in which managers frequently carp about their bosses' general inability or unwillingness to make decisions, and I'll show you one in which hard data is seldom brought into play and hunches are the order of the day.) Solid, relevant, timely customer feedback can reduce—and sometimes eliminate completely—much of the risk element associated with strategic decision making. But in organizations not accustomed to working with data, going with hunches always seems quicker and easier, even if only because it's simply more familiar.

Several years ago I was speaking with an editor at a book publishing house that has since gone out of business. She was bemoaning that only a small proportion of their books ever broke even, and none ever made enough to cover the losses incurred by all the others. "Do you ever survey your readers," I asked, "to ascertain whether a given book being considered for publication might or might not appeal to them?" I was treated to a long, detailed dissertation in response; the short version boils down to, "Naw, it would cost more to do that type of study than it would to publish the damn book. About all we can do is go with our instincts, and hope for the best."

This belief that acquiring customer data is too costly and complex an option to consider is by no means confined to the book-publishing industry. Variations of it can be heard in organizations of all types—that is, in organizations of various kinds that all have one thing in common: They seldom, if ever, actually use customer data to run their business. The "expense" issue is the standard antidata excuse offered by those businesses that have historically relied on hunches for their decision making. In trudging out this lame old excuse, they betray their ignorance of how simply, informally, and inexpensively customer data can be harvested. More important, they ignore the terrible costs that are bound to arise as a result of not doing so.

How many businesses believe themselves to be wildly successful, only to inexplicably find themselves going out of business? What looks like wild success—everybody frantically busy, lots of orders coming in, more customers than you can handle—may only be symptomatic of a temporary lack of competition. When the competition surfaces, as it inevitably must, the sea of customers can dry up frighteningly quickly. Having many customers is not enough; having many *happy* customers is what's required. Finding out they were unhappy after they have defected is of little benefit.

SEARCH AND RESEARCH

How to make any business successful:

1 Find out what your customers want most of all.

2 Find a way to turn a profit while giving it to them.

Note that point number one is not to *guess* what your customers want. Some "finding out" is going to be necessary. Even if your research tells you precisely what your customers want today, things will almost certainly change tomorrow. Customer research is an ongoing process. The good news is that despite widely held hunches to the contrary, the finding-out process isn't always complicated, tedious, and expensive.

In descending order of complexity, tedium, and cost, here are some of the most commonly used methods for acquiring customer data:

- Surveys

- Focus groups (or advisory panels)

- Site visits

- Hot lines

- Casual conversation

Surveys

The traditional "comprehensive" customer survey *is* often expensive, complex, and time consuming to administer. Worse, it can also be distressingly ineffective. In attempting to accomplish everything, it often succeeds in accomplishing little or nothing. Mountains of impenetrable data end up languishing in a dusty corner of some backroom storage cemetery.

Surveys are most useful when there is an urgent need for a lot of fairly general customer data. Designing effective survey questionnaires is a science in its own right. If the survey is to be huge (say, more than fifty questions) consider leaving the design process to the experts. If you're designing the survey yourself, a helpful rule of thumb for what should or shouldn't be included is "Less is always more, shorter is always better, and simpler is always best." The better the design, the easier the task of sifting through the resulting deluge of data to make some sense of it all.

Even if surveys bring in huge volumes of data quickly, for the data to be useful it must be distilled, analyzed, and summarized It can take so long to review and analyze all the information from a giant survey that by the time the data is fully understood it may be outdated.

If you are about to initiate your organization's first formal customer research effort, a survey may be the way to go. Once your need for data is less urgent, one of the simpler options may be more appropriate for regular customer data updates.

Focus Groups

Sometimes called advisory panels, advisory boards, or councils, these are sessions in which a group or cross-section of major customers are invited into the organization to meet with members of the staff and discuss one or more key issues. Such sessions are usually held semiregularly; two or three times a year is typical. Sometimes all relevant and interested employees attend; or some attend visibly while others observe while hidden behind two-way mirrors. Sometimes the sessions are recorded, to be reviewed later by any interested parties.

On the positive side, the name *focus group* suggests generation of data that is highly focused on a minimum number of critical strategic issues, and thus very powerful and useful. A number of high-profile corporations attribute some of their most successful innovations to suggestions and ideas that came out of focus group discussions. At the time of this writing, for example, Microsoft in the United Kingdom is revamping its entire intranet service on the basis of recommendations culled from just two recent half-day focus group sessions. The Quaker Oats Company developed its Center for Excellence in Barrington, Illinois in 1994; according to center director John P. Boes, it is an offshoot of teachings from its 1993 academy, a training center to develop skills and capabilities that Quaker feels give the organization a competitive edge. But the company also brings customers to the center. "We use various learning formats," Boes explains. "In some training sessions, we started bringing customers in to speak directly to people who were in training, to build the awareness. It was very effective. We're still doing it."

A potential downside of focus groups is their notorious tendency to degenerate into "gripe sessions"—a danger that increases as general levels of customer dissatisfaction increase. A corollary pitfall is their potential for creating discord in organizations that have not yet moved beyond a culture of finger-pointing and blame-laying. An important customer, trying to be helpful, tells the entire group that her greatest frustration is having to deal over the phone with "that rude, obnoxious dimwit in sales with the incomprehensible Scottish accent," and all eyes turn to salesperson McKechnie in the back of the room; it's a safe bet he won't characterize this later as one of the glowing moments of his career.

Focus groups work best in organizations with previous experience in using data to drive their business, and with a high enough level of maturity and sophistication not to allow occasionally unflattering or even hostile customer feedback to have any punitive repercussions. If your purpose is to define customer likes and dislikes, the focus group may not be your best forum. If, on the other hand, you would like key customers to participate in isolating specific problems and brainstorming solutions, it's hard to beat the focus-group approach for gathering useful data and ideas quickly.

Site Visits

A kind of focus-group-session-in-reverse, in a site visit a group of key employees arrange to visit an important customer on the customer's own premises. Such visits tend to be project-specific: This customer is using our new product, or applying our new system, or perhaps implementing an older product in some new way, and we want to observe for ourselves how well it is or isn't working, and hear the customer's impressions first-hand. As with focus groups, it is important that employees making site visits feel confident there will be no unpleasant consequences for them, regardless of the nature of the feedback they hear. This is an effective way to obtain useful customer data quickly.

Hot Lines

Creating a toll-free customer hot line represents one of the simplest, most economical means by which organizations can acquire feedback from their customers. Alas, hot-line feedback tends to be almost exclusively negative. It appears that most customers view them primarily as a means to lodge complaints or relate problems ("hot" as in hot under the collar).

Of course, complaints and problems represent extremely important categories of customer feedback. They define specific improvement opportunities. (By contrast, bouquets and compliments provide little more than the glorious feeling that life is worth living, and a general, vague desire to do good deeds and help our fellow man.)

Unless some way is found to give customers an incentive to use the hot line for more than letting off steam, it is likely to remain primarily a vehicle for negative customer feedback. Some other data-collecting mechanism should supplement all that negativity with a more balanced representation of what customers are feeling and thinking.

(In this spirit, I offer a tip for multiplex operators: Since you've already got thousands of people calling hot lines for show times and locations, why not incorporate a recording capability into the system, and invite callers to rate the movies they've already seen, or to offer suggestions on how the whole experience might be improved for them? A tip for all other hot-line users: why not incorporate some sort of useful information into your recorded message, as multiplex operators do, in order to give your customers an incentive to call?)

Casual Conversation

This can be one of the most effective ongoing customer data-gathering methods of all, yet is one of the least frequently used. Its power derives from three factors: keeping things simple and informal and getting everyone involved.

1 *Keeping things simple*: The fewer dimensions being addressed at any one time in any data collecting effort, the better. The most potent and useful customer feedback emerges when only one key strategic question is being asked. As more and more issues are added, the data-collecting mechanism becomes more difficult to administer, and the resulting data is harder to analyze. "Is speedy delivery the most important thing to you, or is there something else that you consider even more important?" That one simple question, if posed to a significant number of customers as part of routine transactions, might save an organization millions of dollars.

2 *Keeping things informal*: When customers are confronted with one or more tough questions that they feel they must ponder at some length, the reliability of the resulting data can suffer. The customer may in effect be searching for the answer he or she feels the organization most wants to hear, as opposed to what most accurately reflects what he or she is feeling. Often, the most useful data trips spontaneously off the tongue, without weighty reflection. The best forum for collecting such data is a relaxed, casual conversation. The question(s) should materialize almost as an afterthought, a casual footnote within a routine interaction: "Oh, and by the way, I'm just curious, may I ask what the main thing is that draws you back to our store again and again, when there are others you could be going to instead?"

3 *Getting everyone involved*: The long, elaborate, complicated customer survey requires experts to design it, administer it, and analyze the results. The ownership factor is very small. By comparison, the "expert" most ideally equipped to solicit customer feedback in casual conversation is anyone who routinely interacts with customers face-to-face or voice-to-voice. Indeed, every customer interaction that does not produce at least one speck of feedback data represents an opportunity missed. The ambassador of change looks for ways to help all employees who have direct dealings with customers to think of their customers as potential repositories of a wealth of useful research data.

If the process of acquiring customer data is kept simple and informal, it can be a pleasant experience for customer and employee alike. By and large, customers actually enjoy being asked about their likes and dislikes, particularly when the question comes from someone they're already dealing with anyway. It shows that the organization cares and wants to do the right thing. What customers enjoy less is being asked to fill in long, complicated, impersonal survey questionnaires by someone whose only dealing with them is to administer the questionnaire. Employees, too, often find soliciting this kind of casual feedback from customers personally gratifying, since it affords the customer an opportunity to recognize commendable behavior on the employee's part. Customers who are asked what *would* delight them often take a moment to acknowledge what *has* delighted them as well, something they might not comment upon if not given the specific opportunity.

An example illustrates the simple, informal, everyone-involved style of data gathering. The Eats-a-Pizza chain of restaurants is contemplating setting up self-serve salad bars in all of its outlets. But is this really something Eats-a-Pizza's customers want and would use? (Or is it merely some VP's pet hunch?) To find out, over a two-week period every cashier in every restaurant is encouraged to ask departing customers, as they pay their bill, one basic question: "If we were to install a self-serve salad bar, do you think you'd ever use it?" The replies can be recorded with tick marks on a sheet of paper under *yes* or *no* headings, or tokens deposited in *yes* or *no* piggy-bank-type containers, or any number of other similar options. At the end of the two weeks, the leadership team reviews the results: Eighty-seven percent of respondents say they would not use the self-serve salad bar. A costly strategic error avoided.

How about making buffet-style premade pizzas available during the lunch period? Would the speed and convenience make these more attractive to customers than the traditional order-at-the-table-and-wait variety? Let's ask them! What kind of background music do customers prefer while dining on our premises? Let's ask them! Let's find out as much as we can about things they do and don't like, and see where we might change things to make the experience more pleasant for them. Most important, each time we introduce any sort of change let's be especially diligent about asking them how they feel about it. We need to confirm that we're still moving in the right direction, and if not, we need to make a midcourse correction as soon as possible.

Once an organization develops a taste for decision making driven by hard data, it's typically difficult to return to a hunch-based approach. "We think this is what's important to our customers" simply cannot compete with "We know this is what's important to our customers, because they have told us so."

DATA FROM INTERNAL CUSTOMERS

Admittedly, having a pet hunch disproved by data is sometimes a humbling experience. Years I go I was among those who thumped the pulpit advocating the term *internal customers* as a means of describing employees. Like others in my profession, I subscribed to the hunch that this phrase was bound to catch on, because it did such a nice job of blurring the distinction between customers and employees and reinforced the need to provide an equally satisfying experience to both groups. The data, however, is in. The phrase has not really caught on in a big way, despite more than a decade of effort by true believers to help it along. It simply raises as many ambiguities as it tries to resolve.

Among my current pulpit-thumping favorites is Art McNeil's "internal partners" concept. He describes the "partner chain" as made up of internal partners (employees), external partners (suppliers, joint-venture associates, etc.), funding partners (shareholders or investors), and customers (users, consumers, those who ultimately vote with their dollars to buy or not buy what we sell). I find myself also, from time to time, shifting from a partnership context to the metaphor of sports teams by referring to employees as "players." (In many situations, I find the actual word *employees*, though lacking the trendy appeal of newly minted jargon, also serves to describe employees quite nicely.)

As organizational decision making becomes increasingly driven by data, employees become an ever more valuable source of such data.

Obviously, if customer-contact personnel in particular are encouraged to solicit data from their customers, this data from them has to be harvested. Unless employees see that the data they are gathering on the organization's behalf is repeatedly collected and used meaningfully, their data-gathering activities will surely be short-lived.

In terms of building a more receptive, less cynical organizational culture, feedback originating directly from employees themselves is particularly useful. Almost as commonplace as the universal battle cry of the full-time cynic, "Nobody ever tells me anything about what's going on around here" (a perception that the second big question attempts to dispel), is the corollary echo-response, "Nobody ever asks me for my opinion about anything around here" (which this chapter's big question is now poised to address).

Indeed, from a plan-building standpoint, a number of the big questions to come benefit directly from employee feedback. The objective with the fifth big question ("How will we make things better for our employees?") is to remove organizational obstacles and make it easier for employees to do the things that help achieve the vision. But what are the key obstacles for employees? Rather than acting on hunches about what they might be, how much safer and simpler it is to simply ask the employees directly. In looking at the eighth big question ("How will we celebrate our successes?") we find it semicomical to observe a management team comparing hunches about the kinds of recognition and celebration that are most meaningful to employees. "I think an 'Employee of the Month' photo, prominently displayed, would really mean a lot to them," one manager suggests. "Oh, no," another protests, "I think most people hate having their picture taken. I know I do. No, I think cash awards would be much more appreciated." And so goes the discussion, on and on, without anyone ever proposing that they actually ask the employees for their input.

As with customer surveys, elaborate employee surveys can be something of a mixed blessing; unless kept simple, they tend to generate more data than can easily be digested. Once again, casual conversation may in many cases be the least complicated and most effective way to give employees their say.

Whatever method is chosen, it is important for the ongoing success of the organization that decisions be fueled by data culled from internal as well as external sources.

FEEDING FEEDBACK BACK

If those responsible for collating customer or employee data retreat to closed chambers to do so; if early findings are kept strictly hush-hush; if an aura of secrecy and high drama surrounds the whole process of sifting through all of the accumulated feedback, then the conclusion is inescapable: Data is a mighty scary thing. Furthermore, if few or none of the findings are ever openly disclosed, the rumor mills go into rotating-shift, round-the-clock overtime.

Let us once again learn from those experts in information retrieval and transmission, the purveyors of television news. Consider how live broadcasts of election coverage hold viewers transfixed for hours while voting results come in and are tallied. Trends are plotted. Forecasts and projections are made, and revised, and revised again. Speculators analyze, while analysts speculate. Commentators try to make sense of it all for us.

Why not treat the collation of incoming customer data the same way—as engaging news, as an open, ongoing process, complete with projections and speculative analysis? Whereas the results of an election are finalized within hours, the process of sifting through customer data may take weeks; but otherwise both activities can be treated in much the same way.

Now imagine if there were no election-results coverage whatsoever. Imagine if, after voting, the voters go home and hear nothing until at some point in the future it is suddenly apparent that a new political leader has taken office. By what margin did the incumbent lose the election? Did the new leader even win at all, or did he take office by force? Who's to know?

This is the feeling of noninvolvement, of helplessness, that employees experience when they participate in gathering data that subsequently vanishes into a black hole. They find themselves wondering if the changes around them are in any way related to the data that vanished without a trace. Could it be that the changes actually *contradict* the data? Who's to know?

The true mark of a data-driven organization is the effort it makes to demystify the data itself. In setting out to acquire and use customer data in the daily operation of the business, and in openly and unhesitatingly making all of the data findings public knowledge, the members of the leadership team take a giant step toward engineering genuine transformational change within their organization.

BIG QUESTION 3 PLANNING EXERCISE

From a planning standpoint, ambassadors of change begin by defining the vital strategic questions for which the organization requires answers. The objective is to acquire and use customer data to validate (or discredit) hunches and assumptions, and thereby minimize the element of risk in strategic decision making. A key part of planning also involves looking for new, different, and better ways to keep the acquisition of customer data simple and informal, and to give all customer-contact personnel ongoing involvement. Finally, methods for gathering vital data from employees also need to be considered.

In some instances it makes sense to tie these third-question concepts to the approach of the second big question: How will we spread the word internally so that our customer-contact people better appreciate the value of customer feedback in the first place? How will we train these people to best use our chosen data-gathering tools and techniques? How will we summarize and communicate the content of the accumulated data back to the workforce?

∙∙∙

PHASE ONE: STATUS-QUO QUESTIONS

For no more than ten minutes and without any discussion or analysis, list on a flipchart as many answers as you can think of to these two questions (approximately five minutes per question):

1 Strengths: What do we currently do well to acquire and use customer data?

2 Weaknesses: What prevents us from more effectively acquiring and using customer data?

The first question really asks: With what existing mechanisms do we presently solicit feedback from our customers? What are examples of ways in which we use data from customers to guide our decision making?

The second question asks: What impediments make it difficult for us to consult more regularly or more effectively with our customers? What factors get in the way? What obstacles complicate our efforts?

PHASE TWO: BRAINSTORMING QUESTIONS

For no more than fifteen minutes, review the list of strengths and weaknesses created in phase one, and for each, without evaluation or discussion, list on a flipchart as many ideas as you can think of to answer these two questions (approximately seven minutes per question):

1 What can be done to amplify our strengths?

2 What can be done to overcome our weaknesses?

For each strength listed, the question becomes, If we had unlimited resources, time, and authority, what could we do to derive even more benefit from this? How could we make this even more effective? What would it take to give this even more impact?

For each weakness: If we had no constraints whatsoever, how could we eliminate this problem? What could we do to get around this obstacle? How might we turn this weakness into a strength?

PHASE THREE: ACTIVITY-PLANNING QUESTIONS

Spend no more than a minute or two selecting one idea that seems a suitable candidate for inclusion in the plan from the list generated in phase two. For this one idea, take no more than twenty minutes to answer all of the following questions on a flipchart. (It's prudent to allow five full minutes at the end for the final question.)

▶ What exactly will be done? (Distinguish between objectives and activities, and concentrate on the latter. The response to this question should begin with a verb, such as *create, establish, communicate*, etc.)

▶ How will it be done? (If it is not immediately obvious, describe in broad terms how this activity will be implemented. Make note here of any implementation details or issues that remain to be resolved.)

▶ Who will do it? (Use actual names where possible.)

▶ Who will ensure that it gets done? (In most cases, the person who will be held accountable should be a member of the leadership team.)

▶ When will it begin, or be completed? (Specify an actual date.)

▶ How will success be measured? (By what means will we confirm that this particular activity has truly helped us derive more and better feedback from our customers? Has reduced risk in our strategic decision making? Has made our decision making easier by replacing competing hunches with facts?)

At the conclusion of each three-phase round of the plan-building exercise, those flipcharts bearing content destined for inclusion in the final plan must be separated from the rest and put safely aside for preservation.

Begin by collecting the flipcharts bearing the responses to the phase-three activity-planning questions. Using a marker of a different color than already appears on the charts, "brand" them by inscribing *BQ3* prominently on each sheet, wherever space permits; this indicates to the creator(s) of the final planning document the section to which this activity should be assigned. The answer to the *what* question thus becomes the descriptive heading for this particular activity, the first entry in the section of the plan devoted to the third big question, "How will we acquire and use customer data?"

Next, isolate the flipchart from phase one that bears the list of strengths. This chart, too, needs to have *BQ3* inscribed upon it. During the creation of the planning document, it may be appropriate to include in the section on the third big question certain items from this list of strengths, under the heading "Things We Will Continue to Do."

Once the content flipcharts have been separated from the rest, branded, and put safely aside for preservation, the team can elect to do one of the following:

▶ Take a break.

or

▶ Select another item from the existing brainstormed list of ideas for the third big question generated in phase two, and subject it to the phase-three activity-planning questions, for no more than twenty minutes.

or

▶ Proceed to the fourth big question, and begin by answering the phase-one status-quo questions, for ten minutes or less.

••

As always, there is no hard-and-fast rule for determining when a given team is ready to proceed to the next big question. If in doubt, however, it's always wise to err on the side of plenty; it's easier to omit a fully planned-out activity from the final plan than to reconvene the entire team after the fact for a remedial planning session.

Once the third big question has been addressed to the team's satisfaction, it's time to begin thinking about how to bring new employees up to speed.

4

How Will We Bring
New Employees Up to Speed?

The world's biggest names in hamburgers frequently have restaurants in close proximity to one another. In the busiest areas of the larger cities, it's not uncommon to see competing outlets virtually across the street from each other. For the student of corporate culture, how illuminating it is to be able to observe their different approaches in side-by-side comparison. In one city, I saw two such restaurants advising passersby, with large portable signs on display out front, that they were seeking to hire new staff.

> ### HELP WANTED—APPLY WITHIN

> ### NOW HIRING FRIENDLY PEOPLE

Each sign has only four words. Yet each speaks volumes about the values of the organization it represents. The implication of the second is clear: If you're not friendly, then please apply within that outfit down the street. If you *are* friendly, however, come and talk to us, because we recognize that it's probably going to be a lot easier for us to teach you to take the fries out of the fryer when the buzzer goes off than to teach you how to be friendly to customers. In order to operate successfully, one restaurant believes that it requires staff; the other believes that it requires friendliness.

ENLIST HERE

Once an organization articulates its core values, defines its mission, and establishes its vision, these cultural markers should begin showing up in everything it does—including recruiting new employees. Indeed, the ambassadors of change within the organization must carefully plan to *ensure* that the recruiting, hiring, and orienting of new employees all clearly reflect what the organization stands for and is striving to achieve. An infusion of new players can lead to dilution of the team's basic cultural character and shared sense of purpose, unless thoughtful steps are taken to guard against it. This is what ambassadors of change need to consider as part of their planning process.

EXPANSION VERSUS ATTRITION

The recruitment net has to be cast in times of prosperity and organizational expansion. Because the drafters of the corporate vision anticipate success, once the anticipated reorganization or expansion becomes imminent it is entirely appropriate to consider strategies for recruiting new employees. But this is not the only time the company feels the need to bring new players on board.

Inevitably, any sort of change introduced into an organization causes some people to resent it, to strive to undermine it, or to resist it bitterly. The more profound the change, the greater the unrest it engenders in a certain—small, one hopes—portion of the employee population. "Time to update the old resumé," the disenfranchised are likely to grumble, and not entirely in jest, when the despised change initiative shows no sign of going away. The good news is that through a natural process of attrition, many of those least disposed to support the organization's stated values (or mission, or vision, or change effort) tend to remove themselves from the picture on their own initiative, thus sparing the organization from having to do it later. They simply recognize their growing discomfort as a basic conflict of ideologies and undertake on their own to find for themselves a more suitable cultural environment in which to work. The bad news, if we can call it that, is that unless this attrition is anticipated, the organization suddenly finds itself scrambling to fill key vacancies that seem to be materializing out of the clear blue. The time to plan for bringing new employees on board is *now*.

Since every member of the leadership team should play an active role in making the final selection of new players for his or her corner of the organization, it makes eminent sense for the entire team to participate in planning the overall strategy for bringing the best possible new employees on board and getting them up to speed as quickly and effectively as possible.

HIRING FOR A VALUES FIT

Pick up a copy of today's newspaper, and turn to the classified ads. Observe the recruitment ads in particular. What proportion of them convey anything at all about the culture of the organization in question, what it believes in, the guiding principles it holds dear? Now think back on recruitment ads your own firm has run in the past, or perhaps is even running at present. What can prospective job applicants glean about your organization's cultural values from its recruitment efforts?

The success of any recruitment program should not be measured by the number of applications received. The notion that the greater the number of candidates to choose from, the better the odds of finding the right one is just plain dumb. It's like saying that your chances of finding the right postcard to send home from vacation improve if you find a store that stocks postcards by the millions. Even after you squander your entire vacation evaluating hundreds of thousands of postcards and narrow the field down to the most promising two or three hundred, how can you be sure there won't be an even better one somewhere in the next million?

A far more sensible approach is to determine what the various criteria for the right candidate are and then apply a process of elimination to "disqualify" all those that do not meet the criteria. In a parlor-game context, many people are surprised to discover how few questions can reveal the one word another person has chosen at random from among hundreds of thousands of possibilities. If, for example, the first question is, "Does your word begin with a letter that falls between A and M inclusively in the alphabet (that is, within the first thirteen of the alphabet's twenty-six letters)?" and the answer is no, approximately half of the words that make up the entire language are eliminated right off the bat. A succession of similar questions to arrive at the word's first letter, the total number of letters, and the presence of particular vowels, etc., leads to the chosen word in a matter of seconds.

The postcard-hungry vacationer should enter the postcard shop, for example, intent on finding a color photo of palm trees, beach, and sea, with no people in sight, and only the name of the resort appearing as text. Thus, all black-and-white postcards, all those using illustration media other than photography, all those displaying humorous text, and so on, are disqualified at once. The vacationer is left choosing from six candidates, all of which meet the criteria, and is free to go with the one that adds a little something extra that wasn't initially identified as nice-to-have but that is now appreciated.

Similarly, in recruiting new players for the team, let the tone of the recruitment effort itself eliminate most of the potential applicants. Suppose you need a new typist. How does it benefit you to find and hire the speediest, most accurate typist in the world, listed for the past nine consecutive years in the *Guinness Book of Records*, if it turns out she is so cranky and unpleasant to deal with that most people never bring her anything to type and instead prefer to do it themselves, hunt-and-peck style? By filtering out undesirable applicants at the outset, you have a much smaller number of candidates to evaluate, each of which is a potentially good choice; you then review only the best and select the best of the best.

Along with all the necessary skill and experience requirements, emphasize the kind of values your organization espouses, the kind of ideological fit you're looking for. Scare away the misfits by making it obvious they would feel uncomfortable in your working environment. As much as possible, strive to attract only applicants who are predisposed to support the organization's efforts and fit comfortably into the culture. The more detailed the picture you paint of who you are and what makes you tick during the recruitment phase, the fewer surprises for the new employee once he or she is on the job, and thus the fewer early defections. High employee turnover is as often a sign of sloppy hiring practices as a sign of substandard working conditions.

An additional benefit to be derived from values-driven recruitment efforts is that their positive effect is not limited to people actively looking for work. In creating a depiction of your organization's culture intended to appeal to a certain kind of potential job applicant, you transmit a message that is likely to resonate for a certain kind of customer as well. An investment made to attract new employees often serves as well to attract new customers for the new employees to do business with.

ASSUME VICTORY

One surefire way to discourage deadbeats from applying for work in your shop is to let prospective applicants know there is little opportunity for dragging their feet or lollygagging; your business is a whirlwind of activity, a dynamic organization crackling with a positive sense of motion and progress. To dissuade those who live in terror of change of any kind, describe how nothing is static at your place, how everything is constantly in an exciting state of evolution and transformation. If appropriate, enumerate your values; if not, hint at them; either way, let the prospects know what matters to you. If feasible, outline your vision; if not, imply it; give them a sense of where you're going.

A feeling of optimism for the organization's future should emerge from your recruitment message. To scare away those harboring any sort of self-defeating fear of success, make it unmistakable that you are determined to succeed. Make it clear that this business is embarking upon an exciting journey to victory and triumph; you're inviting applicants to be part of the voyage, but only those who are most personally enthusiastic and committed to reaching the destination will ultimately form the traveling party.

This same sense of determination and optimism should also pervade the interviewing process. While you're evaluating candidates at close range, it's useful to remember that they are also evaluating you. If, by the time you finally decide they turn you on, they have come to a simultaneous conclusion that you turn them off, it may be too late to begin pouring on the charm. Anyone who survives the initial filtering mechanisms and makes it to the interview stage is a potentially valuable addition to the team; from the very first point of contact, the objective is to make them want to join. They should feel that they are being considered for membership in a highly desirable, highly exclusive, winners-only club. It is their amazing good fortune to find themselves (as so seldom happens in life) at the right place at the right time. Here's an exciting organization poised to achieve wonderful things in the not-too-distant future, and here they are, right on the doorstep, just a stroke of the pen away from ground-floor admission as an important part of it all. The more intensely membership is coveted, the more it is prized if conferred.

CULTURAL IMPRINTING

Important as a tone of optimism is for recruiting and selecting new players, it should figure even more prominently in the formal orientation the new employees receive as part of their induction into the organization.

Animal behaviorists describe a phenomenon known as imprinting. Upon first entering the unfamiliar environment that is the outside world, the newly born or hatched young of certain species—geese are the most well-known example—tend to follow the first moving (or call-producing) object they see as if it were their parent. Such an imprint can remain with the individual animal for some time.

The first day of work for a new employee places the individual in an unfamiliar new environment. Here too there is an opportunity to imprint, to make a lasting impression.

Ask an employee at the end of the first day in a new workplace to describe what the culture of the new organization is like, and in most cases he or she has no difficulty elaborating at considerable length in response. (Interestingly, words often come more easily to the new recruit than to a veteran who is asked the same thing and should be expected to better grasp the organizational culture.) In contrast with the culture of a previous workplace, the differences and similarities of the new one stand out in sharp relief. If a conscious effort is made to impress certain values and feelings upon the new employee, these surely figure in his or her account. If no such effort is made and the new worker is basically abandoned and forced to fend for him- or herself, this too leaves a clear and sharp impression about the kind of organization he or she is now dealing with.

The ambassador of change recognizes the potential, at the very start of a new employee's tour of duty, to create a cultural imprint that stays with the individual for a long time. In particular, the new employee has a significant advantage over the veteran: For the new hand, the change effort that the plan is designed to facilitate does not represent any actual change at all! There is no personal experience with the way things "used to be around here," so every aspect of the organization—even the constants that go back to the original founding of the business—represent an equal challenge for the newcomer in terms of personal adjustment. The object of the orientation exercise, therefore, is not to draw attention to new elements of change being introduced into the culture but rather to present the so-called new along with the so-called old as one seamless cultural tapestry: "This is who we are, and this is what we're about, and this is where we're going, and this is how we intend to get there, and this is how your contribution is going to make a difference."

Central to the orientation is the vision. In terms of cultural imprinting, this one element above all others must make a lasting, meaningful impression. The vision, as presented throughout the orientation, should impart exhilaration to the new employee, a feeling that he or she has clearly joined a winning team and will personally be participating in exciting victories leading to a major triumph. Essentially, an orientation is effective if the answer to a friend's question "So, what's your new outfit like?" revolves around the vision and what it means. Ideally, it should be possible to approach the new employee on day six (or day sixty, or day six hundred), point to whatever task he or she is engaged in at that moment, and ask, "How does what you're doing relate to the vision?" and hear an immediate, logical response that ties the activity directly to the vision.

Next in importance as part of orienting new employees are the values the organization espouses. These become the behavioral guidelines for the new employee, a code of conduct defining what is and isn't acceptable. The values begin to answer a question many new employees have in the back of their minds, even if they refrain from asking it directly: "What are the kinds of things that score big brownie points around here?" (The converse is, "What are the big no-no's to avoid?") The sooner these become imprinted, the sooner they are likely to start being lived.

The orientation should next summarize the organization's mission. This is the tactical nitty-gritty by which the strategic vision is being realized. It is through the details of the mission that the occasionally mundane day-to-day elements of one's job are seen to relate directly to the grandiose vision.

Only if the orientation has satisfactorily covered vision, values, and mission (all elements that look to the future) does it make sense to elaborate on the organization's proud heritage and the legacy of the past. Sadly, many orientation efforts neglect vision, values, and mission altogether and focus almost exclusively on the past. It's like entering a car with the front windows painted over and providing passengers only with rear-view mirrors.

In planning ways to bring new players up to speed, ambassadors of change need to consider all three aspects—recruitment, hiring, and orientation—as frequently overlooked opportunities to make important strides toward realizing the vision.

BIG QUESTION 4 PLANNING EXERCISE

The three-tiered nature of the fourth big question (recruitment, hiring, orientation) means that in a sense, each of the subquestions represents three questions. The temptation, therefore, is to assume that plan building must take three times as long for this issue. This is not the case. (If it were, we would deal with each as a separate big question on its own.) The objective is to think of the entire operation of bringing new employees up to speed as a single process in which vision, mission, and values are emphasized and reinforced; the three tiers are means for the plan builders to pinpoint where, in the overall process, the greatest opportunities for improvement lie.

. . . .

PHASE ONE: STATUS-QUO QUESTIONS

For no more than ten minutes and without any discussion or analysis, list on a flipchart as many answers as you can think of to these two questions (approximately five minutes per question):

1 Strengths: What do we currently do well to bring new employees up to speed?

2 Weaknesses: What prevents us from more effectively bringing new employees up to speed?

The first question really asks: With what existing mechanisms do we presently recruit new employees? What do we currently do well in terms of selecting and hiring candidates for jobs? What works well in our existing orientation efforts?

The second question asks: What makes it difficult for us to recruit new employees more effectively? What causes some of our selecting and hiring efforts to miss the mark? What are some of the shortcomings in our orientation of new employees?

. . . .

PHASE TWO: BRAINSTORMING QUESTIONS

For no more than fifteen minutes, review the list of strengths and weaknesses created in phase one, and for each, without evaluation or discussion, list on a flipchart as many ideas as you can think of to answer these two questions (approximately seven minutes per question):

1 What can be done to amplify our strengths?

2 What can be done to overcome our weaknesses?

For each strength listed, the question becomes, If we had unlimited resources, time, and authority, what could we do to derive even more benefit from this? How could we make this even more effective? What would it take to give this even more impact?

For each weakness: If we had no constraints whatsoever, how could we eliminate this problem? What could we do to get around this obstacle? How might we turn this weakness into a strength?

....

PHASE THREE: ACTIVITY-PLANNING QUESTIONS

Spend no more than a minute or two selecting one idea that seems a suitable candidate for inclusion in the plan from the list generated in phase two. For this one idea, take no more than twenty minutes to answer all of the following questions on a flipchart. (It's prudent to allow five full minutes at the end for the final question.)

▶ What exactly will be done? (Distinguish between objectives and activities, and concentrate on the latter. The response to this question should begin with a verb, such as *create, establish, communicate*, etc.)

▶ How will it be done? (If it is not immediately obvious, describe in broad terms how this activity will be implemented. Make note here of any implementation details or issues that remain to be resolved.)

▶ Who will do it? (Use actual names where possible.)

▶ Who will ensure that it gets done? (In most cases, the person who will be held accountable should be a member of the leadership team.)

▶ When will it begin, or be completed? (Specify an
actual date.)

▶ How will success be measured? (By what means will
we confirm that this particular activity has truly
helped us attract better candidates for job openings?
Has improved our ability to select the best candidate
from among the applicants? Has made our orientation
more effective for new employees? Has otherwise
helped us do a better job of bringing new employees
up to speed?)

At the conclusion of each three-phase round of the plan-
building exercise, those flipcharts bearing content destined for inclusion in the final plan must be separated
from the rest and put safely aside for preservation.

Begin by collecting the flipcharts bearing the responses
to the phase-three activity-planning questions. Using a
marker of a different color than already appears on the
charts, inscribe *BQ4* prominently on each sheet, wherever space permits. Next, isolate the flipchart from
phase one that bears the list of strengths; inscribe *BQ4*
on this chart, too. (During the creation of the planning
document, it may be appropriate to include in the section on the fourth big question certain items from this
list of strengths, under the heading "Things We Will Continue to Do."

Once the content flipcharts have been separated from
the rest, branded, and put safely aside for preservation,
the team can elect to do one of the following:

▶ Take a break.

or

▶ Select another item from the existing brainstormed
list of ideas for the fourth big question generated in

> phase two, and subject it to the phase-three activity-planning questions, for no more than twenty minutes.

or

▶ Proceed to the fifth big question, and begin by answering the phase-one status-quo questions, for ten minutes or less.

....

If the team is not sure it's ready to proceed to the next big question, it's usually wise to err on the side of plenty.

Once the fourth big question has been addressed to the team's satisfaction, it's time to begin thinking about how to make things better for employees.

5

How Will We Make Things Better for Our Employees?

I n terms of the sheer magnitude of the issue it represents, the fifth big question potentially encompasses more aspects of organizational culture than any of the other 8 Big Questions. This is the part of the planning process that forces the leadership team to take a hard look at a huge canvas entitled The Way We Do Things Around Here, and to begin to challenge some of those cherished traditions. These are the tough questions: Is the traditional way of doing things making it more difficult—or even impossible—for employees to live the corporate values day-to-day, achieve the mission, and therefore realize the vision? If so, how do we go about making the appropriate changes? How do we make this organization a more benign environment for its employees?

THE BIGGEST OF THE BIG QUESTIONS

The canvas is vast because aside from touching upon established operational procedures at the employee level it also addresses policies, structures, and systems at the management level. It includes, but is hardly limited to, such cultural fixtures as performance appraisal systems, the process by which expenses are submitted for reimbursement, the compensation scheme, how job promotions are handed out, purchasing processes, information technology systems, policies governing operating hours, vacation policies, even the telephone system. . . . It's quite a can of worms.

This probably represents the part of the plan with the greatest potential for management-level resistance. Over the years, some of these long-standing traditions might have taken on the status of sacred cows. Some of them might once have been brilliant brainwaves of managers who are still part of the organization, whose idea or innovation propelled their own rapid rise within the ranks, perhaps to the level of senior leadership, where they may now still reside. Who are we to come along and challenge such ideas, threatening to gore such sacred cows?

Or these traditions might once have been the product of managers hoping their inspiration was a ticket to the executive suite. These disillusioned managers have come to consider their "babies" as their only real claim to fame in the organization. Will they cheer our announced intention of putting their babies to the sword?

It is this part of the plan that may have the most need for tact and diplomacy. It is here that educational efforts (as outlined in the chapter on the second big question, spreading the word internally) take on particular importance. The managers who own the policies, processes, or systems that require revision need to understand that the rules of the game have changed, that yesterday's brilliant strategy is precisely what enabled us to survive until today, but now a new and different strategy must be devised if we are to survive until tomorrow.

Big question number five is a delicate balancing act. We want to avoid upsetting our middle managers unnecessarily with all of this; their support is absolutely vital to our success. At the same time, our determination to succeed obviously implies removing all obstacles to success. When Peter Drucker points out in *The Changing World of the Executive* that "so much of what we call management consists of making it difficult for people to work," he's highlighting the magnitude of the problem. For the ambassador of change, the objective is not only to make it easier for people to work in the general sense but also to make it easier for them to implement the plan in particular, and ultimately to realize the vision.

HOW'D THIS DRAGON GET IN HERE?

In the fancy restaurant at the large resort hotel at which I am staying as I write this, upon entering the dining area it is necessary to report to the lecternlike "hostess desk" in order to be shown to a table. Last evening my wife and I joined a line of several other guests waiting to be seated. None of the restaurant's tables were occupied as yet. There were a total of five restaurant employees huddled around the hostess desk, all of them hunched over sheets of paper taped to the top of the desk, all of them engrossed in some intense activity that involved pointing to the representation of tables on a printed floor plan, and to names on a reservations list, and to other documents the purpose of which was not self-evident. Check marks were being made on one sheet, and handwritten names highlighted in bright yellow on another; through it all, not one of the five employees took even a moment to lift his or her head and acknowledge the guests waiting to be seated. (Of course, in more technically sophisticated restaurants, where the floor plan is on a computer screen, it takes *seven* employees to huddle around and ignore arriving guests.)

It would not be fair to say that these employees were indifferent. In such a beautiful tropical setting, any number of things would have been more pleasant for them to do, I suspect, than to remain stooped in an uncomfortable position over a small desk, struggling to make sense of a bunch of papers. The fact that they continued fiddling with the papers, to the exclusion of everything around them, suggests to me that these were highly dedicated employees. And fiddle they did, for quite some time. So great was their dedication that eventually some of the folks in line, my wife and I included, decided to try the more casual eatery in another part of the hotel. The prospect of encountering such dedication even inspired us to decide, on our next visit, to try another hotel altogether.

These employees, like millions more in organizations around the world, find themselves struggling to cope with a policy or procedure designed for the gratification of management, in total disregard of the frustration and difficulties it may happen to create for anyone else. In this case, it happened to be a convoluted seating process; next time, the customer may confront a "Sorry, no exchanges" policy, or a needlessly tedious ordering procedure, or inconvenient operating hours, or an indecipherable automated phone system, or some ludicrous hidden extra charge. Within the organization proper, hidden from customers' eyes, are hopelessly vague job descriptions, ever-shifting priorities, impenetrable accounting systems, and layers of bureaucratic complexity that boggle the mind.

All of these constitute roadblocks, barriers to realizing the vision. They are dragons that lie at the mouth of the cave of success; they scorch with their breath of deadly fire all who dare approach the cave.

It is not enough to rally the employee population around a triumphant vision of success. Even if they are positively infused with eagerness to realize the vision, they quickly learn that their way forward is blocked. If they somehow manage to find a way around the dragon in their path without getting seriously burned, they discover another dragon lurking close behind the first, and yet another after that. Even highly enthusiastic employees quickly tire of fending off dragons, and their eagerness to blaze new trails soon evaporates. They become quite content to focus their energies on the mundane tasks at hand ("Never mind 'customer satisfaction'—I'll be happy if I can just get this ridiculous seating process sorted out in my head."). Instead of dreaming about grandiose visions of future triumph, they dream about making it to quitting time at the end of the day, or about their next weekend, or their next vacation, or of one day finally turning sixty-five, at which time perhaps somebody will give them a gold watch and the whole dreary nightmare will be over.

VALUES AS DRAGON DETECTORS

Organizational roadblocks are so numerous and so familiar that they almost fade into invisibility. These dragons are masters of camouflage; when the decision is taken to rout them, one discovers that they are everywhere, yet paradoxically quite hard to see.

Would-be dragon slayers require special viewing goggles that, like night-vision technology, make the quarry easier to find. The organization's core values provide such a viewing mechanism. Instead of looking all around to spot where dragons may be hiding, ambassadors of change pick one of the organization's values and then look for elements within the culture that appear to violate the particular value. Such violations are often markers indicating the presence of a dragon or two.

Many organizations, for example, cite trust as one of their guiding principles. A roving dragon-slayer, with the concept of trust uppermost in mind, may stop in front of the punch clock and gaze at it in a new way. Just what purpose does this device actually serve? These elaborate time sheets that employees are required to fill in daily or weekly: Tell me again, why were they instituted? The lock on the storage cabinet in which office supplies are kept, the fact that a doctor's certificate must validate certain kinds of sick leave, the need to secure authorization before making purchases on behalf of the department, all these so-called control measures: Why are they felt to be necessary? The dragon slayer observes the time employees waste, standing in long lines at the punch clock, or doing without needed office supplies until the storage cabinet keyholder returns from pursuing a doctor's certificate or a purchasing authorization; the dragon slayer contrasts this with the often-heard employee lament that there just isn't enough time in a day to do everything that needs doing. The dragon slayer concludes that a significant, multiheaded, fire-breathing cultural roadblock has been uncovered.

Time-consuming, complicated, tedious, pointless, insulting, demotivating: These are the marker words that, when applied to systems, policies, or procedures, alert ambassadors of change to the possibility of dragons lurking nearby. The fifth big question affords a splendid opportunity to demonstrate leadership commitment to the organization's values: "What we identify as our values, the guiding principles by which we intend to operate our business, are not empty words; we intend to 'live' them. It seems to us that this particular procedure (process, policy, system) is in violation of one of our core values. So, as of today, it is being rescinded."

In another example of how the 8 Big Questions tend to reinforce each other, question five often gives rise to powerful first question (ambassador of change) activities. That is, when we undertake to remove an organizational hindrance and make things simpler, easier, and more pleasant for our employees, at the same time we lead by example, changing our own systems or behaviors before expecting anyone else to change theirs. In effect we demonstrate, in the most persuasive way possible, our determination to realize the vision. We combat organizational cynicism with the most powerful tool in our entire arsenal: results. It is extremely difficult for the cynics to find listeners for their war chants of "Nothing's going to change around here, it's all just a lot of hot air . . ." when something very visibly does change for the better.

The opposite is also true. Implementation efforts in which little or no conscious effort is made to visibly live the values—or to eradicate cultural impediments to success— tend to fail (surprise!). This is another reason why the fifth big question can be thought of as the biggest of the eight; in terms of securing required levels of employee support and involvement, bringing values to life, demonstrating determination to succeed, and creating a more benign organizational culture, this one has momentous implications. It is here that ambassadors of change get to put their money where their collective mouth is.

FEEDBACK AS A DRAGON DETECTOR

There is, of course, another surefire way to find out what constitute the main obstacles as far as employees are concerned: Simply ask them. An obvious approach; what may be less obvious, however, are some of the hazards attendant to doing so.

In many organizations, the employees' list of things that make doing the job difficult is quite extensive. The line between difficult and unsatisfying is often a subtle one, as is the distinction between "things everyone finds difficult" and "things I personally find difficult." In effect, inviting employees to enumerate obstacles amounts to throwing open the floodgates; the risk is great of being swept away and drowning. Furthermore, every employee who contributes to the torrent will expect his or her pet grievance to be at least acknowledged, if not acted upon. Meeting this expectation could keep a small army of data processors occupied for months; failure to meet it raises general levels of cynicism a full peg or two. ("I knew they had no intention of doing a darn thing with any of these problems we pointed out for them. Just another attempt to con us into thinking they really care.")

Is there a way to solicit employee feedback that helps identify key obstacles while avoiding these pitfalls?

Encouraging employees to pinpoint all those things that, in Drucker's phrase, make it "difficult for people to work" is far too broad an undertaking. Linking it to the *plan* narrows things to manageable proportions. Ask not "What makes doing your job difficult?" but rather "What might make doing some of what's in the plan difficult?"

A logical part of sharing the contents of the plan with the employee population is to invite comments and questions, big question by big question. A logical way to invite such comments is to ask such things as: "Do any of these proposed activities seem to you to be in conflict with established policies or procedures? Can you foresee impediments to doing any of these things? Can you think of any reason why doing this might be more difficult than we anticipated?"

As part of planning around making things better for employees, ambassadors of change may want to add something to spreading the word internally and acquiring and using (internal) customer data, concerning the use of educational plan-sharing sessions as a means of identifying potential impediments to implementation.

Some impediments aren't difficult to find at all, of course. They're the ones that are so big no one could possibly miss them, the ones never eliminated precisely because they're so big that no one even knows where to begin.

SLAYING THE BIGGER DRAGONS

Adapting the old parable of the blind men examining an elephant reveals how difficult it is for people to blindly examine portions of a really big dragon. The procedures or processes that typically make life most difficult for employees (and customers!) are the big, clumsy, complex ones, those that cut across a number of divisions or departments or functions. Individual employees see only part of these processes, whatever relates to their own area within the organization. Very few people, if any, are likely to know what the whole dragon looks like. Only a specialist can lead the effort to exterminate a dragon of this size. Only a true ambassador of change has the specialized skills and knowledge to personally take ownership of such an assignment.

The dragon slayer needs help. He or she must put together a team made up of individuals from various parts of the organization who are each familiar with the part of the process passing through their area. The team then sets to work correcting the problem, usually by following a sequence of steps such as what follows here.

Map Out the Existing Process

The members of this cross-functional team begin by mapping out on paper exactly what the complete process looks like. That is, they create a composite view of the entire process, linking together a flowchart of the sequences of events that unfold within their respective areas. The flowchart must include every step that occurs, sensible or not, along with an indication of who is involved in each step. It also includes a time line: How long does this step usually take? What is the typical interval between this step and the next? This produces a reasonable portrait of what the beast looks like today.

Map Out an Improved Version of the Process

The team then creates a second flowchart, one that depicts what the entire process *should* look like if it is operating smoothly and efficiently. They do this by analyzing the first portrait, looking for needless steps, duplication of effort, unnecessary complications, detours, and delays. Every step is challenged: Is this really essential? What happens if it is removed? Can it be done any more quickly, any more simply? They remove as many of the steps as possible and attempt to simplify those that remain. If necessary, they create new transition steps to move the simplified process from one phase to another, revising the time lines to reflect all the changes.

Anticipate Side Effects

The team reviews their new, streamlined process flowchart, trying to discern whether it inadvertently creates unexpected problems or complications in other areas, or otherwise generates undesirable side effects. If any are anticipated, the process is modified to eliminate them.

Implement the Improved Process

If necessary, those who actually use the process are given appropriate training or education to prepare them to work with the modified version. The modifications are then implemented in the workplace, with team members closely monitoring the results. If there are problems, it's back to the drawing board to attempt to resolve them; if all runs smoothly, a major dragon has been successfully slain. (Why not celebrate the fact with a special "funeral" for the deceased?)

The Payoff of Teamwork

Of course, such a highly condensed simplification of process-management or process-reengineering practice cannot convey every possible technique or potential pitfall. For the purposes of planning for transformational change within an organization, however, it is usually sufficient for the members of the leadership team to appreciate, in broad terms, the kind of effort that is required to remove cross-departmental impediments to the vision, and make things better for employees on a large scale. The effort can be considerable, but the payback is proportionately large. In fact, in many cases the cultural payback is disproportionate in that a major roadblock to the vision is removed and, additionally, ongoing relations among areas of the organization tend to improve greatly.

DOWN WITH TURFDOMS

Cross-functional efforts to remove organizational obstacles lead to slain dragons; they also promote healthy erosion of the stone walls that close off various areas within the organization from one another, like so many fortresses or silos.

There is a mantra, a chorus that rises chantlike from every organization in which I have ever observed cross-functional teams as they begin working together: "We had no idea you (or they) were struggling with the very same problems we have." It is surprising how intensely this simple realization affects cultural relationships among different parts of an organization. Nothing unites disparate groups more effectively than a common enemy. Within organizations, the various divisions—the word itself could hardly be more divisive—are unknowingly doing battle routinely with a number of obstacles they all have in common; when this is discovered, they begin to see each other in a new light. Where there was always a certain degree of suspicion, a certain aloofness, a tendency to form cliques in the cafeteria or at company social events, a certain we-they mentality pervading all cross-functional dealings, suddenly there develops a refreshing sense of just "we": "Hey, we're all in this together"; "A win for you folks means a win for us too."

Suddenly it's OK for someone in engineering to be on friendly terms with someone in manufacturing. Suddenly it's no longer treasonous for sales personnel to consort with marketing personnel. The new clique is the organization as a whole. "They" are no longer the folks down the hall or on a different floor in the same building; "they" are the competition. Such a cultural realignment has profound implications in terms of how business is conducted day to day. In my experience, one of the fastest and best ways to generate such cultural realignment is to charge members of the senior leadership team to put together one or more teams of representatives from different areas, set them to work selecting one of the biggest dragons they all have in common, and figure out how best to go about slaying it.

BIG QUESTION 5 PLANNING EXERCISE

In planning for ways to make things better for employees, ambassadors of change look for cultural obstacles that can be removed. The fundamental objective is to make it easier—and therefore more enjoyable—for employees to do all that must be done to accomplish the mission and realize the vision.

Because there are potentially so many systems, policies, procedures, and traditions making things needlessly difficult, it is not uncommon for this fifth section of the plan to contain more actual content, in terms of proposed activities, than any other section. This need not be cause for concern. As we'll see in discussing "storyboarding" the plan in the chapter "Finishing Touches," it is useful once the entire planning process is completed to review the time frames allocated to the planned activities. In the case of the fifth big question in particular, it may make sense to push some of these activities back to year-two time frames, if not later. Thus, having lots to do does not necessarily mean having lots to do *right away*. Also, question-five activities are often more subtractive than additive in nature; they tend to involve removing elements rather than adding new ones: simplifying procedures by eliminating steps, for example, or discontinuing practices, or abolishing certain policies. Thus, a heavy concentration of ideas on this question may well translate into an ultimate *lightening* of the total activity workload. Implementation of many of these ideas may require no more than the stroke of a pen.

....

PHASE ONE: STATUS-QUO QUESTIONS

For no more than ten minutes and without any discussion or analysis, list on a flipchart as many answers as you can think of to these two questions (approximately five minutes per question):

1 Strengths: What are some of the existing systems, policies, procedures, or traditions that will help our employees achieve the mission and realize the vision?

2 Weaknesses: What are some of the existing systems, policies, procedures, or traditions that may act as obstacles or otherwise make it difficult for our employees to achieve the mission and realize the vision?

The first question really asks: What existing systems, etc., do employees currently use to good advantage? What do we currently do well in terms of supporting our employees and making it easier for them to do their jobs? What works well in terms of helping employees move us closer to realizing our vision?

The second question asks: What are the existing systems, etc., that may (or clearly do) get in the way? What causes the most frustration for our employees?

....

PHASE TWO: BRAINSTORMING QUESTIONS

For no more than fifteen minutes, review the list of strengths and weaknesses created in phase one, and for each, without evaluation or discussion, list on a flipchart as many ideas as you can think of to answer these two questions (approximately seven minutes per question):

1 What can be done to amplify our strengths?

2 What can be done to overcome our weaknesses?

For each strength listed, the question becomes, If we had unlimited resources, time, and authority, what could we do to derive even more benefit from this? How could we make this even more effective? What would it take to give this even more impact?

For each weakness: If we had no constraints whatsoever, how could we eliminate this problem? What could we do to get around this obstacle? How might we turn this weakness into a strength?

....

PHASE THREE: ACTIVITY-PLANNING QUESTIONS

Spend no more than a minute or two selecting one idea that seems a suitable candidate for inclusion in the plan from the list generated in phase two. For this one idea, take no more than twenty minutes to answer all of the following questions on a flipchart. (It's prudent to allow five full minutes at the end for the final question.)

▶ What exactly will be done? (Distinguish between objectives and activities, and concentrate on the latter. The response to this question should begin with a verb, such as *create, establish, communicate*, etc.)

▶ How will it be done? (If it is not immediately obvious, describe in broad terms how this activity will be implemented. Make note here of any implementation details or issues that remain to be resolved.)

▶ Who will do it? (Use actual names where possible.)

▶ Who will ensure that it gets done? (In most cases, the person who will be held accountable should be a member of the leadership team.)

▶ When will it begin, or be completed? (Specify an actual date.)

▶ How will success be measured? (By what means will we confirm that this particular activity has truly removed obstacles to realizing the vision? Has made it easier or more enjoyable for employees to do their jobs?)

At the conclusion of each three-phase round of the plan-building exercise, those flipcharts bearing content destined for inclusion in the final plan must be separated from the rest and put safely aside for preservation.

Begin by collecting the flipcharts bearing the responses to the phase-three activity-planning questions. Using a marker of a different color than already appears on the charts, inscribe *BQ5* prominently on each sheet, wherever space permits. Next, isolate the flipchart from phase one which bears the list of strengths; inscribe *BQ5* on this chart, too. (During the creation of the planning document, it may be appropriate to include in the section on the fifth big question certain items from this list of strengths, under the heading "Things We Will Continue to Do.")

Once the content flipcharts have been separated from the rest, branded, and put safely aside for preservation, the team can elect to do one of the following:

▶ Take a break.

or

▶ Select another item from the existing brainstormed list of ideas for the fifth big question generated in phase two, and subject it to the phase-three activity-planning questions, for no more than twenty minutes.

or

▶ Proceed to the sixth big question, and begin by answering the phase-one status-quo questions, for ten minutes or less.

••

If the team is not sure it's ready to proceed to the next big question, it's usually wise to err on the side of plenty.

Once the fifth big question has been addressed to the team's satisfaction, it's time to begin thinking about how to make things better for customers.

6

How Will We Make Things Better for Our Customers?

E ven if your organization's mission and vision do not make specific reference, even implicitly, to raising levels of customer satisfaction—which would be something of a rarity—the fact remains that you certainly do not wish for your change initiative to drive customer satisfaction levels down. Yet if the issue is not a key element of your vision, there is a real danger of this happening.

PARDON OUR DUST

Change often entails temporary periods of transition characterized by considerable disorder and confusion. When a hospital decides it's time to refurbish one of its wings, or a town finally gets around to repairing a well-worn section of street, it is usually not a matter of the bad situation gradually being replaced with a better one. More often, for a short time the bad must get considerably worse before any dramatic improvement can be seen. The dingy and drafty hospital wing is temporarily full of workers and dust and noise, with bits of scaffolding and plastic tarpaulins and building materials scattered everywhere. The potholed streets are closed off and torn up altogether, and for a while motorists must negotiate muddy, unpaved, back-road, torture-test detours while work progresses. (If the hospital and town in question have skilled ambassadors of change in their employ, of course, then handsome billboards soothe raised hackles by depicting what the refurbished wing or improved roadway will look like, along with trumpeting anticipated dates of completion.)

During this time of transition, the danger of alienating customers is greatest. The organization's collective focus is on the task at hand: implementing the various changes that make it possible to achieve the mission and realize the vision. The stresses and pressures associated with attempting to maintain some sort of business-as-usual normality while coping with a variety of new, unfamiliar, and confusing elements frazzle nerves and shorten tempers. If customer satisfaction is not a central element of the mission and vision, then during this stressful time it is in danger of being overlooked altogether, to the organization's potential long-term detriment. ("Hurray! We've successfully made the move to work teams! Boo! Half of our key customers have taken their business elsewhere in the meantime!")

Planning around the sixth big question gives ambassadors of change a means of ensuring that customers are not inadvertently driven away during the noisy, dusty, detour phase of implementation. The strategy involves maintaining a business-as-usual focus while actually setting out to incorporate some business-*better*-than-usual elements into the customer experience during the period of transition. (Positive results constitute the most potent antidote for cynicism of the external kind as well: "Folks, not only do these changes in our policy *not* represent any sort of 'slipping' or 'slacking off' on our part, or any worsening of the experience you the customer can expect from us; but rather, as you can see, they will actually serve to make things easier and better for you.") If raising levels of customer satisfaction is a key element of the mission and vision, then the planning exercise of this sixth question defines how it will be done, when, by whom, and so on.

MANAGING CUSTOMER PERCEPTIONS

Customer satisfaction is a fairly scary concept, when you get right down to it. Everyone knows it's important; no business can long survive without it. But it's an intangible, slippery thing. It's interwoven with the even-less-tangible business of perception, which is about as substantial as a bag of smoke. How can such abstractions be managed systematically?

Consider a five hundred dollar gift. Would such a gift be "perceived" by most people as a good thing or a bad thing? The answer, of course, is that it all depends; we begin to understand how perceptions can be managed when we understand the kinds of things it depends on.

Imagine if one-third of the people in your neighborhood received a letter from the tax office announcing that thanks to a general region-wide overpayment of taxes each of them is entitled to a five hundred dollar rebate; all they have to do is show up at the tax office next Tuesday during business hours to collect. Good news?

What if another third of the neighborhood population received a letter announcing a rebate of a thousand dollars, but two days later got a second letter stating, "Oops, sorry, due to a clerical error, you will actually be required to split your rebate with another person. But hey, never mind, that's still five hundred bucks that's all yours." Does the gift feel as good to the second group as to the first?

What if the final third of the folks in your neighborhood received a letter promising a gift of $250, but when they went to collect it they were told, "Good news, we are able to make the rebates larger than anticipated—you're actually getting five hundred!"

Which group would feel best about the five hundred dollar gift? A basic tenet of managing perceptions is to always *underpromise and overdeliver.*

The same dollar amount, the same experience, can be perceived very differently. It isn't just because people are different; a bigger factor is what surrounds or accompanies the amount or the experience. A swatch of a certain color seems to change when it is surrounded by fields of contrasting colors. Things can be made to appear quite different simply by changing the field of surrounding elements.

Price, for example, is often isolated as the primary determinant in most buying decisions. Whenever a manager or CEO tells me the firm competes "on price," I always ask, "Are you sure?" If the answer is yes, I then ask for some advice. "I haven't been able to make up my mind about something," I announce, "and I'm hoping you can help me. As far as you're concerned, would you say seventy-five dollars is a good price?" "For what?" they ask.

Precisely. Price by itself is just a random number. The only conceivable scenario in which it is accurate to say a business is competing on price is one in which two perfectly identical businesses, equivalent in terms of the size and decor of their premises and the number (as well as knowledgeability) of staff, and every other imaginable attribute, are selling perfectly identical merchandise to exactly the same potential customers in exactly the same area for exactly the same price, and one of the businesses suddenly decides to lower its prices. Unless all of these factors are identical, competing businesses are not competing on price; they're competing on *value*, which is the cost-benefit ratio. All those nonidentical attributes—convenience of location, size of parking lot, helpfulness of staff, etc.—tip the cost-benefit scales in favor of one business over the other. There is no such thing as a good price or a bad price; but there is the perception of good value and of poor value. Price is an important part of the equation, but not the only part. If the perception of value is high, customers don't mind paying the price; if the perceived value is low, any price is too high.

A THREE-RING CIRCUS

How can we represent this notion of the perception of value in simple, graphic terms to simplify and better understand the idea? In the mid-1980s, Art McNeil and I adapted an idea that originated with Theodore Levitt and created a conceptual model using three concentric rings: the larger the ring, the greater the perception of value. It has been gratifying to see this simple model reproduced graphically in several business books, on posters and videos in a number of internationally distributed training programs, and to see it adopted into the language and thinking of hundreds of organizations around the world over the years. Briefly, the Three Rings of Perceived Value model, as it is formally known, works as follows.

The smallest, innermost ring represents the *basic product*, that which the organization supplies to meet its customers' basic requirements. Amazingly, in many organizations there is uncertainty about what precisely constitutes the basic product. When I ask hotel employees what their basic product is, for example, I'm often given "beds" as a response. It is only after I ask them "Does this mean you are in direct competition with Charlie's Bed Store down the street?" that they begin to appreciate the distinction between selling a bed and selling the use of a bed. Further challenges help them distinguish between the use of a bed and the use of a room. The object is to help them appreciate how all aspects of the customer experience that relate to the room—availability on a specific date, bed size, smoking and nonsmoking policies, and so on—are "inner ring" issues; they are directly related to the basic product. The comparative size of this inner ring reflects the perception of value the customer attaches to the basic product, based on how well it meets his or her requirements.

Surrounding this innermost ring is a larger second ring representing *support elements*: those activities and processes designed to support, or add value, to the basic product by meeting customer expectations. In this model, the distinction between requirements and expectations, which can be thought of as needs versus wants, is typically that requirements are stated aloud (or otherwise specified outright) whereas expectations are not. A person making a reservation at a hotel, for example, indicates what type of room is required on what dates but as a rule does not bother asking such things as "Will there be hot and cold running water?" "Will there be linen on the bed?" "Can I count on a minimum of insect life visiting me in the night?" Yet failure to meet these unspoken expectations can have a devastating effect on the perception of value. In a hotel, the second ring would encompass a wide range of activities, including parking, housekeeping, reception, billing, room service, etc.

In most organizations, the bulk of the employee population is engaged in second-ring activities. It is in the second ring, too, that most customer dissatisfaction typically originates: "You make a great widget, but your delivery was late, plus you shipped the wrong quantity, plus you overcharged me, plus you misspelled my name on the invoice." If all of the second-ring support elements work properly, however, and the all of the customer's expectations are met, the perception of value expands; hence the larger ring.

The third and largest ring of all represents *enhanced service*: those rare but delightful "wow factor" elements that exceed customer expectations and expand the perception of value as far as it can go. In our hotel example, this might be a basket of fruit bearing a personalized welcome note hand-signed by the manager, or willingness to stock the minibar with items specifically requested by the guest. It is supremely ironic that third-ring elements are often the simplest and least expensive to implement yet tend to have the greatest positive impact by far on the customer's perception of value. When travelers fly cross the ocean, their most lasting impression is not that they have been safely transported a great distance at great speed and at great altitude—even though such a feat might leave their great-grandmothers nearly catatonic with awe and terror. It's the fact that the in-flight crew baked a batch of fresh cookies from scratch during the flight that really wows them, though that's a rather humdrum accomplishment from great-grandmother's point of view. The third ring has the greatest perception of value attached to it (hence its even larger size); it provides businesses with maximum market differentiation and competitive advantage.

The power of a model as simple as this one lies in the clarity it brings to the language that various parts of the organization use to communicate with each other. Suddenly everyone begins to understand that customer satisfaction does not revolve solely around the basic product but rather depends on the total experience represented by the combination of all three rings. If someone refers to a "second-ring problem," everyone knows that it does not refer to a deficiency in the basic product but instead to a breakdown in one or more of the support elements. If someone describes a third-ring experience, everyone knows this refers to a case of customer delight, the wow factor, expectations exceeded.

The model is sufficiently adaptable to permit some deeper understanding as well. For example, it makes it easier to explain why change by its very nature must be constant. What happens to a wow-factor idea immediately after it's introduced into the third ring? It becomes expected. Put another way, it migrates to the second ring as a standard expectation. For their part, second-ring elements often become so identified with an organization, or so integral to the way it operates, that they essentially become part of the basic product; that is, they migrate to the inner ring. The three rings are dynamic. Nothings stays put; everything is constantly moving inward. In addition, once an innovation has been introduced into the third ring, it's often a simple matter for competitors to appropriate the idea for their own use. How, then, is an organization to maintain the competitive advantage the third ring gives it? By continuously adding new third-ring innovations, of course; hence the need for constant change.

As an educational tool, the model also allows ambassadors of change to illustrate how everyone within the organization has a vital role to play in realizing the vision (or in delighting customers). Who owns the inner ring? That is, who makes the big decisions that involve the basic product offering? Usually the senior leadership team does. Who owns the second ring? That is, who's responsible for all of the support elements and how they work? In most cases, middle management. Who owns the third ring? That is, who's responsible for what happens at the coal face, in the trenches, in direct contact with customers? For the most part, frontline employees. Of all three rings, which has the biggest impact on the perception of value? But which segment of the organization's workforce in most cases receives the least amount of training, attention, and recognition? Is it just me, or is there something wrong with this picture?

To realize the vision, the organization must make improvements in all three rings; everyone therefore needs to be involved. From the point of view of spreading the word internally, the three-ring model makes it easy to convey how each part of the plan, each of the activities related to the 8 Big Questions, has a direct bearing on the total customer experience, and therefore on the customer's ultimate perception of value.

Armed with the language of the three-ring model, ambassadors of change could say that one of the objectives of making things better for employees (Chapter 5) is to introduce some third-ring elements into employees' working conditions within the organization. It becomes so much easier for employees to embrace the whole strategic philosophy of wowing customers if they themselves have occasion to personally experience what being wowed feels like. Indeed, making things better for employees almost always ends up directly or indirectly improving things for customers as well.

STUMPING THE RINGS

Naturally, the benefits to be derived from sharing a common language can only be enjoyed if the language in question is known and fully understood by all. What's the best way to spread the word vis-á-vis the whole concept of the customer's perception of value?

Enter the humble stump speech. In the first big question, becoming ambassadors of change, we outlined exercises to develop two stump speeches, one for the mission and vision and a second one dealing with indicators for change (the four Cs: customers, competitors, changes, and costs). What follows is a similar exercise, designed to produce the content for a third stump speech, on the theme of perception of value. Although a large number of client organizations have built educational modules for the three rings into their formal internal communication efforts, many of them acknowledge that it is through informally delivered stump speeches that the message ultimately takes hold most effectively.

For those organizations in which customer satisfaction is not a key element of the mission or vision, this exercise can be thought of as a potentially useful supplement to the overall internal communication strategy. For the rest, this could be one of the most useful tools in the entire ambassador-of-change toolkit.

....

STUMP SPEECH THREE: THE PERCEPTION OF VALUE

As with the stump-speech exercises outlined in Chapter 1, this one is intended for the members of the senior leadership team. A stopwatch or countdown timer is required. A prepared visual aid (flipchart or overhead transparency), described below, should be created beforehand.

▶ The facilitator supplies the team with a brief overview of the three-rings concept, making reference to this prepared visual aid.

> ### THE PERCEPTION OF VALUE
>
> ▶ Meeting requirements
>
> ▶ Meeting expectations
>
> ▶ Exceeding expectations
>
> ▶ Continuous improvement
>
> ▶ Everyone has a role

Experience has taught that when explaining the concept for the first time, it's preferable to use a neutral business example to illustrate—that is, an example removed from the organization's own industry. This avoids unproductive debate about whether, in "our particular case," such-and-such an element "truly" qualifies to be thought of as belonging in the first or in the second ring, and so on. The best neutral examples are those everyone is familiar with: a hotel, an airline, a hamburger restaurant, etc.

▶ The context for the five points listed on the visual aid might be paraphrased as follows:

1 The basic product (inner ring) is perceived to have value to the extent that it meets the customer's stated *requirements*.

2 The support elements (second ring) expand the customer's perception of value to the extent that they meet the customer's typically unstated *expectations*. It is in the second ring that most customer dissatisfaction originates.

3 The wow-factor elements (third, largest ring) expand the perception of value to the maximum by *exceeding expectations*.

4 Of course, once a third-ring wow-factor enhancement is introduced, the customer expects it thereafter; it immediately migrates to the second ring. To maintain competitive advantage, we need to constantly add new third-ring innovations, *continuously improving* all aspects of the customer experience. In short, this improvement effort is an ongoing part of how we do business.

5 Ownership of the basic product (inner ring) and the decisions made around it typically reside with the senior leadership team. Control and decision making around the second ring support pieces typically come from middle management. The third ring is clearly in the hands of frontline employees who interact directly with customers. We thus *all have a critical role* to play in this ongoing improvement effort

▶ At the conclusion of the facilitator's presentation, team members are given ten minutes, working alone, to determine how to incorporate the five points into a stump speech of their own, using three concentric rings along with a neutral example to illustrate how the customer's perception of value can be made to expand beyond the basic product. They record their key points on a crib sheet.

▶ When the ten minutes are up, the facilitator instructs the team members to select a partner and form pairs. Listeners are encouraged to keep paper and pen at hand and make notes during the speech, recording key words to help them recall elements that worked well and opportunities for improvement, so as to feed these back to their partners. Speakers are advised that a stopwatch or timer will be set in motion as the various speeches get under way, and that once three minutes has elapsed all speeches are to be concluded—even if not all of the speakers' intended points have been covered. Speakers are allowed to refer to their crib sheets during their speeches. They are to imagine that they are responding to a question from an individual employee, along the lines of, "If our basic product (or basic service) gives customers what they want, isn't that enough?"

▶ The clock is set in motion, and the speeches begin.

▶ Three minutes later, the speeches are brought to an end. Listeners are given two minutes to provide feedback.

▶ When the feedback is concluded, listeners and speakers exchange roles. The clock is once more set in motion, and another round of speeches begins.

▶ After three minutes, the speeches are concluded. Listeners are given two minutes to provide feedback.

▶ The facilitator asks if anyone was unable to cover all of the intended points within the time limit and encourages those who were not able to do so to think about how they can shorten their speech.

▶ The facilitator asks whether any listeners would like to nominate their partner to come to the head of the room and provide an instant replay of the speech for the whole team's benefit. If nominations are made and time permits, the group hears one or more model perception-of-value stump speeches. Afterwards, the facilitator asks whether listeners recall any particular highlights from their partners' speeches that they would like to offer to the team. If so, these are heard.

Particularly inventive or amusing three-ring stump speeches are often fondly remembered long after the event. (I'm quite confident that none of us who were at one particular public academy session several years ago in Georgia is ever going to forget Rhonda Lawson's persuasive use of a bordello as her neutral example of how exceeding expectations might enhance the customer's perception of value.)

••

Clearly, the first step in making things better for customers involves helping employees better understand how customer perceptions work. But how is such understanding translated into action?

THE CUSTOMER-FOCUS PROCESS

Empowerment, involvement, ownership: what lofty ideals. What worthy pursuits.

We do not want our employees to become paralyzed with indecision when we are not around. We want them to feel empowered to take initiatives on their own, to delight customers, and to do what needs to be done to realize the vision.

They mustn't be denied a voice in matters that affect their work. We want them to feel a sense of personal involvement in the pursuit of success for the organization.

It's not good if they feel that management's ideas are being forced down their throats. They must experience the pride associated with a sense of ownership that can only come if it is their own ideas being acted upon, their own approaches contributing to the organization's success. Yes, how true.

Alas, easier said than done. Of the 8 Big Questions, this one alone, the sixth, focuses on applying the third-ring wow factor to customers. The third ring is the province of the frontline employees; what better place, therefore, in all of the planning for change, to concentrate on enhancing the sense of empowerment, involvement, and ownership among these employees? But how to do it?

Join me now, in a nostalgic journey down memory lane, as we revisit yesteryear's ineffectual methods and approaches for "training" employees to make things better for customers.

Here we see a group of listless employees attending a corporate customer-service training program entitled The ABCs of Customer Service. This one is the third of twenty-six sessions the group is attending, focusing this time on the letter *C*, specifically on Complaints. Note the printed wall chart bearing the heading "Basic Steps for Dealing With Angry Customers." Note that there are nine basic steps listed beneath the heading. Note that the instructor is using a long pointer to indicate the first of these basic steps, which reads "Carefully pry the customer's teeth from your lower calf." Note in particular that most of the employees in attendance are creating elaborate doodles in their training workbooks while the instructor drones on; note that while some of these doodles are quite imaginative, a few are somewhat risqué and in questionable taste.

We could visit a couple of hundred "customer service training sessions" in a couple of hundred corporate training rooms over a couple of decades, and the scene wouldn't be significantly different. This is pretty much the essence of traditional customer service training: Here are the things we (or the faceless experts) want you to do from now on. In terms of fostering empowerment, involvement, and ownership, such efforts score zero across the board.

The customer-focus process (CFP) is not "training" in the conventional sense. No new skills are taught, nor is any new knowledge imparted. Instead of the facilitator telling the participants what they could be doing to delight customers, the participants tell the facilitator what they could be doing. A wide range of ideas are recorded and preserved through a highly interactive brainstorming process.

The double paradox of CFP is that first, while no actual teaching happens during the session, significant learning nevertheless does take place. Participants come to realize, through their own process of discovery, that there are a great many opportunities for improving the customer's experience that are being consistently overlooked, and that in many cases making things better for customers almost certainly makes things better for themselves as well. They develop a heightened sensitivity to customer expectations and a greater appreciation of the effect the wow factor has on customers' overall perception of value. In a word, they become more customer-focused, without a wall chart, video monitor, workbook, role-play exercise, or list of basic steps anywhere in sight.

The second paradox is that whereas traditional training programs mandate a change in behavior on the part of participants, those programs are notoriously ineffective in terms of producing genuine behavior change. CFP, by comparison, keeps behavior change at the purely voluntary level yet holds an impressive track record for producing profound and lasting changes in behavior. This, I believe, is largely because in CFP the sense of empowerment, involvement, and ownership is at a maximum.

Elements of CFP

The customer-focus process is designed as a highly interactive team brainstorming session, typically of approximately three hours' duration. The participants should all be part of the same functional workgroup. Twelve participants make an ideal-sized group, though the process works with as few as three and as many as twenty. The individual to whom the participants report should act as facilitator.

All that is required in the way of materials for each participant are one pad of Post-it Notes® (preferably of the two-by-three-inch size) and one marker that produces a heavy, highly visible line for maximum legibility.

The CFP facilitator's main tool is the matrix, a rows-and-columns arrangement by which ideas written on Post-its are displayed for the group's ongoing reference. Essentially, headings are posted in a horizontal row extending from left to right; entries related to these headings are posted in vertical columns beneath the relevant headings.

Facilitation Guidelines

First of all, ideas must be stated out loud. The facilitator promotes ideas by asking a series of key questions. Participants are not to write their ideas on a Post-it until the entire group has had the opportunity to hear the idea and perhaps improve upon it.

Second, participants write down their own ideas. It is important that the workers see their *own* ideas posted in their *own* words and in their *own* handwriting; this emphasizes the ownership aspect of the process.

Third, the facilitator ensures that all ideas are captured and posted. This is the facilitator's primary challenge. CFP sessions typically generate a rapid flow of ideas; the facilitator may need to do some fancy footwork merely to receive all of them and post them within the matrix.

Fourth, the matrix is to be preserved for future reference. However the matrix is displayed, think about how it can be preserved for use in follow-up sessions. One popular solution is to tape blank flipcharts to the wall and affix the Post-it Notes to the flipcharts, which can then be rolled up for storage or transport.

Opening Remarks

The facilitator needs to explain to the participants the nature and purpose of the session they're about to participate in. These opening remarks should, at a minimum, cover the following points:

■ Why the need to improve? This is an excellent opportunity to use the Indicators for Change stump speech described in "How Will We Become Ambassadors of Change?"

■ How will ideas be captured? This involves explaining how CFP differs from conventional training, and stipulating that answers to questions must be spoken aloud before being written down and added to the matrix.

■ Implementing ideas is strictly voluntary ("Nothing you come up with will be used against you.").

Customer Categories

Throughout the CFP session, the facilitator generates ideas from participants by asking a series of key questions. For this first section, which serves as a kind of warm-up exercise, the first key question is, "What different categories of customers do we do business with?" The answers to this question are posted left to right in a horizontal row along the top of the matrix, to serve as headings.

The second key question is, "What kinds of unique expectations do [customers of a particular category] have when they do business with us?" The answers to this question are posted in columns below the customer-category headings that apply.

Transaction Sequence

The facilitator identifies which particular type of customer transaction the session is focusing on. Then the key question is asked: "What are the various steps our customers typically go through as part of this type of transaction?" The answers are posted left to right in a horizontal row along the top of the matrix, to serve as a new group of headings.

Brainstorming, Phase One

At this point the facilitator begins the actual creative brainstorming process. The key question for the first phase of brainstorming is, "What could be done in each step of the transaction sequence to *exceed customers' expectations*?" The answers to this question are posted in columns below the steps in the transaction sequence to which they apply.

Brainstorming, Phase Two

The key question for the second phase of brainstorming is, "What could be done in each step of the transaction sequence to *make the customer feel important*?" Once again, the answers to this question are posted in columns below the steps in the transaction sequence to which they apply.

Brainstorming, Phase Three

In the third and final phase of brainstorming, the facilitator refers participants back to the customer-categories section of the matrix, created at the outset of the session. The first expectation posted in the column below the first customer category is removed and posted anew in a clear area to the right of the matrix, as a new heading. Two key questions, each related to the expectation under consideration, are then asked:

(Action-related):	"What could be done to better meet or exceed this particular expectation for [this category of customer]?"
(Communication-related):	"What could be done to ensure that [this category of customer] recognizes we're [addressing this expectation] specifically with them in mind?"

The answers to these questions are posted in columns below the expectation to which they apply.

Each of the remaining expectations under the original customer-category headings are in turn repositioned as new matrix headings and the two key questions above are asked for each, with answers posted below. When the questions have been answered for the last of the expectations, the brainstorming element of CFP is concluded.

Turning Ideas Into Actions

It's important that participants understand they are under no obligation to implement their ideas. If they decide they would like to do so, however, it is the facilitator's responsibility to keep a record of the activities being committed to and later celebrate successes in some conspicuous and meaningful way.

BIG QUESTION 6 PLANNING EXERCISE

Since the lion's share of activities identified as answers to the *fifth* big question in all probability address a range of second-ring elements, adding a third-ring customer component to many of them is often quite straightforward. Misaligned systems, inefficient processes, needlessly complex procedures all are second-ring issues. Fixing them so that they create less of a hindrance for employees is an objective of the fifth big question; but as a rule this means that by default employees are also able to better and more consistently meet customer expectations, a goal of the present big question. Fixing these problems to meet expectations is the hard part; the relatively easy part is to add the little something that exceeds expectations, the little something that, for customers, makes the big difference. Question five involves baking elaborate cakes; this big question involves adding the icing.

A useful starting point for planning around the sixth big question, therefore, is to review the activities planned in response to the fifth question, activities intended to make things better for employees, and to investigate whether something might be added that would also serve to wow customers.

....

PHASE ONE: STATUS-QUO QUESTIONS

For no more than ten minutes and without any discussion or analysis, list on a flipchart as many answers as you can think of to these two questions (approximately five minutes per question):

1 Strengths: What do we currently do well to make things easy, convenient, or pleasant for customers?

2 Weaknesses: What prevents us from making things easier, more convenient, or more pleasant for customers?

The first question really asks: What are the existing sources of customer satisfaction or delight in our business? In what aspects of the customer experience are we judged to be better than our competitors? By what means do we currently strive to improve things for customers?

The second question asks: What are the existing sources of customer dissatisfaction or frustration in our business? What factors make it difficult for us to consistently deliver a delightful customer experience? What obstacles make it difficult for us to improve things for customers?

PHASE TWO: BRAINSTORMING QUESTIONS

For no more than fifteen minutes, review the list of strengths and weaknesses created in phase one, and for each, without evaluation or discussion, list on a flipchart as many ideas as you can think of to answer these two questions (approximately seven minutes per question):

1 What can be done to amplify our strengths?

2 What can be done to overcome our weaknesses?

For each strength listed, the question becomes, If we had unlimited resources, time, and authority, what could we do to derive even more benefit from this? How could we make this even more effective? What would it take to give this even more impact?

For each weakness: If we had no constraints whatsoever, how could we eliminate this problem? What could we do to get around this obstacle? How might we turn this weakness into a strength?

PHASE THREE: ACTIVITY-PLANNING QUESTIONS

Spend no more than a minute or two selecting one idea that seems a suitable candidate for inclusion in the plan from the list generated in phase two. For this one idea, take no more than twenty minutes to answer all of the following questions on a flipchart. (It's prudent to allow five full minutes at the end for the final question.)

▶ What exactly will be done? (Distinguish between objectives and activities, and concentrate on the latter. The response to this question should begin with a verb, such as *create*, *establish*, *communicate*, etc.)

▶ How will it be done? (If it is not immediately obvious, describe in broad terms how this activity will be implemented. Make note here of any implementation details or issues that remain to be resolved.)

▶ Who will do it? (Use actual names where possible.)

▶ Who will ensure that it gets done? (In most cases, the person who will be held accountable should be a member of the leadership team.)

▶ When will it begin, or be completed? (Specify an actual date.)

▶ How will success be measured? (By what means will we confirm that this particular activity has truly improved customers' perception of value? Has made things easier, more convenient, or more pleasant for customers? Has given us a mechanism for continuously improving the customer experience?)

At the conclusion of each three-phase round of the planning exercise, those flipcharts bearing content destined for inclusion in the final plan must be separated from the rest and put safely aside for preservation.

Begin by collecting the flipcharts bearing the responses to the phase-three activity-planning questions. Using a marker of a different color than already appears on the charts, "brand" them by inscribing *BQ6* prominently on each sheet, wherever space permits. Next, isolate the flipchart from phase one that bears the list of strengths. This chart, too, needs to have *BQ6* inscribed upon it. During the creation of the planning document, it may be appropriate to include in the section on the sixth big question certain items from this list of strengths, under the heading "Things We Will Continue to Do."

Once the content flipcharts have been separated from the rest, branded, and put safely aside for preservation, the team can elect to do one of the following:

▶ Take a break.

or

▶ Select another item from the existing brainstormed list of ideas for the sixth big question generated in phase two, and subject it to the phase-three activity-planning questions, for no more than twenty minutes. Or review the activities generated in response to the fifth big question; investigate whether any obvious "third ring" ideas spring to mind to make the employee-oriented improvements beneficial for customers as well, and subject one or more of these ideas to the phase-three activity-planning questions, for no more than twenty minutes.)

or

▶ Proceed to the seventh big question, and begin by answering the phase-one status-quo questions, for ten minutes or less.

••

If the team is not sure it's ready to proceed to the next big question, it's usually wise to err on the side of plenty.

Once the sixth big question has been addressed to the team's satisfaction, it's time to begin thinking about how to measure successes.

How Will We Measure Our Successes?

We who are accustomed to driving those more "boring" conventional cars may find that the absence of gauges and dials actually gives rise to more fretting than ever. As soon as we accept the idea that it is possible to measure some aspect of our car's performance, we begin to routinely monitor it. When indications are that all is well, we're reassured. If, suddenly, that measurement mechanism is removed, we tend to miss the reassurance it gave us.

DRIVING BLIND

Many organizations navigate almost exclusively by their rearview mirrors. Their dashboards are clutterfree. Their sales figures and financial results, when eventually tabulated, tell them if where they have been is really where they want to go. It is, shall we say, a somewhat dangerous way to drive, even on a straight and flat highway in beautiful weather. Add the storm clouds of change and the unexpected twists and turns of transitional detours, and the danger is greatly magnified.

At a minimum, the organizational dashboard should include two additional gauges beyond financial results: operational performance, and customer satisfaction. These measures, as with all others, can be as broad and general, or as detailed and involved, as the situation warrants. Operational measures, for example, can be a simple reflection of overall quality: product quality (as in number of errors, defects, or other slipups over a period of time), and process quality (levels of waste, general throughput). Or they can delve into highly specialized elements of the operation and measure extremely fine variabilities within separate aspects of product or process quality. Similarly, measures of customer satisfaction can range from generalized evaluations (such as might be derived from feedback cards that customers fill in and submit at their own discretion) to frequent, highly focused surveys endeavoring to plumb the depths of customer expectations and perceptions.

The object of building measurement components into the plan is to minimize the danger of wrong turns and fiery crashes by establishing effective early warning systems. The most important object, though, is to confirm progress, bring successes to light, and create opportunities for celebration.

DATA VERSUS MEASUREMENT

"How do you know if you're improving if you're not measuring?" asks Mimi Andrews, vice president of quality at Advanced Environmental Technical Services (AETS), a seventy-thousand-employee waste management firm in Flanders, New Jersey. "We found we had lots of data," she observes, "but we weren't really measuring anything at all."

The distinction is subtle. Generally speaking, when you set out to measure something, you always end up with data; but when you set out to simply collect data (as in the sense of acquiring and using customer data, big question number three), you do not always end up with a useful measure of anything. To illustrate: the statement *There are nine people in my company who are over six and a half feet tall* is an example of raw data. (Though it would have been necessary to measure everyone to arrive at this data, this is not the precise meaning of measurement in the context of the big question of this chapter. One might prefer to say the height of everyone was "recorded," to avoid confusion.) This data does not tell us if this is remarkable in some way, however; to answer that, we need additional data. What is the total number of people in your company? What are the national population statistics in terms of height? Only when we put all these related bits of data together do we come up with a meaningful measure: X percent of the people in my company are over six and a half feet tall; this is more than triple the national average of Y percent.

In the case of AETS, each time there were "discrepancies" with incoming processing drums of waste material, the discrepancies were duly noted. These records constituted the existing data. The discrepancies being recorded might be incorrect manifest numbers, errors in the shipping code, other faults in the paperwork, or even cases where the wrong material was inside the drum. If such discrepancies went unnoticed and the drums were turned over for disposal, the state could levy stiff fines against the firm.

Andrews and her team put on their measurement hats. First order of business: Measure what proportion of all incoming drums have discrepancies, and among these which types of problems are most prevalent. The answers turned out to be 5 percent, with the bulk of problems of the faulty paperwork variety. The team set a target: to cut the discrepancy rate in half within six months. They simplified some of the forms and took other corrective actions; six months later, the discrepancy rate was down to 2.2 percent, slightly better than the target. "When you start measuring things, everyone gets involved," says Andrews. "It makes people aware. We began measuring sales calls, too. Six months later, the original number of sales calls had doubled, just because people were aware it was being measured. If you aren't measuring, how are you going to get people excited about their progress?"

One way for ambassadors of change to think about measurement, as distinct from data gathering, is to remember that an effective measure answers the basic question, "Is this good news or bad news?" A student driver, observing a red illuminated notice on the dashboard, instinctively turns to the instructor and asks, "Is this supposed to be there?" A patient, after listening to a lengthy explanation of his or her symptoms from a doctor, timidly asks, "Should I be worried?" In dozens of everyday situations, the question is always fundamentally the same: How does the observable data at hand compare or relate to established norms? It may be interesting to discover that in April, we received a total of eleven complaints regarding billing errors; but how does this compare to February and March? Are we improving, staying the same, or getting worse? How does it compare to the previous April, or even the previous three Aprils? How does it compare with the billing-error performance of our competitors? In short, is it good news or bad news?

Measurement is the process of gathering data and then working it: looking for patterns, making comparisons, plotting trends. All kinds of interesting information is hidden inside raw data; when we work it, the hidden information begins to emerge. ("Hey, this is interesting, look at this. All through April, there were never any billing-error complaints on Wednesdays. Let's check the other months. Look, same thing. It's the only day of the week on which there are never any complaints. Let's find out who handles the billing on Wednesdays. I think somebody may be in line for some kind of recognition.")

Of course, as the data yields its secrets, it can uncover as much mischief as gallantry—which is why the whole notion of systematically measuring organizational performance strikes terror into the hearts of many.

THE LEGACY OF SNOOPERVISION

Deeply entrenched in the collective corporate psyche is the archetype of suspicious, mistrustful higher-ups who feel a need to be constantly checking up on their "underlings," sometimes openly, sometimes sneakily, to reassure themselves that there's no malfeasance taking place in any hidden corners of the organization. This book is not the place to open a psychosociological debate about whether such surveillance-style tactics are ever justified, or even whether they might in some ways foster the very attitudes and behaviors they're ostensibly aimed at discouraging. Employees by and large have a natural tendency to get uneasy the moment anything even vaguely Orwellian rears its head in their vicinity. When well-intentioned ambassadors of change proudly unveil their elaborate measurement strategies, it sounds to some ears like the very voice of Big Brother himself.

In Chapter 3, on acquiring and using customer data, we emphasized the danger of focus groups being perceived by employees as having potentially punitive implications; with measurement issues, the danger is at least as great. The best way to minimize it involves a one-two approach: some education before the fact, and some dramatic positive steps afterward.

SETTING THE STAGE FOR MEASUREMENT

It follows: If the outfit I work for intends to measure some element of organizational performance in the area where I work, or related to the work I do, then at least to some extent my own personal performance is bound to be directly or indirectly measured as well. This may be a somewhat unsettling prospect, not because I have anything in particular to hide but because the measurement results could very easily be misinterpreted, and not necessarily in my favor. I'm certain, for example, that my productivity was down noticeably the month before last, but will anyone remember, or even care, that it's because I was putting in dozens of extra hours on that huge rush job that came in at the last minute? I worked like a dog to help the company out on that one; is this now going to be held against me? Will we be given the chance to comment on these measures, and clarify what they really say, or does someone just put a big black mark on my personnel file and I don't even find out about it until I get some kind of dock in pay or something?

The key message ambassadors of change need to get across is that the object of the measurement initiative is not to keep tabs on performance; it is rather to keep tabs on *improvement*. This is not at all the same thing. Not how fast are we going, but how much faster than before; not how many errors were made this month, but how many fewer than last month. Most dieters would probably be eager to share with friends the fact that they've successfully shed over twenty pounds on their new diet, but some of the glow is lost if a well-intentioned spouse chimes in with the additional tidbit that " . . . in fact, Honey, you're down to what, about 340 now, something like that? It's the lowest Chris has been in years!"

Naturally, it is not possible to track improvements without tracking performance. It means measuring current speed, current error rates, current body weight. The difference lies in the basic intent: how the measures are used. The ambassador of change becomes the sensitive partner who shares in the dieter's jubilation, while at the same time exercising discretion to avoid causing any embarrassment or discomfort.

The greater the cynicism within the organization, the greater the fear associated with measurement. In planning for success-measurement activities, therefore, it may well be advisable to return to the second big question and strategize how best to spread the word internally regarding the measurement objectives. To exorcise the fear-demons of change, as outlined in Chapter 2, we must first give them a name and then speak their name aloud. A key element of any such communication effort regarding measurement, therefore, is to state outright, in words to this effect: "Some of you may be worried about what such measurements might bring to light, in terms of personal productivity or other personal performance issues. This is understandable. But our sole purpose is to verify that changes we are implementing to bring about certain improvements are in fact doing so. We have no interest whatsoever in finding out 'who's to blame' for this or that problem; if the planned improvement isn't there, our focus will be on '*what's* to blame', in terms of systems, policies, or procedures that we may need to further refine in order to see the desired improvement."

Obviously, no amount of before-the-fact reassurance will succeed in eradicating all traces of concern on everyone's part; but a concerted effort by the entire senior leadership team to consistently reinforce the message, both formally and informally (do I feel a stump speech coming on . . . ?), goes a long way to minimize overt resistance and make overall implementation of measures smoother and simpler. Then, when the after-the-fact elements begin to kick in, their positive impact is that much greater.

MAKING MEASUREMENT SOMETHING TO CHEER ABOUT

The next chapter explores the theme of celebration, recognition of achievement, reward for good work. For the purposes of the seventh big question, it must be clearly understood that the real key to deriving the greatest possible organizational benefit from measurement is to tie it to celebration. If my disdain of measurement is proportional to my fear that it will lead to the stick, then conversely I am likely to welcome it to the extent that I believe it will lead to the carrot.

Remember, the 8 Big Questions provide means of ensuring that all of the elements necessary to achieve the organization's mission and realize the vision of success are addressed. The measures collectively serve as the corporate instrument panel, indicating increments of progress toward ultimate success. On an Apollo lunar mission, each milestone in the journey was an occasion for cheering and celebrating: a smooth launch from the gantry, the firing of each of the rocket's stages, the entry into earth orbit, the recovery of telemetric signal beyond the dark side of the moon, the separation and docking of the command and lunar modules, the successful landing on the lunar surface. If the corporate instrument panel similarly reports successful passage of various critical milestones, is it not appropriate for the same sort of cheering to take place?

Measurement and celebration should become so tightly linked in people's minds that the organization eventually comes to see them almost as one. It's as if management is so darned eager to find some reason to celebrate something that they keep poking around with these measures of theirs, hoping to turn up some excuse for a party. (Such a perception may be absurd, and even somewhat disadvantageous, but in the grand scheme of things it is also a far better problem to have than its opposite: "Management is so determined to blame something on somebody that they keep poking around with these blasted measures of theirs, hoping to turn up a scapegoat.")

Add a third strand to the rope, to make it even stronger: Measurement must be linked not just to celebration but unmistakably to the vision as well. To be truly compelling, as we suggested in the chapter entitled Learning to See the Future, the vision of success should depict a defining moment of triumph that can be seen to be drawing ever nearer. That can only be seen, of course, if we are continuously measuring our progress forward. The celebrations at each milestone become more elaborate, the emotions more intense, as the final goal looms ever larger on the horizon. Each time a new measure is reported, the view of the destination becomes a little bigger and clearer. With each new measure, the excitement mounts.

Achieving a strong link between vision and measures is one of the easiest tasks facing ambassadors of change. Remember that every single activity identified within the plan under each of the 8 Big Questions is chosen because it moves the organization closer to achieving the mission, and thus to realizing the vision. Remember too that a measure has already been assigned to each of these activities, as a response to the subquestion, "How will success be measured?" In effect, much of the planning around success measurement has already taken place, and the link to the vision is strong and clear: This is what we intend to do (activity) to move us closer to the vision, and this is how we'll know it's working (measure).

By the time the triple link between measurement, celebration, and the vision is clear in most people's minds, measures usually cease to be a source of anxiety; if anything, they tend to become more like a refreshing tonic for the whole organization. At least, this is true for as long as the improvements are there to measure. But what happens if instead of improvement the measures uncover deterioration, a worsening situation, a view of the anticipated triumph receding into the distance? What does that do for morale?

MEASURES AS PORTENTS OF FAILURE

Imagine two families undertaking a trip from Boston to New York. Family C. will make the journey by car; family F. will fly. Both families leave their homes at the same time on the same day, family C. in their car, family F. in an airport-bound taxi.

Nine-year-olds Charlie C. and Freddy F. are in the same class at school. They have told each other of their families' plans to travel on the same day, and in their own minds have come to think of the trip as a race between the two families. Freddy is something of a junior measurement nut and intends to carefully monitor his family's progress toward New York.

Almost as soon as the taxi departs, Freddy is dismayed; for most of the trip to the airport, his pocket compass indicates that the taxi is actually moving away from New York City. In effect, the taxi ride is increasing the distance between family F. and its destination. To make matters worse, Freddy's stopwatch indicates a grand total of one hour and forty minutes' elapsed time before the plane even leaves the ground. Still worse, on takeoff the compass confirms that the plane is climbing in the wrong direction altogether, once again increasing the total distance that must be traveled. These measures, combined with the anticipated delay while awaiting baggage in New York, finding a taxi to the hotel, and checking in at the hotel, lead Freddy to fear the worst.

Ultimately, of course, family F. arrives well before family C., which both sets of parents knew in advance would certainly be the case, barring any calamities. The one most critical measure—the air speed of the plane, compared to the land speed of the car—inevitably tips the scales in favor of family F. But for measurement-conscious Freddy, the apparent conclusion to be drawn from his various measures is that the prospects for success are not good.

As organizations measure their own progress toward realization of the vision, they too occasionally observe that they are heading in the wrong direction. Certain measures appear to indicate that success is by no means a foregone conclusion and may even be somewhat in doubt. How are ambassadors of change to respond to such measurement results as they arise?

There are two types of "discouraging" results that need to be recognized: those that don't make much difference in the bigger picture, and those that do.

You see, Freddy, the fact that the airport is in the quote-unquote wrong direction is actually immaterial. If we lived across town, so that the taxi ride to the airport was in the right direction but took as long to complete, the result would be no different. The direction the airport is in is not relevant; how long it takes to get there is. Now if our flight were *delayed* by an hour or so, that would be a different story. Our plane-speed-to-car-speed advantage would be greatly weakened by delays in departure time.

As part of their ongoing education and communication efforts in answering the second big question, ambassadors of change help the rest of the organization distinguish between so-called negative measurement results that represent potentially significant setbacks and those that do not. The compelling vision has an element of suspense built into it: Will we or won't we make it? Occasional real setbacks serve to raise the stakes, suspensewise, which heightens attention and keeps the whole organization focused on the target ("Well, well, it appears that cracking this particular nut is not quite as easy as we imagined at first. All right then, let's try *this* approach and see if we have any better luck."). The trick is to strike a balance between rising suspense and diminishing confidence. Nothing must be perceived as a weakening of the leadership team's overarching conviction that success will ultimately be achieved, regardless of how numerous—or how serious—the various setbacks are that arise.

WHO'S TO BLAME VERSUS WHAT'S TO BLAME

Sooner or later a negative measure surfaces that points a clearly incriminating finger at someone within the organization. The ambassador of change awaits this moment with eagerness, because of the dramatic opportunity it affords to counter the forces of cynicism and shape a more benign organizational culture.

This is one of those moments of truth, an acid test for the leaders' stated ideologies regarding values and eradication of a blame-oriented culture. This is where the ambassador of change clears his or her throat to speak (while the rest of the organization collectively holds its breath) and proceeds to *exonerate* the hapless employee(s) whom the measures appear to betray. This problem, the ambassador explains—like every other problem, oversight, omission, or error that our measures bring to light—represents a breakdown at the system level. (Even if the problem is a clear-cut case of personal incompetence; malicious neglect; or even outright sabotage, theft, or vandalism, it still ultimately represents a flaw in the hiring system, or the personnel evaluation system.) It is we, the members of the leadership and management teams, who are responsible for the systems by which this organization operates. If anyone at all is to blame for this, it is we who are to blame. Therefore, the responsibility now rests upon us for ensuring that a fair solution is found.

Does this mean, some cynics may wonder, that no one is ever going to be blamed for anything around here anymore? Does this mean that as of now, anything goes?

Of course it does not. If anything, adopting a less blame-oriented approach tends to be part of a larger cultural change that in the long run *increases* the sense of personal accountability felt by employees. Putting an end to public executions does not represent abolishment of civil law. As the benign organization moves toward greater levels of personal empowerment, involvement, and ownership, so too must feelings of personal responsibility increase in direct proportion. In such a cultural environment, most employees genuinely want to help the organization succeed; if they mess up, they blame themselves far more effectively than anyone else could do on their behalf. Those who wish to do the right thing must be allowed to occasionally do the wrong thing by mistake, without being made to feel that their personal stock in the organization has suffered as a result.

As for those few who hold no particular interest in helping the organization succeed, of course they need to be culled out, but as quietly and undramatically as possible. These are the folks itching to cry wrongful dismissal at the drop of a hat, so the organization's case against them must be ironclad and watertight, full of written and clearly dated admonitions of increasing severity spanning months, and always accompanied by written acknowledgments of receipt and promises of reform. When these folks finally do leave, they leave smiling, knowing well that if they make even the slightest fuss, the organization can easily make public a well-documented justification for dismissal that would haunt them for years to come.

If measures bring incriminating problems to light, the fair solution that the ambassador of change promises to find is one in which nothing and no one is allowed to prevent the organization from realizing its vision of success. All obstacles are overcome or removed, even if some people, despite every invitation extended to them to board the train, insist instead on taking up a sitting position, with arms firmly crossed, in the middle of the tracks.

UNITED BY A COMMON ENEMY

In the fifth big question, on making things better for employees, the topic of cross-functional teams working on cross-functional problems was cited as an example of the unifying power of combating a common enemy. The measurement process is another source of this same sort of unifying effect.

Once measures disclose a setback and all of the baggage associated with blame-laying and attendant protestations, recriminations, and vilifications are sidestepped, what remains is basically a potential impediment to success: an enemy to the vision, pure and simple.

The film *Apollo 13* nicely captures the effect that a serious and unforeseen setback has on a team of highly motivated individuals sharing a common sense of purpose. The mission is to reach the moon, but a serious accident quickly changes it to a whole new mission of bringing the endangered crew members back alive. The mission flight director does not waste time demanding to learn the name of the moron responsible for designing the cryogenic tank that exploded and created the crisis; his and everyone else's attention goes directly to problem solving. Once the threat is successfully averted, the ensuing celebration and sense of accomplishment is possibly greater than would have been the case if the original mission had been achieved!

In the film, ambassadors of change use the methods of Chapter 2 to spread the news about the glitch that threatens the mission and rally the whole organization around the effort to stave off the threat. Regular reports keep everyone informed of progress. And after the obstacle is removed and the danger past, there is appropriate cheering and celebration. A potentially negative situation can generate a highly positive outcome.

Measuring the organization's progress toward success provides many occasions for celebration—even when the measures disclose problems and obstacles.

DERIVING PERFORMANCE STANDARDS FROM MEASURES

Such terms as *job standards* and *standardization* tend to worry many people. They convey the notion that standards make their jobs so regimented, consistent, and unvarying in tightly controlled execution that a terrible monotony and sameness sets in. With "standardized" jobs, all opportunities for flexibility, personal initiative, and innovative experimentation disappear; people doing the work become like robots, automatons expected to go on endlessly repeating the same dreary tasks in the same dreary ways until they drop.

This is not the purpose of standardization at all. At the process level, any repetitive process can be said to be "under control" if the output stays within well-defined control limits; that is, if unwanted variability is minimized. Standardization at the process level seeks to eliminate errors, waste, and all the other evils that ensue if things very simply don't go the way they're supposed to. A process under control is one that consistently does what it's supposed to.

An apt analogy concerns driving a car to work in the morning. For many of us, this is almost an autopilot activity; when we arrive at our workplace we may have little conscious recollection of how many red lights we encountered en route, or which parts of the drive featured lighter traffic than usual. The activity has become so standardized for us that we can do it without thinking, which permits us to turn our attention to other matters, such as learning a second language from tapes. But what would happen if, for a two-week period, we were assigned a different car to use for the drive to work every morning, and an unfamiliar route to take? How useful would our second-language tapes be on those mornings?

In reality, it is the standardized tasks that free us to become more creative, flexible, and innovative. Processes that churn out of control and spring new kinds of leaks and develop unexpected problems from day to day require our constant attention; we are forever engaged in firefighting, problem solving, and crisis management. Once everything is brought under control and runs smoothly and as expected, we are free to step back and take a leisurely look at the operation and question whether there might be even better, simpler ways to get the job done.

The function of job standards is to establish some performance baselines. When we speak of things going the way they're supposed to, job standards serve to define how they're supposed to go. If employees have to consult with supervisors to find out how well they're doing their work, it probably means there are few if any job standards in place. If, for instance, the standard is that telephones are answered before the fourth ring, then a receptionist hearing the sixteenth ring while finishing her nails does not need a supervisor to tell her that the job isn't being done as well as it might.

One of the benefits that derive from ongoing measurement of organizational performance is that it provides the baseline from which job standards can be established. Within each area of the organization, once the measures provide some sense of current performance levels, it becomes relatively easy to use these as the basis for establishing a range of performance standards.

Ambassadors of change, however, recognize the importance of fostering employee empowerment, involvement, and ownership and are not inclined to simply impose job standards like some sort of new legislation. Rather, their approach is to share the results of the performance measures with the employee group in question and then allow them to propose the related job standards that seem most appropriate. Old-school managers are often surprised to find that given this freedom, employees quite often tend to set the performance bar at a higher level than what the managers themselves would choose.

What happens if ongoing measurement indicates that the performance standard is being consistently met? Naturally, a new standard is proposed. The bar is raised. The element of challenge is introduced anew. This is continuous improvement in action. This is change as a way of organizational life.

BIG QUESTION 7 PLANNING EXERCISE

Much of the plan-building around the seventh big question has already taken place, in terms of the existing answers to the subquestion "How will success be measured?" for each of the other big questions.

What remains to be explored here are the more general types of organizational measures: financial measures, for example, or operational indices that measure certain aspects of organizational performance such as on-time delivery or billing accuracy. Also important are qualitative-type measures, such as complaint-tracking systems, product defects, process variabilities, and so on.

In essence, the object in brainstorming this seventh question is to create new measurement systems or improve existing ones that help track progress toward the vision and yet are not covered in the measurement elements of the other big-question activities.

. . . .

PHASE ONE: STATUS-QUO QUESTIONS

For no more than ten minutes and without any discussion or analysis, list on a flipchart as many answers as you can think of to these two questions (approximately five minutes per question):

1 Strengths: What do we currently do well to measure our performance as an organization?

2 Weaknesses: What prevents us from more effectively measuring our organizational performance?

The first question really asks: With what existing mechanisms do we presently measure our results? What do we currently do well in terms of tracking our progress relative to our own past performance and to industry standards? What works well in our existing measurement efforts?

The second question asks: What makes it difficult for us to use measures more effectively? What causes some of our measurement efforts to be ineffective? What prevents us from making more and better use of measurement data?

. . . .

PHASE TWO: BRAINSTORMING QUESTIONS

For no more than fifteen minutes, review the list of strengths and weaknesses created in phase one, and for each, without evaluation or discussion, list on a flipchart as many ideas as you can think of to answer these two questions (approximately seven minutes per question):

1 What can be done to amplify our strengths?

2 What can be done to overcome our weaknesses?

For each strength listed, the question becomes, If we had unlimited resources, time, and authority, what could we do to derive even more benefit from this? How could we make this even more effective? What would it take to give this even more impact?

For each weakness: If we had no constraints whatsoever, how could we eliminate this problem? What could we do to get around this obstacle? How might we turn this weakness into a strength?

PHASE THREE: ACTIVITY-PLANNING QUESTIONS

Spend no more than a minute or two selecting one idea that seems a suitable candidate for inclusion in the plan from the list generated in phase two. For this one idea, take no more than twenty minutes to answer all of the following questions on a flipchart. (It's prudent to allow five full minutes at the end for the final question.)

▶ What exactly will be done? (Distinguish between objectives and activities, and concentrate on the latter. The response to this question should begin with a verb, such as *create*, *establish*, *communicate*, etc.)

▶ How will it be done? (If it is not immediately obvious, describe in broad terms how this activity will be implemented. Make note here of any implementation details or issues that remain to be resolved.)

▶ Who will do it? (Use actual names where possible.)

▶ Who will ensure that it gets done? (In most cases, the person who will be held accountable should be a member of the leadership team.)

▶ When will it begin, or be completed? (Specify an actual date.)

▶ How will success be measured? (It may feel like a box within a box, but by what means will we confirm that this particular activity has truly helped us do a better job of measuring our progress toward the vision? Has given us valuable new information about our performance? Has in some way helped build a stronger, more unified culture within the organization?)

At the conclusion of each three-phase round of the planning exercise, those flipcharts bearing content destined for inclusion in the final plan must be separated from the rest and put safely aside for preservation.

Begin by collecting the flipcharts bearing the responses to the phase-three activity-planning questions. Using a marker of a different color than already appears on the charts, inscribe *BQ7* prominently on each sheet, wherever space permits. Next, isolate the flipchart from phase one that bears the list of strengths; inscribe *BQ7* on this chart, too. During the creation of the planning document, it may be appropriate to include in the section on the seventh big question certain items from this list of strengths, under the heading "Things We Will Continue to Do."

Once the content flipcharts have been separated from the rest, branded, and put safely aside for preservation, the team can elect to do one of the following:

▶ Take a break.

or

▶ Select another item from the existing brainstormed list of ideas for the seventh big question generated in phase two, and subject it to the phase-three activity-planning questions, for no more than twenty minutes.

or

▶ Proceed to the eighth big question, and begin by answering the phase-one status-quo questions, for ten minutes or less.

•••

If the team is not sure it's ready to proceed to the next big question, it's usually wise to err on the side of plenty.

Once the seventh big question has been addressed to the team's satisfaction, it's time to begin thinking about ways to celebrate successes.

8

How Will We Celebrate Our Successes?

The last of the 8 Big Questions involves celebrating successes, cheering the players on, recognizing individuals and teams for their contributions to the organizational effort, and rewarding contributors for their good work.

Why do so many organizations remain so stingy with their praise for employees? The industrial revolution may seem like ancient history, but the long, sad chronicle of warfare and mistrust between labor and management haunts us still. It's utterly appalling to hear present-day managers defend their stinginess with the infantile riposte that they're giving their employees the best type of recognition possible: "continued employment." Or that they cannot see a need to recognize people for simply doing the high-quality work they were hired to do in the first place: "Isn't that what their salaries are for?" These are the managers who still cling to the notion that the only way to compel workers to improve their performance is by expressing perpetual dissatisfaction with it; in this view, to give voice to approval is tantamount to giving employees formal permission to start slacking off. Even in more enlightened circles, only a small minority of organizations have made a decisive effort to promote a genuine "culture of celebration," to fashion a workplace environment in which employees are routinely made to feel like winners, like part of a winning team.

MAKING FUN OF BUSINESS

Of all the big questions, this one may represent the most powerful culture-shaper that ambassadors of change have at their disposal. No other

big question does so much to bring a spirit of fun, play, and general optimism into the workplace. No other is so closely linked to employee
motivation and the forging of a strong esprit de corps. This is the feel-
good part of planning for change.

"It's important to make the organization feel good about the
things it's accomplishing," points out Bob Heberling, certified quality
engineer at Triangle Auto Springs in DuBois, Pennsylvania. "When we
achieved zero past-due production orders for the first time in our history,
we held a hot dog roast for the whole organization to celebrate."

"We receive some heart-wrenching letters from our customers,"
says Pamela Miller of Blue Cross Blue Shield of New Jersey:

> Someone may write in and say something like, "Maureen is
> really fabulous. My child is dying of leukemia, and I had
> half a million dollars in claims, and Maureen spent a whole
> day with me going through everything and helping me fig-
> ure it all out. She's the greatest." That kind of thing. We'll
> arrange to take a picture of the customer, publish excerpts
> from the letter, and stuff it into the payroll envelopes for
> everybody in the company to see. And then once a year, we
> invite 150 customers to lunch. We give them a chance to
> present flowers or a gift (which we pay for) to the person
> they wrote about. These lunches are standing room only.
> We do it once a year, and we get so many beautiful letters
> it's hard to decide who to invite.

Celebration is a powerful source of cultural energy. As with any
powerful technology, though, a certain amount of caution must be exer-
cised in its application.

CELEBRATING THE RIGHT THINGS

A last-minute crisis erupts. If it is unchecked, an important customer
will be disappointed. A group of dedicated employees work late on a Friday night to correct the problem, and thanks to their diligence the satisfied customer remains unaware of how closely disaster loomed. The
employees are heroes, and they receive some sort of formal recognition
for their dedication.

In most organizations, this type of heroic-rescue scenario is the
most frequent catalyst for recognition. Dedication of this sort deserves to

be acknowledged and recognized, of course. But when this is the predominant stimulus for celebration, it creates a problem at the cultural level.

The problem stems precisely from the fact that such celebration is crisis-dependent: "If the only way I'm ever going to be made to feel that my contribution is worth anything around this place is through averting crises, then bring on the crises. It may even prove to be worth my while to help a few crises materialize from time to time, just to make sure I get regular opportunities to do my heroic-rescue bit. If some hotshot ambassador of change comes along to triumphantly announce that henceforth a great effort will be made to put an end to crises once and for all, this is hardly going to fall upon my ears as welcome news. This clown intends to remove the one chance I have of ever earning a few strokes for my good work around here. Why on earth would I want to help achieve that objective?"

Bad news always seems to get priority over good news, as a glance at this evening's newspaper or TV newscasts confirms. But for the benign organization to shift its cultural bias away from pessimism toward optimism, this balance needs to be altered. In Chapter 2, on spreading the word internally, I made a plea to communicate good news internally with the same urgency and fanfare accorded to bad news. This plea applies as well to the eighth big question. If a crisis can be thought of as bad news and heroic rescues necessitated by the crisis as good news, then avoidance of the crisis in the first place must be the best news of all. Let us celebrate crisis *prevention* with at least as much hoopla as is typically lavished on crisis correction.

Of course, it's difficult to imagine news about a devastating earthquake that didn't happen, and about all the fires and destruction and loss of life associated with it that never took place, ever commanding the same kind of media attention as a calamity that does occur. That is, it's difficult to imagine this if you are in the bad-news business, which the mainstream news media are on the whole. But in the good-news ambassador-of-change business, such a story should be big news indeed. Then the challenge becomes this: If an event doesn't happen, how are we to even know about it? The short answer, of course, is that our success measures (Chapter 7) tell us it *could* have happened, it *nearly* happened, it *would* have happened if not for the prevention efforts of our crackerjack team of troubleshooters. Bring on the champagne.

As emphasized in the previous chapter, measures and celebration need to be tied together, and tied to the vision as well. Measures tell of heroic rescues after crises have struck, and of crises avoided. "Our major new client, Global Digiplexonix, is notorious for its zero-tolerance policy with regard to late deliveries. As you know, late deliveries have been our bane for the past several years. When we began moving to a team-based approach last spring, one of our high-priority objectives was to solve and eliminate the late-deliveries problem once and for all. Thanks to the superb work done by our cross-functional task force, we achieved 'zero late deliveries' in July and have maintained it since that time. If not for the work of this task force, the large last-minute order that we shipped to Global earlier this week would most assuredly have gone out late. This would have cost us the highly lucrative contract, which, as you know, our competitors are dying to get their hands on. Losing the Global contract would have put a stranglehold on us, financially. It would have placed our vision of market dominance within three years in serious jeopardy. We owe the fact that Global remains our very satisfied customer to the great work of our team." Let us celebrate a crisis averted.

Woven into the whole issue of celebration is the related question of reward, one that has given rise to a lot of confusion and frustration over the years. The terms *celebration* and *reward* are not synonymous and should not be used interchangeably. The former is a public acknowledgment, an occasion of festivity to honor employees for meritorious achievement; it is a largely symbolic act of tribute. The latter represents an occasion of awarding something real and tangible, of calculable value, to employees in recognition of achievement. Reward may be part of celebratory events, of course, but it need not be. Indeed, one could even argue that it should not be. The entire question of reward is a thorny one.

REWARDS AS BRIBES

"No ice cream for you, Young Man, until you finish every bit of that spinach on your plate."

This is the traditional approach to reward at its simplest and purest. If you do this unpleasant thing I want you to do, I will give you this reward in return. It seems fair enough, doesn't it? Granted, it is a form of control, a form of gentle coercion, but how else are we to get people to do unpleasant things? It is certainly better than using threats, isn't it? What harm can there be in it?

The possible harm is in the attitude that this may encourage the young man to develop toward spinach—and toward ice cream. (Not to mention the additional questionable element of rewarding overeating with more food.) In a similar vein, parents continue to drum into their children's minds the importance of good grades at school: "If your grades improve enough, Young Lady, we might look into getting you that new bike (or car)." No mention of getting any good "knowledge," you'll notice, or doing some good "learning." It isn't the quality of the education that's important; the "grades" are all that matter. Grades are what gets this young lady her new bike or car. What is this doing to children's attitudes toward formal education, toward learning as a worthwhile human activity in and of itself?

In an experiment published in the *Journal of Personality and Social Psychology* in 1982, a team of researchers led by Mark Lepper of Stanford University divided a group of preschoolers in half. One subgroup was told that if they were willing to draw using felt-tip markers for a certain period of time, their reward would be permission to use pastel crayons to draw. The other subgroup was told the opposite: If they consented to using crayons for a while, they would be rewarded with access to markers. Some weeks later, the children were observed to see which type of drawing tool they favored. Can you guess the results? In most cases, the type of drawing tool that had originally been held up as a reward had more appeal than the one to be "put up with" while awaiting the reward.

The conclusion these and many other researchers have come to is that, as Alfie Kohn puts it in his book *Punished by Rewards* (Boston, Mass.: Houghton Mifflin, 1993), extrinsic rewards tend to reduce intrinsic motivation. That is, applying an external reward to any activity makes the activity itself less appealing and the reward more so. How many avid amateur painters, musicians, golfers, cooks, model train buffs, etc., have gone professional and turned their hobby into a money maker, only to discover that they subsequently lose interest in doing it for free anymore, or doing it on weekends, now that it is something they can be paid for nine-to-five?

Consider the implications of the word *compensation* as it applies to monetary reward for employees. One might as well come right out and tell the worker, "I realize the job you have is dull, dreary, and unfulfilling, but here, to 'compensate' you for forcing yourself to endure it, is some cash. Buy yourself something nice." What effect does this have on the employee's view of the job?

Consider the so-called incentive plan. "These are the vouchers (or tokens, or points) you can earn by doing better at your dreary job, and these are the great prizes you can redeem them for; this way, even if the time you spend at work is intolerably tedious, at least you can add a little zip to your life away from work." Historically, just how effective are incentive plans over the long term? Typically, the moment the carrot is withdrawn, all forward motion ceases.

So what's the answer? If bribery does more harm than good, are we never to reward deserving employees for anything? Is there no way to extend tangible rewards constructively?

REWARDS AS JOB ENHANCERS

In the context of celebrating successes, the term *rewards* should not be assumed to include basic salaries or wages. "Continued paid employment" simply does not qualify as a dandy motivation builder in recognition of exceptional effort or results. (On the matter of the whole salaries-wages question, a host of experts recommend that every effort be made to allow employees to feel that they are being well and fairly paid, and that thereafter the question should be put aside and not revisited unless employees raise the matter themselves.) For the purposes of this discussion, therefore, monetary rewards other than salaries or wages (such as bonuses) are treated as no different, in principle, from the nonmonetary sort.

The principle is as follows: Replace extrinsic rewards with intrinsic ones. That is to say, replace "If you do this we'll give you that" with "If you do this we'll make doing it more satisfying for you." Replace "Because you did your job really well, we'd like to give you this" with "Because you did your job really well, we'd like to make doing your job easier and more fun for you."

If the meritorious job were done on a computer, perhaps an appropriate reward is an upgraded computer, or some new software, or a new and more comfortable chair to use when sitting at the computer. If it involved staying late and standing for hours at the photocopy machine, perhaps the reward is to give the recipient a budget for redesigning the area around the copier and incorporating some seating into the area. If there is to be some sort of tangible reward associated with a celebration event, the simplest way to minimize its potentially demotivational effect is to look for ways to enhance for the recipient(s) the very activity that made the employee(s) deserving of reward in the first place.

Interestingly, the value of a reward is highly subjective. An inexpensive "World's Greatest Mom" trophy can have tremendous sentimental value, far beyond its modest purchase price. Symbolic rewards often carry far more positive impact than their tangible counterparts. Peggy W. may love the idea that she can arrange for seating to be installed near the office copier, but a plaque affixed to the wall proclaiming the area the "Peggy W. Photocopy Station" may be a reward she will privately treasure for many years. The unique, the customized, the personalized tends to be more appreciated than the generic, the standard, the one-size-fits-all.

Where reward is to be part of celebration, the guiding principle might be to keep it as intrinsic, symbolic, and personalized as possible. Of course, when pure, straight celebration is done well, it tends to feel very much like a reward in its own right.

THE LAUGHTER BAROMETER

How can ambassadors of change ascertain how well a given celebration event is going? How can they determine whether, in a broader sense, the culture of their organization is truly changing, and for the better?

The answer is laughter. This is a virtually foolproof indicator of progress. I have attended corporate celebrations in which various people make speeches, during which the audience is quiet and attentive and generous with its applause afterwards. At others, there is so much boisterous wisecracking and spontaneous shouting of support from the audience that speakers can barely make themselves heard; applause comes frequently and is always accompanied by piercing whistles, loud whooping, and general tumult. In the former, the attendees smile a lot; in the latter, they laugh a lot, sometimes uproariously. In terms of sheer civility, the first type is by far the more orderly; the second type is brash and unruly. But in terms of overall success, I have to go with the second type as the winner. You see, they're laughing.

It is very difficult to make artificial or insincere laughter sound real. Even professional actors have a hard time producing convincing laughter on cue. They often have to try thinking of something that strikes them as genuinely laughable to pull it off. In social situations, forced laughter tends to be painfully obvious.

For real laughter to happen in group situations, a host of stringent conditions have to be met. The mere fact that something humorous is being said or done guarantees nothing (as rookie stand-up comedians have frequent occasion to discover). The audience has to feel comfortable, relaxed, and predisposed to allow laughter to emerge. On the other hand, if conditions are just right, laughter seems to erupt of its own accord.

These are the conditions that are created when organizational celebration unfolds successfully. The more widespread and intense the laughter, the more successful the event. It simply means people are having a good time. They are happy to be a part of the event, they feel good about what the event stands for, and they want the event to be a success. In short, they want the *organization* to be a success. Ambassadors of change can't hope for much more than that.

As part of celebrating successes, anything that can be done to encourage laughter is worth considering. It doesn't mean leaders must learn to behave like buffoons, or that propriety and decorum must be discarded in favor of madcap high jinks. It does mean, however, that a relaxed, casual mood works better than stiff formality, and that thinking creatively about how a sense of fun and play might be injected into the proceedings usually proves to be a good investment of time and effort. It's hard for an employee population that spends Thursday evening cheering and laughing together to plunge into dark mutterings and sinister plots against the organization on Friday morning.

Beyond special celebratory events, laughter provides a reliable means of taking the organization's cultural pulse. The various success measures of the seventh big question give you detailed X ray and blood test results; but if you just want to quickly check the patient's heartbeat, walk around the organization during normal work hours and listen for laughter. The more of it you hear, the healthier your patient is.

Ah, a question from the cynic in the back of the room: "Isn't there such a thing as malicious laughter? Couldn't employees be laughing at what they consider to be the stupidity of their leaders and of this whole change initiative? Is that kind of laugher still a sign of good health?"

If it is real laughter, the laughter of mirth and pleasure, and not just a forced cackle to placate some bully who happens to be making snide comments, then I have to stick with my diagnosis. If mistakes and human fallibilities provoke genuine laughter from the belly, there is good reason to remain hopeful. It's when the perceived shortcomings of leaders or their initiatives produce silence or softly grumbled mutterings of discontent that one might be inclined to suspect a turn for the worse in the patient's condition.

TOO MUCH OF A GOOD THING?

Can this celebration thing be taken too far? Is there a danger that the more celebrations take place, the less meaning each of them has? Does the impact of celebration diminish with overly frequent exposure? Are employees in danger of becoming blasé about the whole thing? All this constant laughter, these endless celebrations . . . when is anybody going to get around to doing any real work?

This line of inquiry always intrigues me. Only those who have intimate knowledge of poverty and whose fortunes begin to improve are likely to worry whether there might be such a thing as having too much money; such a concern never crosses the minds of the wealthy. Too much comfort, too much security, too much opportunity for advancement, too much sheer happiness: These are the worries of those who have long had to do without.

Too much recognition for good work? It's a complaint I have personally never encountered. In all my travels, no employee has ever confided to me that he or she is feeling a little "overappreciated" on the job ("As employees, I feel we're just simply having a little bit too much fun around here all the time."). It's never come up.

Oh, all right; let's agree that in theory it may be possible to overdo it, especially if there's something forced, contrived, and not quite sincere about the whole thing. (In my mind, this represents a case of not celebrating *effectively*, which creates problems no matter how often it is done.) But to generate too great a sense that people's contributions are being acknowledged and appreciated? This concern reminds me of Uncle Scrooge's money bin. For readers unfamiliar with the old comic books featuring Donald Duck's wealthy uncle, imagine a large, hollow, windowless, cube-shaped concrete building large enough to contain Scrooge's "three cubic acres" of cash, a structure no less imposing than NASA's Vertical Assembly Building at Cape Canaveral. Now outfit it with a depth gauge, so that the owner can estimate current cash holdings in terms of so many hundreds of feet deep. Outfit it with a power shovel and a bulldozer, for piling up the cash, and a diving board, for swimming in the currency. This is Scrooge's money bin.

When I hear managers voicing concerns about too much celebration in their organization, I picture them standing in their own huge, empty version of the money bin, tossing a pocketful of change onto the bare floor in a corner of the cavernous place, and knitting their brows as they fret about what they're to do once the bin is full to overflowing. Folks, relax: You've got a long way to go before this is in any danger of becoming a problem.

CELEBRATING INDIVIDUALS VERSUS TEAMS

Another quote-unquote troublesome issue that crops up on occasion, especially in organizations that have historically been stingy with celebration, concerns the "hazards" associated with conferring recognition upon deserving individuals, as opposed to entire teams. The traditional arguments against celebrating individual achievement refer to perceptions of favoritism, the danger of generating envy and resentment in those not being recognized, the possibility of the recognized individual receiving cruel taunts from peers for having somehow curried favor from the boss in some unwholesome way, and so on. It is probably safer, the thinking usually goes, to distribute recognition more widely at any given time by focusing on team achievements rather than on individual initiatives.

Interestingly, those organizations that successfully create for themselves a culture of celebration usually discover after a time that all of these supposed hazards somehow evaporate without a trace, as if by magic. The magic, I suggest, stems from the fact that the hazards exist in the first place only because recognition is such a rarity to begin with. If the mob is starving, the one who is thrown a crust of bread is set upon by all the others, sometimes viciously. If all are consistently well fed and confident that their future appetites will be satisfied as well, they feel freer to applaud a fellow's good fortune in being accorded a piece of chocolate cake—especially if they have good reason to believe that sooner or later, all of them will receive some equivalent treat of their own.

To recognize the individual, or the team: The determining factor should be very simply the answer to the question of who is responsible for accomplishing what is being celebrated. In clear-cut cases where the organization is moved closer to realizing the vision thanks to something one employee accomplishes, recognizing this employee's entire peer group diffuses and greatly devalues the recognition element for everyone involved. The individual responsible for the accomplishment senses that his or her efforts are not genuinely being acknowledged, since those not responsible seem somehow eligible for the same kind of pat on the back. Similarly, the message to the rest of the team is that it's not really necessary to do anything special in order to receive recognition—which means, of course, that there is nothing at all special about the recognition itself.

Even when team recognition is a frequent occurrence, it is still appropriate to celebrate outstanding personal achievements. One particularly effective way of doing so, as mentioned in our discussion of spreading the word internally, is to use the internal communication media to treat the individuals as "celebrities." Rather than simply placing these employees in front of peers and expecting them to take bows in a potentially awkward or embarrassing setting, this approach treats their accomplishments as news stories. The employees are featured in an interview format, in which they're allowed to describe their achievement in their own words, interspersed with additional expositional material that clarifies the significance of the achievement. The power of this technique is that it places maximum emphasis on the link between their achievement and the organization's vision, and it creates celebrity for the employees almost as an incidental by-product; yet this media exposure is often the most personally rewarding element for the employees so honored.

CELEBRATING QUICKLY AND SUPERFICIALLY

As a rule, the overall effectiveness of celebration initiatives, whether directed toward individuals or teams, can be improved by adhering to two simple principles:

1 Sooner is better than later.

2 Specific is better than general.

Recognition, like bread, tastes best when fresh. The longer the time lag between success milestone and corresponding celebration, the weaker the impact—especially when the delay is visibly and clearly a function of scheduling convenience for management or anyone other than the intended recipients of the proposed recognition. (The exception is if the celebration event is so elaborate and extravagant that no one could reasonably expect something of this complexity to be organized in a hurry.)

Overall effectiveness of celebration initiatives is enhanced when they are clearly linked to a specific activity that produces a specific benefit. In other words, a vague, general form of celebration ("This is in recognition of the really excellent work all of you have done in the past six months.") delivers far less impact than one clearly perceived to be in response to a particular achievement and which spells out the organizational benefit of that achievement in unmistakable terms. ("I know many of you already had plans for the long weekend, and had to cancel when the calibration problem came up. Because of your willingness to give up some of that precious free time to come in and correct the problem on a Saturday, we were able to resume normal operation on Monday without a glitch. Thanks to you, we not only avoided a drop in productivity but actually enjoyed a gain because of the fine-tuning to the calibration. This has put us over a week ahead of schedule in terms of our progress toward achieving the mission. So, to show our appreciation for your high level of dedication, it gives me great pleasure to. . . . ")

The only way I know for sure that you are truly aware of my contribution, and that you truly appreciate it, is if I sense that you just can't wait to tell me how pleased you are, and if you spell out for me why you consider my contribution so valuable or helpful. Let me know that you know, and I will know it's real. You will have made me feel good.

BIG QUESTION 8 PLANNING EXERCISE

In planning to create a culture of celebration, ambassadors of change must consider the particular kinds of accomplishment or achievement that they most want to celebrate and the systematic means by which they will learn of them on an ongoing basis (which may involve some of the internal data gathering of Chapter 3 or the measurement elements of Chapter 7). They may also consider soliciting some employee suggestions in terms of the kind of recognition or celebration that would be most meaningful (Chapter 3).

The central objective of celebration planning, however, is to find answers to the basic question, "How will we make it unmistakably clear to our employee population that their good work, particularly as it relates to moving the organization closer to successful realization of the vision, is consistently being both acknowledged and appreciated?"

PHASE ONE: STATUS-QUO QUESTIONS

For no more than ten minutes, list on a flipchart, without any discussion or analysis, as many answers as you can think of to these two questions (approximately five minutes per question):

1 Strengths: What do we currently do well to celebrate our successes?

2 Weaknesses: What prevents us from more frequently or effectively celebrating our successes?

The first question really asks: With what existing mechanisms do we presently recognize employees for their good work? What do we currently do well in terms of making employees feel acknowledged and appreciated?

The second question asks: What makes it difficult for us to celebrate more frequently or effectively? What causes some of our recognition efforts to be ineffective?

....

PHASE TWO: BRAINSTORMING QUESTIONS

For no more than fifteen minutes, review the list of strengths and weaknesses created in phase one, and for each, without evaluation or discussion, list on a flipchart as many ideas as you can think of to answer these two questions (approximately seven minutes per question):

1 What can be done to amplify our strengths?

2 What can be done to overcome our weaknesses?

For each strength listed, the question becomes, If we had unlimited resources, time, and authority, what could we do to derive even more benefit from this? How could we make this even more effective? What would it take to give this even more impact?

For each weakness: If we had no constraints whatsoever, how could we eliminate this problem? What could we do to get around this obstacle? How might we turn this weakness into a strength?

....

PHASE THREE: ACTIVITY-PLANNING QUESTIONS

Spend no more than a minute or two selecting one idea that seems a suitable candidate for inclusion in the plan from the list generated in phase two. For this one idea, take no more than twenty minutes to answer all of the following questions. (It's prudent to allow five full minutes at the end for the final question.)

▶ What exactly will be done? (Distinguish between objectives and activities, and concentrate on the latter. The response to this question should begin with a verb, such as *create*, *revise*, *increase*, etc.)

▶ How will it be done? (If it is not immediately obvious, describe in broad terms how this activity will be implemented. Make note here of any implementation details or issues that remain to be resolved.)

▶ Who will do it? (Use actual names where possible.)

▶ Who will ensure that it gets done? (In most cases, the person who will be held accountable should be a member of the leadership team.)

▶ When will it begin, or be completed? (Specify an actual date.)

▶ How will success be measured? (By what means will we confirm that this particular activity has truly helped us do a better job of making employees feel acknowledged and appreciated? Has had a positive motivational effect on employees? Has made them feel more like winning players on a winning team?)

At the conclusion of each three-phase round of the planning exercise, those flipcharts bearing content destined for inclusion in the final plan must be separated from the rest and put safely aside for preservation.

Begin by collecting the flipcharts bearing the responses to the phase-three activity-planning questions. Using a marker of a different color than already appears on the charts, inscribe *BQ8* prominently on each sheet, wherever space permits. Next, isolate the flipchart from phase one that bears the list of strengths; inscribe *BQ8* on this chart, too. During the creation of the planning document, it may be appropriate to include in the section on the eighth big question certain items from this list of strengths, under the heading "Things We Will Continue to Do."

Once the content flipcharts have been separated from the rest, branded, and put safely aside for preservation, the team can elect to do one of the following:

▶ Take a break.

or

▶ Select another item from the existing brainstormed list of ideas for the eighth big question generated in phase two, and subject it to the phase-three activity-planning questions, for no more than twenty minutes.

or

▶ Begin applying the finishing touches to the plan.

If the team is not sure it's ready to conclude its brainstorming, it's usually wise to err on the side of plenty.

Once the eighth big question has been addressed to the team's satisfaction, it's time to begin to thinking about applying some finishing touches to the plan.

Part

III

BREAKAWAY PLANNING

Next Steps

Finishing Touches

Michelangelo is credited with saying that a work of art is never actually completed; it is merely abandoned at some point. Once the leadership team has answered all of the 8 Big Questions to everyone's satisfaction, there understandably will be a considerable shared sense of accomplishment; the team could easily be forgiven for assuming that their work is done and that the academy is over. However, the work of art that is their "completed" plan is not yet quite ready to be "abandoned" and set loose upon an unsuspecting world. A little fine-tuning is required before it is circulated for final ratification.

FINE-TUNING AND OTHER PRELIMINARIES

Steps that remain to be dealt with in the actual academy include:

- Identifying activities to be discontinued

- Creating an "overview storyboard"

- Deciding on a kickoff strategy

- Assigning responsibility for creation of the plan document (if necessary)

Following the academy, the sequence of events for the plan as it moves toward implementation typically unfolds as follows:

- The actual plan document is cleaned up and completed

- (If necessary) training-plan elements are added

- The plan is circulated for final review and ratification

- (If appropriate) the contents of the plan are formally communicated to the organization as a whole

- Copies of the plan are turned over to relevant parts of the organization for implementation

We begin by examining the three fine-tuning steps that bring the academy itself to a close. The remaining preimplementation steps are examined in the chapter "Moving Toward Implementation."

HOW TO CREATE A "TO-STOP-DOING" LIST

It's only natural: When people think about introducing change into an organization, when they think about missions that need accomplishing and visions that need realizing, they think of things that must be done to achieve these ends. And so too do the rank-and-file when they first hear about all the change that's a-comin' their way. The introduction of change is automatically assumed to be an additive process: new stuff to be piled on plates already overflowing with things that need doing. Interestingly, it seldom occurs to anyone that change might just as easily be a subtractive process, in which items are *removed* from the plate.

Once the members of the leadership team have captured all of their ideas for new activities to be undertaken in response to the 8 Big Questions, it makes sense for them to review each of the questions in turn with an eye to uncovering existing activities that might profitably be discontinued.

It is sometimes surprising, and always heartening, to discover how many discontinuables turn up once we really start looking for them. For example, as part of slaying a dragon by eliminating or simplifying an internal procedure or process, we inevitably wind up removing steps, tasks, details. If our incoming customer data indicates that customers consider some aspect of our operation too time-consuming or confusing, once again we find ourselves with an opportunity to hack away needless duplication of effort or complexity. By its nature, the pursuit of heightened efficiency implies reduction, simplification, subtraction. As leaders generally become more sensitive to the kinds of behavior and signals required of effective ambassadors of change, they tend to recognize that a host of existing policies and approaches are counterproductive to their mission and vision goals; these, too, simply have to go.

Finally, in virtually every organization one can find a rich assortment of activities that do no real harm, nor cause any real anguish for customers or employees; they simply add no value to anything (despite someone's long-ago hunch to the contrary). These are the countless tasks, projects, and procedures that, when challenged ("Why do we even do it this way?"), fall under that great all-encompassing umbrella heading of Things We Do This Way Simply Because We've Always Done Them This Way. There is often a great deal of accumulated junk under this umbrella that can be discarded quickly and painlessly, with no ill effects.

Ambassadors of change develop highly sensitive noses with which to sniff out discontinuables. Within the structure of the academy, however, the members of the leadership team can sample the refreshing effect associated with creating a "to-stop-doing" list—to balance their weighty to-do lists—by participating in the exercise outlined below.

Under no circumstances should the team feel disappointed or in any way dejected if this exercise fails to yield a rich harvest of things that can be effortlessly jettisoned from the menu of current activities. For one thing, a short list of discontinuables (or even no list at all) suggests that this is an organization with very few immediately obvious nonvalue-added time wasters—an encouraging indication of organizational health. Also, the fact that the team does not bag any trophy fish on their first outing does not mean that superb catches will not follow on subsequent fishing expeditions. What is certain is that no fish ever get caught unless a line is put into the water.

THE STOP-DOING EXERCISE

In this exercise, each of the 8 Big Questions is revisited. Instead of recycling the phase-one status-quo questions and phase-two brainstorming questions as before, however, we use a specialized set of abbreviated subquestions, outlined shortly. From the list of responses thus generated, one or more items may be selected and subjected to a modified and abbreviated version of the phase-three activity-planning questions, as described below. (It's difficult to predict how long the exercise will take to complete, since the amount of material it produces varies widely among organizations; in many cases several of the 8 Big Questions bring no discontinuables to the surface whatsoever. As a rough timing guide, somewhere between one and two hours is typical.)

··

BIG QUESTION 1:
HOW WILL WE BECOME AMBASSADORS OF CHANGE?

For no more than five minutes and without any discussion or analysis, list on a flipchart as many answers as you can think of (if any) to each of these two questions (approximately two and a half minutes per question):

1 What are some things we currently do (if any) that might be interpreted as sending pessimistic or negative signals to the organization in terms of the future, or of change?

2 What are some of the methods or approaches we currently use to prepare the organization for the future, or for change, that are not working well or at all (if any)?

From the list of responses, spend no more than a minute or two selecting one idea that seems a suitable candidate for discontinuation. For this one idea, take no more than ten minutes to answer all of these questions on a flipchart:

▶ What exactly will be discontinued? (What is the specific activity that is no longer to be done or, if appropriate, done less frequently?)

▶ How will it be discontinued? (Who needs to be informed of the discontinuation? How will the news be communicated? Will the news give rise to any concerns that need to be addressed proactively?)

▶ Who will stop doing it? (Use actual names where possible.)

▶ When will it be discontinued? (Specify an actual date.)

▶ How will success be measured? (Which of the measurement approaches already assigned to our planned activities for the first big question will also confirm that discontinuing this particular activity truly helps make us better ambassadors of change; or helps reduce anxiety levels within the organization; or improves the general understanding of our mission, vision, and values, or the reasons behind the changes being introduced?)

With these questions answered, the team can choose to select one or more additional items from the list of potential first-big-question candidates for discontinuation and subject them to the activity-planning questions above for no more than ten minutes; or the team can proceed to the second big question.

BIG QUESTION 2:
HOW WILL WE SPREAD THE WORD INTERNALLY?

For no more than five minutes and without any discussion or analysis, list on a flipchart as many answers as you can think of (if any) to each of these two questions (approximately two and a half minutes per question):

1 What are some things we currently do (if any) that might be contributing to organizational rumors, uncertainty, and anxiety?

2 What are some of the methods or approaches we currently use to communicate to our employees that are not working well or at all (if any)?

From the list of responses, spend no more than a minute or two selecting one idea that seems a suitable candidate for discontinuation. For this one idea, take no more than ten minutes to answer all of these questions on a flipchart:

▶ What exactly will be discontinued? (What is the specific activity that is no longer to be done or, if appropriate, done less frequently?)

▶ How will it be discontinued? (Who needs to be informed of the discontinuation? How will the news be communicated? Will the news give rise to any concerns that need to be addressed proactively?)

▶ Who will stop doing it? (Use actual names where possible.)

▶ When will it be discontinued? (Specify an actual date.)

▶ How will success be measured? (Which of the measurement approaches already assigned to our planned activities for the second big question will also confirm that discontinuing this particular activity truly helps us reduce or eliminate cynicism and anxiety, has raised raises levels of optimism, or helps dispel the impression that people are being kept in the dark?)

With these questions answered, the team can choose to select one or more additional items from the list of potential second-big-question candidates for discontinuation and subject them to the activity-planning questions above for no more than ten minutes; or the team can proceed to the third big question.

. . . .

BIG QUESTION 3:
HOW WILL WE ACQUIRE AND USE CUSTOMER DATA?

For no more than five minutes and without any discussion or analysis, list on a flipchart as many answers as you can think of (if any) to each of these two questions (approximately two and a half minutes per question):

1 What are some things we currently do (if any) that might be encouraging or perpetuating management-by-hunches rather than management-by-data?

2 What are some of the methods or approaches we currently use to acquire and use customer data that are not working well or at all (if any)?

From the list of responses, spend no more than a minute or two selecting one idea that seems a suitable candidate for discontinuation. For this one idea, take no more than ten minutes to answer these questions on a flipchart:

▶ What exactly will be discontinued? (What is the specific activity that is no longer to be done or, if appropriate, done less frequently?)

▶ How will it be discontinued? (Who needs to be informed of the discontinuation? How will the news be communicated? Will the news give rise to any concerns that need to be addressed proactively?)

▶ Who will stop doing it? (Use actual names where possible.)

▶ When will it be discontinued? (Specify an actual date.)

▶ How will success be measured? (Which of the measurement approaches already assigned to our planned activities for the third big question will also confirm that discontinuing this particular activity truly helps move us closer to a fact-driven, rather than a hunch-driven, style of management?)

With these questions answered, the team can choose to select one or more additional items from the list of potential third-big-question candidates for discontinuation and subject them to the activity-planning questions above for no more than ten minutes; or the team can proceed to the fourth big question.

....

BIG QUESTION 4:
HOW WILL WE BRING NEW EMPLOYEES
UP TO SPEED?

For no more than five minutes and without any discussion or analysis, list on a flipchart as many answers as you can think of (if any) to each of these two questions (approximately two and a half minutes per question):

1 What are some things we currently do (if any) that might be encouraging or perpetuating a tendency to recruit, hire, and orient new employees in a way that fails to reflect our values, mission, or vision?

2 What are some of the recruitment, hiring, and orientation methods or approaches we currently use that are not working well or at all (if any)?

From the list of responses, spend no more than a minute or two selecting one idea that seems a suitable candidate for discontinuation. For this one idea, take no more than ten minutes to answer these questions on a flipchart:

▶ What exactly will be discontinued? (What is the specific activity that is no longer to be done or, if appropriate, done less frequently?)

▶ How will it be discontinued? (Who needs to be informed of the discontinuation? How will the news be communicated? Will the news give rise to any concerns that need to be addressed proactively?)

▶ Who will stop doing it? (Use actual names where possible.)

▶ When will it be discontinued? (Specify an actual date.)

▶ How will success be measured? (Which of the measurement approaches already assigned to our planned activities for the fourth big question will also confirm that discontinuing this particular activity truly helps us attract better candidates for job openings, improves our ability to select the best candidate from among the various applicants, makes our orientation more effective for new employees, or otherwise helps us do a better job of bringing new employees up to speed?)

With these questions answered, the team can choose to select one or more additional items from the list of potential fourth-big-question candidates for discontinuation and subject them to the activity-planning questions above for no more than ten minutes; or the team can proceed to the fifth big question.

. . . .

BIG QUESTION 5:
HOW WILL WE MAKE THINGS BETTER FOR OUR EMPLOYEES?

For no more than five minutes and without any discussion or analysis, list on a flipchart as many answers as you can think of (if any) to each of these two questions (approximately two and a half minutes per question):

1 What are some things we currently do (if any) that might be creating obstacles or hindrances for our employees, or may be making it more difficult for them to do their part in achieving our mission and realizing our vision?

2 What are some management rules, policies, procedures, or systems that are not working well or at all (if any)?

From the list of responses, spend no more than a minute or two selecting one idea that seems a suitable candidate for discontinuation. For this one idea, take no more than ten minutes to answer these questions on a flipchart:

▶ What exactly will be discontinued? (What is the specific activity that is no longer to be done or, if appropriate, done less frequently?)

▶ How will it be discontinued? (Who needs to be informed of the discontinuation? How will the news be communicated? Will the news give rise to any concerns that need to be addressed proactively?)

▶ Who will stop doing it? (Use actual names where possible.)

▶ When will it be discontinued? (Specify an actual date.)

▶ How will success be measured? (Which of the measurement approaches already assigned to our planned activities for the fifth big question will also confirm that discontinuing this particular activity truly removes obstacles to realizing the vision, or makes it easier or more enjoyable for employees to do their jobs?

With these questions answered, the team can choose to select one or more additional items from the list of potential fifth-big-question candidates for discontinuation and subject them to the activity-planning questions above for no more than ten minutes; or the team can proceed to the sixth big question.

••

BIG QUESTION 6:
HOW WILL WE MAKE THINGS BETTER FOR OUR CUSTOMERS?

For no more than five minutes and without any discussion or analysis, list on a flipchart as many answers as you can think of (if any) to each of these two questions (approximately two and a half minutes per question):

1 What are some things we currently do (if any) that

might be discouraging employees from taking initiatives to make things better for customers?

2 What are some customer-related policies or practices that are not working well or at all (if any)?

From the list of responses, spend no more than a minute or two selecting one idea that seems a suitable candidate for discontinuation. For this one idea, take no more than ten minutes to answer these questions on a flipchart:

▶ What exactly will be discontinued? (What is the specific activity that is no longer to be done or, if appropriate, done less frequently?)

▶ How will it be discontinued? (Who needs to be informed of the discontinuation? How will the news be communicated? Will the news give rise to any concerns that need to be addressed proactively?)

▶ Who will stop doing it? (Use actual names where possible.)

▶ When will it be discontinued? (Specify an actual date.)

▶ How will success be measured? (Which of the measurement approaches already assigned to our planned activities for the sixth big question will also confirm that discontinuing this particular activity truly improves customers' perceptions of value; makes things easier, more convenient, or more pleasant for customers; or gives us a mechanism for continuously improving the customer's experience?

With these questions answered, the team can choose to select one or more additional items from the list of potential sixth-big-question candidates for discontinuation and subject them to the activity-planning questions above for no more than ten minutes; or the team can proceed to the seventh big question.

· ·

BIG QUESTION 7:
HOW WILL WE MEASURE OUR SUCCESSES?

For no more than five minutes and without any discussion or analysis, list on a flipchart as many answers as you can think of (if any) to each of these two questions (approximately two and a half minutes per question):

1 What are some things we currently do (if any) that might be discouraging some parts of the organization from tracking their progress and measuring their performance?

2 What are some existing measurement tools, practices, or approaches that are not working well or at all (if any)?

From the list of responses, spend no more than a minute or two selecting one idea that seems a suitable candidate for discontinuation. For this one idea, take no more than ten minutes to answer these questions on a flipchart:

▶ What exactly will be discontinued? (What is the specific activity that is no longer to be done or, if appropriate, done less frequently?)

▶ How will it be discontinued? (Who needs to be informed of the discontinuation? How will the news be communicated? Will the news give rise to any concerns that need to be addressed proactively?)

▶ Who will stop doing it? (Use actual names where possible.)

▶ When will it be discontinued? (Specify an actual date.)

▶ How will success be measured? (Which of the measurement approaches already assigned to our planned activities for the seventh big question will also confirm that discontinuing this particular activity truly helps us do a better job of measuring our progress toward the vision, gives us valuable new information about our performance, or in some way helps build a stronger, more unified, and more focused culture within the organization?)

With these questions answered, the team can choose to select one or more additional items from the list of potential seventh-big-question candidates for discontinuation and subject them to the activity-planning questions above for no more than ten minutes; or the team can proceed to the eighth big question.

BIG QUESTION 8:
HOW WILL WE CELEBRATE OUR SUCCESSES?

For no more than five minutes and without any discussion or analysis, list on a flipchart as many answers as you can think of (if any) to each of these two questions (approximately two and a half minutes per question):

1 What are some things we currently do (if any) that might be hampering the development of an organizationwide culture of recognition and celebration?

2 What are some existing mechanisms and practices for recognition and celebration that are not working well or at all (if any)?

From the list of responses, spend no more than a minute or two selecting one idea that seems a suitable candidate for discontinuation. For this one idea, take no more than ten minutes to answer these questions on a flipchart:

▶ What exactly will be discontinued? (What is the specific activity that is no longer to be done or, if appropriate, done less frequently?)

▶ How will it be discontinued? (Who needs to be informed of the discontinuation? How will the news be communicated? Will the news give rise to any concerns that need to be addressed proactively?)

▶ Who will stop doing it? (Use actual names where possible.)

▶ When will it be discontinued? (Specify an actual date.)

▶ How will success be measured? (Which of the measurement approaches already assigned to our planned activities for the eighth big question will also confirm that discontinuing this particular activity truly helps us do a better job of making employees feel acknowledged and appreciated, has a positive motivational effect on employees, or makes them feel more like winning players on a winning team?)

With these questions answered, the team can choose to select one or more additional items from the list of potential eighth-big-question candidates for discontinuation and subject them to the activity-planning questions above for no more than ten minutes; or the team can bring the stop-doing exercise to an end.

•••

STORYBOARDING THE PLAN

At this point in the academy, the actual contents of the so-called plan are scattered throughout a heap of disjointed flipcharts. Before the plan is forwarded to the document-preparation stage to be turned into a package that can easily be scanned for critical evaluation by all interested parties, there is much to be gained by subjecting it to a quick inspection.

An artist steps back from a painting-in-progress to get a better sense of how the colors and shapes and other elements are working together. How are the plan builders similarly to step back and take in a view of their work as a whole? How can they contrive to see the entire plan at a single glance and check it for overall balance and form? They can create an overview storyboard.

Materials Required

Post-it Note pads in four different colors (3-by-3-inch is a good size for this application), felt-tip markers, and two blank flipcharts.

Preparation

Position two flipchart easels side by side (or tape two blank flipchart sheets side by side to a wall). Use a heavy-line marker to create a series of vertical lines, spaced just slightly more than three inches apart, from top to bottom on both flipcharts. Think of these as month columns that proceed from left to right. At the top of the leftmost column, inscribe in large, prominent letters the abbreviation for the name of the month that is three months from today. (That is, if you're doing this in May, write "Aug." at the top of the first column.) Inscribe the abbreviated name of the following month ("Sept.") at the top of the second column from the left, the name of the month after that on the third, and so on, until each column has an identifying month at the top. (It's helpful to also add the year each time "Jan." appears.)

Depending on the width of your columns, this should yield between eighteen and twenty-four month-columns in total; if you have fewer than eighteen, it's advisable to bring a third flipchart into play. In the interests of neatness, it helps to draw a series of horizontal guidelines across the flipcharts as well. The first of these should underline the identifying month-names at the top of the columns; subsequent horizontal guidelines should be spaced just slightly more than three inches apart all the way to the bottom.

These columns represent the *when* aspect of the plan. (The storyboard time frame begins three months from today, recognizing that there is typically a delay of two to three months between the academy and final plan ratification. Implementation cannot therefore formally begin much before then.)

The *who* is represented by a color code. There are four colors of Post-it Notes; let's say, for the purposes of illustration, that these are yellow, red, blue, and green. The four categories of *who* that each have an identifying color assigned to them are the CEO (or general manager, president, senior VP, or whatever handle the top dog wears; for this illustration he or she is assigned yellow), senior leaders (everyone other than the CEO on the senior leadership team who helped build this plan, to whom we assign red), the change agent or agents (anyone who as a part of his or her regular job function is involved in plan implementation activities but who does not fall in either the yellow or red categories, to whom we assign blue), and other (everybody else, assigned green).

Procedure

The members of the leadership team now get busy transcribing summaries of plan activities to Post-it Notes. Each member of the team takes a number of flipcharts bearing the various responses to the phase-three activity-planning questions that have been generated throughout the entire academy, and the transcription process begins.

The first step requires the transcriber to glance at the answer to the *Who will do it?* subquestion on the flipchart, to determine what color Post-it Note to use. (Note that the color reflects who will do the activity, as opposed to who will ensure it gets done.)

The transcriber next transfers the answer to the *What exactly will be done?* subquestion as it appears on the flipchart to the Post-it Note of the appropriate color. (If a verbatim transcript is too long or detailed, the transcriber can condense or paraphrase the wording.)

Next, the transcriber adds, in a lower corner of the Post-it Note, the inscription "BQ3" (or whichever of the 8 Big Questions this particular activity happens to derive from).

Finally, the transcriber glances at the *When will it begin (or be completed)?* subquestion on the flipchart to determine in which month-column on the storyboard the Post-it Note belongs. All that remains is to physically position the Post-it Note in the appropriate place on the storyboard, and the transcriber is then free to begin transcribing the next activity in his or her series of flipcharts.

With everyone on the team working on the transcription process at the same time, it typically takes less than an hour, often less than half an hour, to get all of the planned activities onto the storyboard.

Now the fun begins. It is not at all uncommon to observe, when the whole plan is laid out in this way, that there is a great deal of Post-it Note congestion in the leftmost month-columns, with later columns increasingly underpopulated. Equally typical is the tendency of one color of Post-it Note (usually the designated change agent's, or in organizations that don't have one, the CEO's) to dominate, and another (the senior leaders') to be virtually absent. This, as the saying goes, is not good.

The objective with the storyboard is to strive for an "eye-pleasing mosaic," that is, a relatively even distribution of color and space. The leftward congestion reflects the eagerness of the leadership team to see early progress, which is commendable. (The danger, of course, lies in trying to do too much too soon and failing, and as a result handing ammunition on a silver platter to the cynics throughout the organization lying in wait, eager to seize upon such a failure as proof that the entire change effort is ill-timed, or just plain ill-advised.) The dominance of some colors over others similarly raises the possibility of noble intentions being undone by overly ambitious target levels of activity. This plan, it should be remembered, is *a plan to succeed*. The ultimate goal in creating a detailed written plan is not to create an impressive plan; it's to use a plan to create an impressive success story for the organization. The storyboard provides a means of tweaking the plan to maximize the likelihood of successful implementation.

Of course, it must be admitted that the storyboard, like any tool, is not perfect. It can be slightly misleading. All the Post-it Notes affixed to it are of the same size, which implies that the activities they represent are of roughly the same magnitude or importance. This is often not the case at all. One Post-it Note may allude to the need to revise a customer feedback card, for example—a one-time activity that may take one person an hour to complete—while another refers to launching an internal employee newsletter, an enterprise requiring the participation of dozens of people over many months to bring it to completion. For this reason, the goal of a perfectly even and eye-pleasing distribution of color and space within the storyboard is not entirely realistic. Even so, the more the time lines are spread out, and the more the workload is shared, the greater the chance of successful implementation.

The storyboard tweaking process should be fast, loose, and informal, a matter of revisiting the *who* and *when* elements for each activity; and, through quick discussion, proposing alternatives until a general consensus is reached. A facilitator can speed things up simply by leading the team through the Post-it Notes one at a time, to solicit or propose revisions, and by generally keeping the discussion focused and moving. Revising the *who* element may represent a need for some members of the leadership team to reconsider their personal level of involvement in the change effort, and their willingness to act as ambassadors of change and take on activities that demonstrate support of the mission and vision. The *when* element, of course, becomes essentially a quick reprioritization exercise; since not everything can be done at once, which items need to move to the top of the list and which can affordably be delayed somewhat?

If debate on these revisions appears to getting bogged down, the facilitator may need to remind the team that nothing they agree to during this academy should be thought of as being etched in stone; there remain opportunities during the review and ratification phases to make further adjustments to the plan if necessary. (In fact, it is almost certain that proposals for revisions will emerge from the ranks of frontline and middle managers as they scrutinize with particular attention those sections of the plan that relate to their own areas.)

Note that each time a change is made to the *who* element, it may be necessary to transcribe the item again to a Post-it Note of a different color. The facilitator may want to enlist a helper to handle the retranscription process. (Changing the *when*, of course, simply involves transferring the Post-it Note to the appropriate new month-column location on the storyboard.)

When the storyboard's mosaic appears sufficiently eye-pleasing to suit everyone's taste, all of the *who* and *when* revisions need to be legibly noted on the original flipcharts from which the various Post-it Notes were derived; it is from these flipcharts that the actual plan document is prepared.

Although we make no further use of the storyboard in the academy proper, do not discard it at the end of the session. As an aerial view of the total plan, it is useful later, when proposed revisions come in from the field. How better to assess the impact this or that revision has than to be able to take in the whole plan at a glance? Another useful application of the storyboard is as an implementation tracking mechanism. By replacing all successfully implemented activities with a Post-it Note of a distinct color, or by affixing a prominent colored sticker to each, it's possible to monitor overall progress in an instant. At the end of each month, outstanding items literally stand out.

With the completion of the storyboard, the members of the leadership team have nearly reached the end of their academy. There remain only two decisions to be made. The first, however, is potentially a biggie.

THE KICKOFF STRATEGY

As outlined in the chapter "Learning to See the Future," with regard to communicating the contents of the ratified plan to the organization as a whole, there are a number of different approaches that can be taken. The decisions around how much of the plan to communicate, to whom, when, and by what means do not as a rule benefit from being made in the academy itself. For one thing, the plan is not really completed until it has been formally ratified by the organization's entire management population, a process almost certain to entail some further revisions and perhaps substantial ones. Also, the tone of early feedback from various management quarters may give a useful indication of how the employees in these same areas are likely to react, which in turn affects how the contents of the plan should be publicized (if at all). It is generally prudent to make such decisions only when armed with as much preliminary data as possible.

However, a broader and perhaps more fundamental question needs to be discussed sooner than this. The plan itself has been created to achieve a specific change within the organization. This change may have a formal name (TQM, or process reengineering, or service quality, as examples) or be designated by a reference to the mission or vision statements ("Excellence in Century 21," or "Best in Class," etc.). No matter how it is referred to by the plan builders, the question that must be answered is to what extent (if any) we want to give this change initiative some sort of formal, official kickoff across the organization.

The issue is not how the leadership team's strategic intentions are communicated; that may have already been planned in terms of communicating the mission, vision, and values (as part of answering the first two big questions) and soon may be explored further as part of discussing how best to communicate the contents of the plan. Rather, the issue relates to whether or not it's appropriate to stage some sort of formal organizational event to mark the official launch of the change initiative (at which the communication of mission, vision, and values as well as highlights of the plan may or may not form a central component), and the degree of fanfare and hoopla that should (or shouldn't) surround the event, if there is to be one.

To arrive at a decision on this issue, the leaders must evaluate the balance that exists at the moment within their own organization between two opposing cultural forces: enthusiasm and cynicism. Here is a simple exercise to make the evaluation process a little easier. Its purpose is to arrive at some basic conclusions, but at the should-we-or-shouldn't-we level only. (If the conclusion is that we should, decisions about the many specific design options for such an event probably have to wait for another creative brainstorming session on another day.)

• •

T H E   K I C K O F F   E X E R C I S E

Each member of the team is to assign an enthusiasm rating to the organization's entire employee population as a whole. The rating should be on a scale of 0 to 10, with 0 representing absolutely no enthusiasm whatsoever (maximum cynicism) and 10 representing maximum enthusiasm (no cynicism whatsoever). The following questions are intended to facilitate the process of assigning such a rating.

▶ To what extent do you believe most employees will greet the news of this new strategic initiative with interest and a collective open mind, rather than dismissing it as just the latest "flavor of the month," one more attempt to generate support for some so-called new approach that is as likely to fail as its predecessors?

▶ Do you believe the prevailing response to the change initiative will be more accurately summed up with "This sounds fairly promising" or "Oh no, here we go again!"?

▶ To what extent do you believe a splashy kickoff event will capture employees' imaginations and generally have a positive impact (rather than prompting a lot of snickering and grumbling)?

> If time permits and there is interest in pursuing such a discussion, team members could share their ratings and the reasons behind them. Otherwise, each team member should anonymously inscribe his or her rating on a scrap of paper, fold it, and toss it into a central pile. One team member then adds up the ratings and divides the total by the number of team members, to arrive at an average group rating.

The kickoff strategy is largely determined by this group rating. In general, the lower the level of cynicism throughout the organization is felt to be (that is, the closer the group rating falls to the high end of the range), the greater the likely benefit to be derived by an all-out, "full speed ahead, there's no turning back, it's the moon or bust" kind of exuberant kickoff to generate some excitement and optimism. As the rating drops closer to 7 or 8, a somewhat more subdued event characterized by a "we're serious about this, and we really need your help to make it happen" tone may be more appropriate. At a rating of 5 or 6, some care must be taken not to give the cynics a field day that could seriously undermine the initiative; something along the more humble lines of "we've decided to try this approach, and we felt it was something you needed to know about" might be the safest bet. If the rating falls below 5, the most prudent course of action might be to dispense with a splashy kickoff event altogether and just informally use stump speeches and other low-key communication mechanisms to quietly spread the word.

Bear in mind a number of cautions if the enthusiasm rating registers at 5 or below, and as a result the decision is made not to pursue a splashy kickoff. First, electing to pursue a quieter, more subdued launch strategy does not mean that the demonstrations of determination to succeed coming from the members of the leadership team should similarly be scaled down. If anything, the opposite should be true; in the absence of a high-octane momentum-building launch to dramatically set the initiative in motion, the ambassadors of change have little more than their own personal commitment to draw upon as a means of nudging the organization's culture forward. The inspiring power of their own fierce, unwavering determination alone must compensate for the lack of explosive firepower at any sort of official kickoff, at least until dramatic positive results are felt and observed.

In such a situation, the ambassador of change typically goes about quietly taking action first and then talking about it afterwards. If, for example, a particularly onerous organizational dragon has traditionally made life noisy, hot, and difficult for employees, they arrive at the workplace one morning to find everything strangely quiet and still. There stands the ambassador of change, one foot poised on the dragon's smoldering carcass, hands resting on the handle of a sword deeply embedded in the beast's hide. "Oh," shrugs the ambassador in response to a flurry of questions about what happened, "it's just part of that little change-initiative thing I've been talking about. . . . " He or she proceeds to launch into a stump speech about how everyone has a role to play, and how he or she has simply taken care of one aspect of the ambassador's role, with more to come. In a cynical climate, splashy results can be more effective than the splashiest kickoff; it's much more difficult for cynics to grumble "it'll never work" when it clearly just has. Positive results take longer to work their magic, of course, but this is the cost ambassadors of change incur for finding themselves operating within a highly cynical culture.

The second caution that applies to the decision to tone down or forgo a splashy kickoff event concerns the need to remember that choosing a low-key communication strategy does not mean keeping the initiative a secret or keeping people in the dark. The fact that there is cynicism in the organization does not lessen the hunger for information; if anything, it increases it. Choosing not to formally announce the launch of a change initiative does not represent a decision to withhold information about it; rather, it's a decision about how and when the information is passed along—usually informally, in drips and drabs (as opposed to all at once in some big, official event).

In high-cynicism situations, there is often a great deal to be gained by following a succession of positive early results with a series of mini-academies in which divisional, departmental, or functional heads meet with their direct reports to create their own local plan for success. It might make perfect sense to treat these sessions as the official kickoff and formally communicate the contents of the corporate plan at that time. (More about mini-academies in the final chapter.)

In the meantime, organizationwide awareness of the change effort seeps into the organization's collective consciousness gradually, as if by osmosis. With frequent and casual stump speeches about it, mentions of it in the newsletter and on bulletin boards, references to it in memos and in meetings, before long it becomes a fact of daily life, even if no one can remember just precisely when or how it all began. This is culture change by evolution, rather than revolution.

What if, one might reasonably ask, in the middle of this subtle communication strategy, some of the cynics wise up and start asking tough questions: "Just what in blazes is going on around here, all of a sudden? What's all this talk about 'change'? Is there some kind of new strategy in the works and we haven't been told about it? What gives?"

Such questions are not bad news. It does not mean you have been found out and must now 'fess up. Au contraire; for any leadership team that elects to bypass a splashy kickoff event in favor of a more cautious communication strategy, questions of this sort are very good news indeed. Despite a tone that may sound suspicious, wary, or even hostile, the employees who ask questions such as these are in effect declaring, "Hey, shouldn't there have been some sort of formal announcement about all this?"

Ambassadors of Change, you will never have a better opportunity to put your stump-speech skills to work. You weren't sure if your audience was ready to hear a formal announcement of your strategy for change, but they have just let you know they are. Now, do your stuff.

First, let them know there is nothing even slightly secretive about your approach. Remind them of what they have already heard, seen, and been exposed to. Reassure them that you—and all your leadership colleagues—welcome the opportunity to tell them as much as they want to know about all of it. Be especially forthright about one thing: The only reason there was no official kickoff announcement was that, in view of how poorly some of the earlier efforts to improve things around here have gone, you felt they'd have some difficulty thinking this one was going to be any different—and you can hardly blame them. You and your colleagues decided that before you came to them to outline some of the things they could do to help make this effort a success, you would go ahead and take some initiatives of your own. You've put together a detailed written plan, for example (the contents of which you will share with everyone before too long). You've been looking at some of the management policies and procedures that have historically made it difficult for them to do their job. Your goal is to slay some of those dragons once and for all. You felt that only after you had demonstrated your own willingness to change some things for the better around here would it be fair for you to ask them to consider changing things as well. That's really why there hasn't been any formal announcement yet. But if they have any questions, you would certainly be very happy to . . . etc.

In a cynical organization, communicating the strategy for change informally in response to spontaneous questions is often the most effective of all communication options. If done with skill, it can transform fence-sitters into supporters and reduce the influence of cynics by significantly cutting their numbers.

Whatever the kickoff strategy is to be, once the members of the leadership team reach a consensus on the issue only one final question needs to be resolved, if it has not been resolved already. It has to do with putting a plan in place for creating the plan document itself. It's a question that can usually be put to bed in a matter of a few minutes, provided a designated owner of the plan has already been identified. (If not, then some further discussion is necessary.)

THE KEEPER OF THE PLAN

As we see in our exploration of the implementation process in the final chapter, all members of the senior leadership team have a key role to play in bringing the plan to successful fruition. As with any critical organizational project, though (and implementation of the plan may well be the most critical project of them all), the prospects for success increase significantly if someone takes or is assigned personal ownership for the process of plan implementation.

If the past few decades' struggles with total quality management (TQM), strategic process management (SPM), quality function deployment (QFD), and all the rest of the alphabet soup of organizational change have taught us anything at all, they have certainly taught us one thing. Somebody has to become a process owner or project sponsor or champion of the cause—a nicer way of saying unless someone with a great deal to lose is personally held accountable for the change effort, things have a way of going wrong or falling between the cracks.

Someone has got to be on top of things, and stay on top of things at all times. It's a continuous uphill battle; turn your back even for an instant and everything slides right back down to the bottom. Good intentions alone can't cut it. A solid, well-thought-out plan alone won't do it. Somebody has to diligently oversee the whole thing, watch it from every angle, from top to bottom and inside out, or progress will stall and the organization's attention will turn elsewhere and the plan will become a fond memory. Somebody's got to ensure that it gets done. Somebody must be able to give an accurate report at any time on what has and hasn't yet taken place; what successes have been achieved; what obstacles have been encountered; and what remains to be done, when, and by whom.

To compare the total organizationwide implementation of the plan to a lavish theatrical musical production, this keeper of the plan (KOP for short) acts somewhat like a stage manager, hidden backstage and invisible to the audience (the organization at large) while ensuring that the right performers (the senior leaders) are ready in the wings, ready to leap into view and do just the right things in just the right ways so that the whole production appears seamless and spontaneous and completely natural, yet effective and impactful. If the backstage KOP does his or her job well, it's the onstage performers who get the applause and take the bows. At the end of each big audience-pleasing number, the KOP coordinates traffic between those leaving the stage and those about to go on, and constantly checks against the script in hand (the plan) to ensure that all is in readiness for the next big number.

Note that the KOP does not become the OOP (owner of the plan)! This would indeed be a big mistake. Ownership for the plan's contents must always reside with, and be *seen* to reside with, the entire senior leadership team: This is their baby; they created it; and it reflects their thinking, their personalities, and their collective vision of the future. They remain the authors of the script; the KOP simply takes personal ownership for helping ensure that their wishes are met, their intentions carried out, their vision realized. They own the plan; the KOP owns the implementation process.

In many organizations, this KOP role is a full-time job assignment that lasts as long as the plan's life span. Certainly, in larger organizations (250 employees and up) it can quickly expand into a full-time job. Indeed, the mere fact that someone is given full-time responsibility to oversee the implementation of the plan sends an unmistakable message to the whole organization about the leaders' determination to achieve success; this makes it much more difficult for the cynics to sneer, "Ah, relax, these guys all talk a good line, but they're not really serious about this stuff. Just give it a few weeks and they'll forget all about it and go on to their next big deal, just like they always do." This is especially true if the person assigned to the job is widely perceived within the organization as a person with credibility and real executive potential. To underscore the importance of the role, it is highly advisable to treat the assignment as a plum, a career-enhancing advancement that normally promotes the recipient to a direct reporting line to the CEO.

If your organization already has a designated change agent or quality coordinator (or equivalent), this person is probably your best candidate for the KOP role and has probably been in attendance throughout the academy in preparation for this assignment. In such case, the final round of activity planning in your academy is likely to be very brief; the answer to the *who* question, in terms of overseeing creation of the plan document itself, has already been determined.

Even if no such change agent function exists in your organization, chances are you have come to the academy with someone from the senior leadership team already designated to take on the KOP role over the long term; once again it is a quick matter to reflect this fact in your final activity-planning exercise.

It is only if the whole notion of a project owner for creation and implementation of the plan has never come up at all prior to the academy that this last round of planning may take a little longer. It means some time should be spent selecting a candidate for the KOP, perhaps from among the senior leaders themselves, or perhaps from elsewhere within the organization.

If it seems to make sense for the keeper of the plan to come from among the membership of the senior leadership team, then the quickest way to determine who it might be is simply to inquire whether anyone on the team is prepared to voluntarily take on ownership for the project. If more than one individual volunteers, count your blessings—and then let the multiple volunteers arrive at an amicable agreement around joint custody versus single parenthood. (If the discussion becomes deadlocked, invoke an anonymous vote.)

If no one volunteers, it means the role of keeper of the plan has to be assigned to someone not in attendance at the academy while the very plan he or she will be entrusted with is being created; this is hardly an ideal situation. This person requires a significant amount of hand-holding to be brought up to speed. It therefore becomes necessary to resolve not one but two *who* issues: Who will become the keeper of the plan, and who will help bring this person up to speed?

In my experience, finding satisfactory answers to such important questions from a ground-zero starting point can take time. My recommendation is that the team look at the clock on the wall and, on the basis of what it says, determine for themselves how much time they wish to devote to the issue—with the understanding that if it remains unresolved when time runs out, the entire team is committed (before the academy adjourns) to setting a date and time for a follow-up meeting to find answers to these two critical questions as soon after the academy as possible.

Either in the academy proper or in a follow-up meeting, each member of the leadership team should be prepared to make at least one nomination for the role of keeper of the plan. (It may be useful to review the key elements of the role, as outlined at the start of this section.) If no obvious favorite emerges from the list of nominees, the team must then discuss and debate the merits of one candidate over another. The following questions may be helpful; team members may wish to assign a 0–10 rating value to each nominee for each question, and then tabulate the results.

- Is this individual sufficiently sophisticated in matters of organizational dynamics to appreciate the cultural implications of introducing profound change?

- Would this individual feel comfortable giving senior leaders feedback, and even holding their feet to the fire if necessary?

- Will this individual's ego permit him or her to remain in the shadows while helping others look good in the spotlight?

- Is this an individual who commands respect and credibility in the organization?

Often, the perfect candidate is the person the organization can seemingly least afford to free up for the role!

Once the team makes its selection, all that remains is to determine who is responsible for helping to bring the appointed individual up to speed. This is usually (but not necessarily) the senior leader in whose area the prospective keeper of the plan presently works. The best choice for this mentoring assignment is whichever member of the senior team feels most strongly that he or she has both the time and the inclination to give this important task the attention it deserves. Again, volunteers can be sought; but this time, if none are forthcoming, the CEO has no alternative but to assign the responsibility directly to a member of the team. (I leave for a future book what I believe the CEO should be thinking, feeling, and doing if after three intensive days of planning for success not one of his or her direct reports is prepared to voluntarily take any sort of initiative whatsoever to help bring the plan to successful fruition.)

If all of this is resolved within the actual academy agenda, the team proceeds to their final round of activity planning.

THE WRITTEN PLAN:
CREATING THE DOCUMENT (PART TWO)

The final round of activity planning is typically a quick one in which an accelerated version of the activity-planning subquestions is used to ensure that a plan is in place for creating the plan document itself. Time guidelines are not typically required in this instance; as soon as one subquestion has been satisfactorily answered, the team simply moves on to the next.

■ What exactly will be done? (This is easy: "All of the information presently recorded on flipcharts is to be accurately reproduced within a formal plan document.")

■ How will it be done? (Not as obvious: as suggested in the chapter Learning to See the Future, it may be appropriate to include additional information elements in the plan document, such as a summary of the organization's mission, vision, and values and some historical background to the creation of the plan itself; will any such elements be incorporated into the plan? If so, how will such elements be prepared, by whom, and by when?)

■ Who will do it? (Who will actually design and create the final document? If the organization has a dedicated internal desktop publishing or word processing or document preparation resource, this is the likely answer. If not, then will someone else wing it? Or will an outside resource be contracted for the job? Use actual names wherever possible.)

■ Who will ensure that it gets done? (Who is the official keeper of the plan? He or she is responsible for turning over the all-important flipcharts or some cleaned-up version of their content to the document producer; for briefing the document producer on what is required, and by when; for ensuring that any supplementary background elements are prepared and turned over to the document producer; for providing clarification or guidance to the document producer as such needs arise; for monitoring progress on the document; and ultimately for participating in overseeing all aspects of the actual implementation throughout the plan's entire organizational life span. If no appointed KOP attends the academy and the team is unable to select a candidate for the role in the time remaining, when will the team meet again to finalize the selection process?)

■ When will it begin, or be completed? (What are the target dates for turning any supplementary background elements over to the document producer? For completing a first draft of the document for senior leadership team review? For completing the interim revised draft that will be circulated for review among the organizationwide management team? For completing the final revised draft for ratification? Use actual dates wherever possible.)

■ How will success be measured? (Usually one of the toughest questions, in this case it's the easiest: If and when the plan is ratified by the entire management population, then the goal of creating a written plan-for-success for the organization to follow has been successfully achieved. All that remains is to successfully implement it!)

With the completion of this final round of activity planning, the formal agenda for the academy has been covered in its entirety.

Most leadership teams, at this stage, experience a complex mix of feelings: a great sense of accomplishment, combined with some trepidation over the magnitude of the implementation challenge that lies ahead. There is often, too, a combination of exhaustion and exhilaration, a feeling of being physically and intellectually drained after working hard for three consecutive days, yet a paradoxical urge to whoop and cheer and celebrate their achievement.

In keeping with the spirit of the eighth big question, celebrating successes, many organizations bring their academy to a memorable close with some sort of ceremony or event. If this is to be the case in your session, then please raise your glasses and clink them together once on my behalf, and accept my congratulations for a job well done!

Moving Toward Implementation

T here is no hard-and-fast rule about how long it should take to create a final draft of the plan document suitable for distribution; some organizations are able to turn it around in a few weeks, whereas in others it can take months. As a general principle, anything over two months begins to feel a bit long. Even members of the plan-building team themselves, when it comes time to review the contents for final ratification, may have difficulty remembering some of the fine details that were originally discussed more than two months earlier. On the one hand, a speedy turnaround signals the importance of the document and keeps the content fresh in everyone's mind; on the other, time must be taken to put together a professional-quality document and include whatever supplementary elements are necessary to make the document more meaningful. A document that looks hastily patched together or is rife with errors does as much to discredit the importance of the plan as does a seemingly long interval between the academy and the appearance of the document. A balance must be struck.

REFINING THE PLAN DOCUMENT

The individual designated as keeper of the plan has a role to play in preparing and dressing the plan's raw content before it is turned over to the document producer. There is one technique in particular that the KOP can use that goes a long way toward minimizing the danger of lapses in the plan builders' memories before the document is available for review. It involves carefully rereading the flipcharts with the eyes of someone who did not attend the academy, looking for details that can be added as clarification or elaboration to help refresh peoples' memories. If the KOP did not himself or herself attend the academy, of course, then this task falls on the shoulders of the senior leader who is acting as the KOP's mentor.

To illustrate, suppose one of the flipchart entries reads "Advise them of all changes." It is listed among several other points under a How Will It Be Done? heading. But who does *them* refer to in this context: employees? customers? At the time, in the hurly-burly of brainstorming, someone raised the topic of suppliers, and someone else pointed out the desirability of keeping them advised of all changes; the scribe, already scrambling to capture ideas on the flipchart as quickly as they were emerging, was content to capture the last speaker's words verbatim without sensing that this wording would later be unclear. Now several months pass before the plan builders review the plan contents, but will they recall that *them* is neither employees nor customers? They will, if a conscientious KOP, reviewing the flipchart before submission to the document producer, revises the entry to read "Advise suppliers of all changes."

As an idea for celebrating successes, someone else proposed "personalized parking spaces" as a means of recognizing special employee achievements. But the flipchart entry reads "Parking spaces." The KOP changes the entry to "Personalized parking spaces for deserving employees." (This is therefore how the plan builders will remember the idea, unaware that the keeper of the plan has even made a change at all. That is the KOP's lot in life, to be doing all kinds of invisible things that no one will ever know about but that help move the organization ever closer to realizing the vision of success.)

Another way in which the keeper of the plan greatly enhances plan content and makes the document more user-friendly is making links between the various big questions that are not otherwise obvious to users of the document. For example, suppose as part of activity planning regarding ambassadors of change the members of the leadership team make a commitment to spend one-half day per week in face-to-face contact with key customers. Naturally, an important reason for these interactions is to hear, from the customers' own lips, about their experiences, preferences, suggestions, etc.; in other words, all manner of feedback.

A perceptive KOP recognizes this as fitting just as appropriately under acquiring and using customer data as under the first big question;

why not, therefore, have it appear in both places in the plan document? This way, if someone is looking for information on that particular idea in the plan but cannot recall under which of the two possible big-question headings it happens to fall, it doesn't matter; whichever one is consulted first is where the idea is found.

A proposal to highlight employee successes in the internal newsletter (the eighth big question) should also appear in the plan under spreading the word internally. The survey designed to measure customer satisfaction (the seventh big question) also belongs under question three, customer data; if the resulting data inspires some changes or simplification in internal procedures (making things better for employees) and leads to higher customer satisfaction (making things better for customers), it may be appropriate to publicize (the second big question) and celebrate the fact (big question eight).

Even casual perusal of the plan's contents should indicate that the various items listed do not represent a disjointed collection of busy-work activities; rather, it should be obvious that all of these items are interlinked and interdependent, all directly related to achieving the vision of success.

In some cases, an astute keeper of the plan can actually revise plan content to allow the organization to derive significantly greater benefit from the implementation than was originally anticipated. In one instance, for example, an idea about one way to improve things for customers (the sixth big question) is recorded on a flipchart during academy brainstorming; as the words are being written, one member of the leadership team quips to another, "Of course, this idea only applies if there's actual data confirming that this is something customers really want." It is a casual remark, made in the midst of a whole series of comments flying back and forth, but the KOP remembers it. Since that particular idea has been selected to be turned into an activity plan under the sixth big question, the KOP turns to the question-three flipcharts (acquiring and using customer data). There, under an entirely different activity dealing with asking customers a series of key questions, the keeper of the plan adds a new question about whether the selected sixth-question idea is in fact "something customers really want." The senior leader thus gets his actual data confirming (or not confirming) that this idea will please customers. The KOP even proposes a revision to the completion date on the question-six idea so that it falls after the third-question data-collection effort; that way, if the data happen to invalidate the idea, it isn't implemented for nothing.

Under ambassadors of change, the plan calls for senior leaders to periodically visit the front lines to "walk in their shoes," that is, to actually work alongside frontline employees, doing the same work they do. But the keeper of the plan anticipates that if senior folks just show up unannounced and start pitching in, the frontline people will be terrified, wondering what they did wrong and why they are being scrutinized at such close range, which will surely hamper their performance. So an item is added to the plan under spreading the word internally stipulating that the purpose behind the walk-in-their-shoes program (to enable senior leaders to better appreciate what the frontline folks are up against) be well publicized before the program itself gets under way.

Or, under the eighth big question, an item calls for "creating an effective, meaningful internal recognition program." So the keeper of the plan adds an item under the third big question, acquiring and using customer data, soliciting employee suggestions about the form of recognition that would be most meaningful for them. A talented KOP can do a great deal to strengthen plan content even before the document is produced.

If there is to be supplementary background material in the plan, whoever is assigned the task of preparing this material should be advised that it is to go to the keeper of the plan when ready, not directly to the document producer. This way the KOP can review the material and look for ways to tie it directly to the listed activities. If the 8 Big Questions are listed in the introductory material, for example, the KOP can insert notations advising readers on which pages they can survey the activities related to each. If elsewhere there is, say, a discussion about the importance of customer feedback, then a note can alert readers to the pages on which activities related to acquiring and using customer data are found.

The theme that runs throughout all supplementary material in the plan should be the vision. If the vision is "the liberation of Europe from Nazi oppression," and the mission is "the invasion of Europe by allied forces at Normandy on June 6," and the entire operational plan outlines a wave of predawn paratroopers followed by amphibious landings at dawn and so on, then even the soldier checking the laces on his boots needs to see a clear connection between his laces being tight and the liberation of Europe. It is a mistake to assume that employees at large make these connections on their own; such links can never be spelled out too often. The ideal place to spell them all out, in writing, is in the plan.

The KOP needs to sift through all background material intended for inclusion in the plan document, attempting to find as many opportunities as possible to make the links: "On this page is the vision, on these pages is the rationale behind the vision, and on all of these pages are the activities by which we will realize the vision."

Even after all the raw content is submitted to the document producer and initial proofs of content pages begin to make their way back to the KOP, he or she will continue to have ideas about how content, layout, or general design can be improved to make the plan easier to use. The document producer should be prepared to expect an ongoing process of fine-tuning and cycles of revision right up to final ratification.

ADDING A TRAINING SCHEDULE

Even if employees catch religion and find themselves suffused with a sincere desire to do their part in realizing the vision, they often discover impediments. We've already discussed the organizational dragons that frequently block their paths; another equally serious impediment is the gap between wanting to do the right thing and knowing how to do it.

Give any eleven-year-old permission to sit behind a set of drums, and observe the rise and fall of enthusiasm that ensues. At first the racket is indescribable; no drum can be struck hard enough, no cymbal lambasted with anywhere near enough force. This is the sheer exuberant joy of making big noise. Gradually, though, the sonic onslaught becomes wearisome even to eleven-year-old ears. No longer content just to generate an unstructured uproar, the would-be drummer attempts to create something resembling rhythm, something that might qualify as a musical beat of some kind. Frustration quickly sets in, however; the desired beat is vaguely audible in the mind's ear, but the limbs simply cannot be persuaded to properly work together in order to produce it. It's like attempting to pat one's head while rubbing one's tummy—a simple enough goal, yet infuriatingly difficult to do on the first try. Before long the attempt to actually play the drums is abandoned. The sticks are unceremoniously put down as the kid remembers something good is about to start on television.

Children are not the only people who become frustrated and discouraged when they discover that they are unable to do what they would like to do. The challenge for organizations undertaking to introduce change into their culture is to ensure that employees find themselves able to do what the change initiative asks of them. It is no good to plan for employees to become involved in process-improvement teams if the employees have no understanding of process analysis, or even of classic problem-solving techniques. It's going to be difficult to get managers to build a less blame-oriented, more celebration-oriented culture if they themselves do not have the skills to give recognition effectively or acknowledge good work meaningfully.

Naturally, for any training to be effective the trainees must have an opportunity to practice using the new skills as soon after the training session as possible. The classic organizational blunder is to provide highly specialized training far in advance of any occasion to apply the learnings, so that by the time it is called for the training is all but forgotten. (A second undesirable by-product of this ill-timed approach is that the actual training sessions are perceived to be unrelated to any actual organizational issues; they are just so many isolated time eaters that interfere with getting one's real work done.) These negative effects can be largely avoided by carefully scheduling all training on a just-in-time basis, by which new skills are introduced just before they are needed on the job.

If your organization has any sort of formal training department or function, during the interval between the academy and the completion of the plan document it is highly advantageous for the training specialist to sit with the keeper of the plan and go through the list of proposed big-question activities one by one. The object is to identify which activities are likely to require some sort of training support to be implemented effectively. It's then a question of reviewing the *when* targets for each, and using this as the basis for creating a just-in-time training schedule tailor-made to reflect the plan's overall structure and objectives. (If there is no established training resource in your organization, then your keeper of the plan needs to create some sort of training strategy on his or her own, perhaps with the help of an expert from a respected outside training firm. In some cases, it may be advantageous to conduct a formal training needs analysis, to help identify areas of greatest skill deficiency.)

Once the bare outline of the training schedule has been laid out, it needs to be integrated into the plan. As before, the object here is to make the links, to permit even casual browsers to plainly see how every training element relates to a specific component of the plan and ultimately to realizing the vision. It cannot be overemphasized: "From now on, everything we do around here is geared to moving us closer to the vision." The various training sessions cannot by any stretch of the imagination be dismissed as pointless time eaters; they clearly form a definite part of the overall strategy for success.

There are two ways to integrate the training schedule into the plan document. First, each training session is listed within the body of the plan under the particular big-question activities to which it relates, with some sort of graphic design element to help distinguish it as training and not one more "activity." I favor this approach. Or the entire training schedule can appear as one separate section of the plan, much like an appendix (which may make more sense if the schedule is long and convoluted). If the latter option is favored, then care will need to be taken to ensure there is extensive and highly-prominent cross-referencing between "big question" activities in the body of the plan, and the related training sessions in the appendix.

With the supplementary background material (if any) and training schedule integrated into the document design, the creation of content for the plan is complete. Now begins the sequence of events leading up to ratification.

REVIEW AND REVISION

Among the first few pages of the completed plan document should be two or more separate pages designed for inscribing signatures. The first page or two contain a series of horizontal lines, under which are printed the names of the CEO and the other members of the senior leadership team. Beneath these spaces is a paragraph of text to the effect that the signatures indicate that these individuals personally took part in the creation of the plan, have reviewed the document to their satisfaction, and thus formally go on record as committing themselves to doing everything they can to support and achieve the plan's objectives, and to realize the corporate vision of "[X], which is explained more fully on page [Y] of this document."

On the next page, or two or more, depending on how many signatures need to be inscribed, are horizontal lines beneath which are printed the names of every person in the organization who has one or more employees reporting directly to him or her. A paragraph beneath these spaces explains that all of these individuals have reviewed the document to their satisfaction, and by inscribing their signatures they formally go on record as committing themselves to doing everything they can to support and achieve the plan's objectives, and to realize the corporate vision of [X], etc.

For the first review phase of the plan document, the audience is the original team of plan builders: the CEO and his or her direct reports. Their objective, beyond obvious checking for typographical and other errors, is to satisfy themselves that by and large the content still sits well with them. They should be encouraged to make as many marks and annotations on these preliminary copies of the document as they wish, and to append additional written notes if there is insufficient space in the document itself to capture all their comments and suggestions. It must be strongly emphasized, however, that no negative remarks are to be acted upon unless in every case a specific alternative is proposed. Also, they must understand that there are not an indefinite number of revision iterations; they have only one additional opportunity to review the revised document and propose further revisions, and then it's signature time.

This means if there are serious differences of opinion that arise between members of the team—which in my experience is extremely rare at this late stage—it may prove necessary to convene a special meeting to resolve the conflict face-to-face, so as not to delay plan implementation and throw all the activity time frames out of whack. Finally, it should be clear that unless their marked and revised copy is returned by a clearly indicated date, usually two weeks after receipt, their particular revisions are disqualified from this iteration, leaving them one last opportunity to propose changes before being asked to sign their names to the document.

Having had several weeks to sleep on it, some members of the team may conclude that some of the time frames are still too ambitious (or not ambitious enough). Some may take issue with certain aspects of the supplementary background material—too wordy, too technical, too casual, etc.—or with elements of the training schedule (which many of them may be seeing for the first time). They may even say they wish the paragraph appearing beneath the endorsement signatures were more toughly worded (or less so).

While awaiting the return of the marked copies of the plan, the KOP should take advantage of the relative lull and proceed to get the word out formally to the organization's management population, advising them that a copy of the plan is headed their way soon, and outlining what they are expected to do with it (see Review and Ratification below).

The senior team's marked copies of the plan are to be returned to the keeper of the plan, who now must sift through all the proposed revisions and record them into a single copy for the document producer to work from. Fortunately, it seldom happens that anything too contentious arises at this point; most recommendations are on issues of prose style or layout design rather than actual content. Nevertheless, if a potentially hot issue surfaces, the KOP may need to make some phone calls and visit some executive offices to get other views before incorporating any change that might trigger a torrent of follow-up protest and counterproposals.

Once all, or at least most, of the proposed revisions have been incorporated into the document, it is distributed to the senior team for the second and final time. On this occasion, they have only one week to review the document and return it. If there are still proposed changes, these are incorporated, but the next time the senior team sees the document it is not be to give it a final once-over; it is to sign their names to it. (Actually, they sign a separate master page that bears all the signatures in original handwriting; subsequent copies of the plan include copies of this master page.)

REVIEW AND RATIFICATION

Once the plan bears the signed endorsement of every member of the senior leadership team, it is ready to be distributed to the management population for organizationwide ratification. This is where things sometimes get interesting.

Before the plan lands in their laps, the organization's managers need to be advised that it will soon be headed their way. A plan for doing so may have been drawn up during the academy, as part of brainstorming how to spread the word internally. If not, some thought must now be given to the best way to proceed.

It is the so-called middle-management population that habitually offers the greatest resistance to organizational change efforts. Not without reason: Speak to any management group about your burning determination to improve efficiency and eliminate waste and redundancy, and what do they hear? When organizations speak of eliminating unnecessary levels of management in order to flatten their structure, how often does this translate into the senior team being handed its walking papers and lower management being left just as it is? It's become a gut-level reflex: "The senior guys go off to 'write a plan, make some changes,' and us lower management guys can probably start counting the days we have left."

The irony is that these frightened, perhaps resentful, perhaps angry souls are the very individuals whom you are about to entrust with the responsibility of implementing the plan, turning it from a handsome document on paper to actual triumph and success. If they support the plan and what it stands for, if they see the logic and wisdom of it and feel proud to be a part of it all, they are in a position to make it happen. If instead they view the whole effort as little more than being politely asked to help engineer their own eventual dismissal, they are also in a position to kill it, pure and simple. Is it safe to say that their buy-in is fairly important?

What's the best way to get somebody to support our idea? Make it their idea.

This is fundamentally the purpose behind the whole ratification exercise. It's important that all the plan builders understand this. They should be perceived as saying: "We ran a three-day brainstorming session to create a list of possible activities that might move us closer to realizing our vision. We now offer this list to you as a series of recommendations, hoping it serves as a starting point for a solid plan that we can all participate in creating or fine-tuning. Any suggestions you have for additional ideas, revisions to the existing ideas, and so on are most welcome, and will be taken very seriously."

The management group must not be made to feel that the plan is a done deal simply being forced down their throats. Rather, the document needs to be emphatically and repeatedly positioned as a work in progress, incomplete until they have added their contributions. Seeing they are expected to inscribe their signatures underlines for the rest of the organization that this plan is not the product of the senior team alone, but rather that the entire management group has been given the opportunity to participate in its creation.

The greater the extent to which management takes the opportunity to participate, the better all around. If the first managementwide review yields a huge number of revisions, good. It means managers are endeavoring to make the plan their own. This what you want. On the other hand, it's dangerous to leave them with the impression that any and all proposed revisions are automatically made without reservation. "Will be taken seriously" does not mean "will be unquestioningly incorporated into the plan"; it means "will be given serious consideration."

If your kickoff strategy is leaning toward the splashy, then some of the biggest splash should be reserved for this management group in particular. They need to understand the process by which the plan was created, the thinking that led to this or that idea, the rationale behind this or that activity, the reasons for giving this item higher time priority than that one, and so on. Some organizations obtain management buy-in not by distributing the plan document and soliciting input but by walking the entire management team through the whole plan at one time, activity by activity, in a workshoplike setting and inviting comments and suggestions right there. Some "cascade" the academy process by holding one- or two-day mini-academies in which members of the senior leadership group work separately with their own management teams to create specialized local or divisional plans to support the corporate plan. (More about cascading academies in the final chapter.)

A more common approach is a variation on the above. The document is circulated for input, but before that, in preparation, the management population receives an educational overview of the 8 Big Questions, how they relate to helping the organization realize the vision, and how they were applied to come up with the activities listed in the plan. Such an event can be staged as a half day or a full day, depending on the depth required. In either case, a central component of the event must be to convey to the audience that they have an important role to play in taking ownership of the plan and finalizing its contents—and ultimately, of course, in helping to implement it.

They are then given their own copies of the plan to take back and review, typically for a two-week period. As with the senior team, they should be encouraged to make as many annotations as they wish, with the understanding that no negative remarks are acted upon unless, in every case, a specific alternative is proposed. They must also understand that this is their only opportunity to formally recommend changes; unless their marked and revised copy is returned within, say, two weeks, their particular revisions are disqualified from inclusion. The next time they see the document, it is not to give it a final once-over; it is to sign their names to it.

(In high-cynicism organizations, where the decision has been made to favor a low-key kickoff, it may be more appropriate to defer securing lower-level management endorsement for the plan until some highly dramatic positive results begin to elicit the right questions. As before, there are few better antidotes to cynicism than results.)

A few thoughts around this signatures business. Sure as shootin', there will be at least one manager who innocently inquires about what would happen if someone didn't want to sign the document—a purely hypothetical question, of course. My recommendation in this scenario is to turn the question back upon the questioner: "How do you think the absence of this individual's name on the list of signatures would likely be interpreted by his or her own people? by the rest of the management team? by the organization at large?" If this still doesn't quite make it clear enough, proceed: "If you were the head of an organization, and you were absolutely determined to achieve some sort of important objective, in fact you were prepared to let nothing stand in your way, and as you set out your strategy to achieve this objective, one of your key team members said, 'I'm not sure I want to personally get behind this particular strategy,' how would you react?" It's usually not necessary to suggest that failure to sign the document could prove to be a career-limiting move; even the most recalcitrant manager has enough survival sense to figure it out for himself or herself.

The happiest possible scenario, of course, is that the members of the management group receive their copies of the plan, and with pen in hand, begin to review the document—only to discover that, try as they might, they simply cannot find any way to improve on what's already there. They each send their copies back, bearing comments like, "Bravo! A masterpiece of creative thinking! I'm extremely proud to sign my name to such an excellent document and look forward to getting involved in the actual implementation!"

In the real world, however, this scenario—while not impossible—does reside in the realm of the profoundly unlikely. As a general rule of human behavior, invite someone to suggest how something might be improved, and they'll usually find something about it that could stand a little improving, totally apart from whether they would feel it needed any improving at all if they hadn't been asked. "This plan the gang created," a manager may say to himself or herself, "actually turned out pretty darn good. But they do expect me to add my own little something to it, so let's see, maybe if I change this part in some way. . . ." Even if some of the proposed changes represent no more than this sort of change for change's sake, they still should be taken seriously; these become the parts of the plan forevermore that, in the managers' minds, make it their own. It's like pointing to a photo of a large audience at a concert and saying, "I was there that night. That little speck right there, just beside the big pillar at the back, that's me."

As a rule, the bulk of the proposed changes are not in any way trivial or frivolous. Some of them may, however, represent a case of placing personal interests before organizational interests. A few of them may even represent one last desperate act of denial, a last-ditch attempt on someone's part to make the whole change effort (or at least that part of it that touches them individually) somehow go away. These are among the proposed revisions that, after being given due consideration, do not make it into the plan. (It is up to the keeper of the plan to determine the best way of sharing with the authors of these recommendations the many solid reasons behind the decision not to incorporate them. At times like these, keepers of the plan most appreciate having a direct reporting line to the CEO.)

There then remains the bountiful harvest of recommended revisions, additions, or suggestions to wade through and deal with. It can be a big job, but trust me on this one: It's one of the best possible problems to have. ("Tough day, Honey?" "You're not kidding. I've been slogging through this huge pile of ideas our managers have come up with for ways to improve our profitability, and strengthen our bonds with customers, and treat employees better, and generally make our company a much happier place to work in. It's absolutely exhausting.")

The more it is possible to incorporate proposed revisions into the plan, the greater the feeling of ownership that is felt by those who must use the plan as a tool, as a blueprint for action. Broadly speaking, proposed revisions tend to fall into one of three categories:

■ *Noncontentious.* These ideas can be incorporated into the plan with ease, make perfect sense, and do not change the intent of the plan builders in any significant way. They simply add precision or otherwise improve on an existing idea. For example: One idea is to give employees prior notification in writing of all scheduling changes; a manager reviewing the plan, and sensitive to the fact that some of his employees cannot read English, suggests changing the notification reference from "written" to "spoken or written, as appropriate." As a rule, the keeper of the plan can authorize these changes to be incorporated into the plan on his or her own, without recourse to higher authority.

■ *Potentially contentious.* These ideas may have a great deal of merit yet also in some way represent a departure from the original intent of the plan builders. For example: The plan includes an idea to assign a peer-group buddy to new employees for a one-week period, to make it easier for new hires to become culturally acclimatized. The reviewing manager proposes that the buddy not be drawn from the new employee's peer-group, but rather from a more senior pool of employees to "help the new hire better appreciate his or her potential career path and thus create a motivational incentive from day one." As a rule, it is not appropriate for the KOP to make unilateral yea-or-nay decisions about including such revisions without consulting the plan builders. (In this example, it may be that the senior team would give such an idea the thumbs up, or they may feel the benefit to be derived from early peer-group bonding outweighs any other considerations.)

■ *Clearly contentious.* Ideas in this category, though submitted in a sincere attempt to be helpful and add value to the plan, nonetheless represent a clear departure from the plan builders' original intent. An example is an impassioned argument against using customer data at all, on the basis that "typical sample sizes, in terms of total number of customers surveyed, are too small to be statistically reliable, and enlarging the sample size to relevant scales would be so expensive it would wipe out any potential long-term gains in revenue." Unlike proposed changes that are the product of self-interest or an attempt to undermine the change effort, these represent reasonable opinions from thoughtful managers who simply do not share one or more aspects of the senior team's view of things. Such proposed revisions are not likely to make their way into the plan, of course, but the senior team does deserve the opportunity to evaluate them. It may be appropriate for one or more members of the senior team to respond to such proposals in person.

The keeper of the plan can speed the ratification process along somewhat by providing the senior team with a streamlined distillation of the proposed revisions to the plan that have come in from managers in the field. One way to do this is to color-code the various proposals according to the three categories of contentiousness.

Rather than submitting this distillation to the members of the senior team individually for feedback (which amounts to creating another review-and-respond cycle within a cycle already in progress), it is highly advantageous for the senior team to meet once more as a body to collectively review the material and agree on which items to incorporate into the plan and which to leave out. Such a meeting may require from one-half day to a full day, depending on the volume of recommendations and their category breakdown. Of course, the keeper of the plan needs to be in attendance as well, to guide the team through distilling the recommendations. Throughout the session, the leadership team must walk a tightrope between building as much management ownership into the plan as possible and doing nothing to compromise the integrity of the plan itself.

Once the leadership team makes its rulings on the various recommendations for revisions to the plan and all the changes are made in the document (and all those whose ideas were not incorporated hear the reasons for rejection satisfactorily explained), it's time to distribute copies to the field for final review and signing off. It must be unmistakably clear to every manager that a signature on the document is intended to indicate several things to the organization at large: (1) personal commitment to carry out those activities assigned to the signee within the plan to the best of his or her ability, at the time and in the manner specified; (2) personal commitment to support the entire plan in principle, and to do or say nothing that could serve to undermine its success; and (3) personal commitment to support the vision and the mission, and to live by the values set out within the plan to the best of his or her ability.

The arrival of the last of the signatures indicates that the plan has been formally ratified, endorsed in writing by the organization's entire management population. It is then appropriate to begin the process of communicating the contents of the plan to the employee population (if such communication is going to take place), and to turn signed copies of the plan over to the various parts of the organization so that actual implementation can officially get under way.

Implementing the Plan

In many ways, the plan can be deceiving, seeming almost to implement itself. Everything is spelled out, like so many recipes in a cookbook. The various chefs entrusted with the task of preparing this lavish banquet need do no more than follow instructions: a simple matter of ensuring that they have all the specified ingredients in the right place at the right time, and that they do all the right things in all the right ways. Right?

Well, not exactly. The difference here is that many of the chefs may not especially want to prepare the particular meal described in the cookbook. This simple fact changes everything. A casual visit to the kitchen may convince the visitor that everything is on hand and in readiness, and that when it is finally served the feast will surely be magnificent. But as the various chefs go about preparing the banquet, their lack of enthusiasm for the task at hand begins to manifest itself in a number of ways. A corner is cut here, a step bypassed there. "We're the chefs, after all. Why aren't we just allowed to get on with what we're good at? Why all this meddling from outside? Don't these meddlers know what happens to the broth when too many chefs get involved?"

Just before the banquet reaches the table, questions begin to arise. Does it have to be asparagus? (This is really not a good time of year for asparagus.) The instructions specify using a high temperature for this, but then that tends to burn, yet if a lower temperature is used, the so-and-so comes out underdone; perhaps we can substitute such-and-such for so-and-so? On it goes, a substitution here, a last-minute change of plans there, until what finally reaches the table looks less like what was in the cookbook and more like what the chefs would have prepared anyway before any cookbook came along.

HAZARDS OF THE ELEVENTH HOUR

A trap many would-be ambassadors of change fall into involves monitoring progress with the greatest diligence early in the implementation and then, satisfied that everything is in place, gradually diverting attention elsewhere as things seemingly unfold on their own. It is typically those last-minute substitutions—which magically crop up when it is too late to do much about them—that cause the dish reaching the table to be so different from the one pictured in the cookbook. Shrewd resisters-of-change know that the most effective resistance is felt not when the change is first announced, but rather just before it is to be actually implemented.

On a visit to a well-known theme park some years ago, I watched with interest as a serious, dedicated amateur videographer set up his camcorder atop a tripod, at a carefully selected curbside location to get the best possible coverage of the nighttime parade, which was not scheduled to begin for another hour or so. During the hour-long interval, the crowds gradually became more dense along either side of the street as people took up their places sitting on the curb to view the parade. Whenever anyone stood anywhere that might obstruct the videographer's line of sight, he would immediately ask them to move, always explaining that he was there first, had been there for some time, precisely to guarantee an unobstructed view, and so on.

The crowd eventually became so dense that those asked by the videographer to move protested that there was nowhere left to move to. At one point, about ten minutes before the parade was due to begin, the videographer chastised a running child for bumping into his tripod, and the child's parent chastised the videographer for chastising the child and for taking up so much room with his contraption, and for a moment it looked as if things might come to blows between them. Tensions were definitely running high. This was supposed to be a happy event, in a happy place; but for the videographer happiness somehow seemed in short supply.

Then the parade began. As the music blared forth and the first of the colorful floats came into view, many of those who were sitting rose to their feet, thereby obliterating the videographer's view completely in an instant. Everyone shifted slightly toward the approaching parade, clapping their hands in time with the bouncy music; everyone, that is, except the tripod-bound videographer, who discovered that he suddenly had a virtually unoccupied space around him, and as a result a luxuriously unobstructed view of the parade. Moral: Once you've got everything in place, don't pour all your sweat into lining things up an hour before the parade. It's what happens in the few seconds before the parade that really counts.

Your plan is designed to introduce profound change into the organization. People don't like change. Nothing personal; it's not because your plan is deficient in some way, or because the particular change you have in mind is especially unattractive in some way. People do not by nature normally welcome profound change of any kind. "You're taking large numbers of people out of their comfort zones," as John Boes of The Quaker Oats Company puts it. "It can be painful, but you have to stick with it. You are changing a culture. You have to continually reaffirm and reassure people that you are doing the right thing."

Even if you do a masterful job at the front end in terms of communicating the plan, building support for the vision, and creating maximum levels of involvement and buy-in, the moment you turn your back everything has a powerful natural tendency to revert to the familiar, traditional, well-established "normal" way of being. You have to reroute a lot of traffic over a long period of time before the new footpath becomes an even more deeply entrenched trail than the existing one; and until it does, unguided traffic always has a tendency to wind its way back toward the well-worn groove of the old path.

The lesson, for ambassadors of change, is to avoid expending all of their personal energy at the front end. All of the tools and tricks of the ambassador's trade must be put to use throughout the entire life span of the implementation—and perhaps most prominently near the end, when a series of early wins might otherwise inspire cockiness that ultimate success has become a magical inevitability.

For the keeper of the plan, it's often wise to constantly track the plan's progress about a month or so ahead of actual dates. That is, if the next big activity milestone on the plan's time line is the launch of a new employee newsletter on November first, the beginning of October is a good time for the KOP to pay a little visit to the parties responsible for creation of the newsletter to see how they're doing. The visits should become more frequent in the final two weeks, and especially in the last few days. Often these visits seemingly serve no real purpose, since all that happens is that everyone assures the KOP that everything is "fine," all is well, no reason to anticipate problems or delays. But that, in fact, is the purpose of the visit. It ensures that no culinary substitutions are sprung on the diners at the last minute. It guards against surprises. Above all, it reaffirms to all parties that "this remains important," that the leadership team's collective attention has not strayed to other matters.

But what is the ambassador of change to do when surprises do spring up? What's the right approach when things start to go wrong or take unexpected turns?

CORPORATE JAZZ

When the jazz ensemble known as the Big Questions Octet takes to the stage for a performance, the musicians know that the opening tune will be Duke Ellington's classic "Satin Doll," which will be followed by "Someone to Watch Over Me," and then the Jobim medley, and so on. The evening's entire program of 8 Big Pieces is mapped out. For each of these pieces, the musicians follow a "chart," a written arrangement that spells out the key, the chord progressions, and even the actual notes to be played in the opening passages, behind some of the improvised solos in the middle section, and in the closing passages. These eight charts, taken together, are the plan for the evening's music; even the slightest departure by only one musician in only one section of one piece will produce a dissonant clash of sounds. If, however, the entire group implements the plan with note-perfect precision, exactly as written, the group's playing will be described as tight, cohesive, highly professional, and highly satisfying.

Yet jazz music is characterized by improvisation. The various soloists take turns weaving an elaborate one-of-a-kind musical tapestry within the highly structured framework of the written charts. There are entire sections in which the soloists are free to wail for as long as they wish in whatever manner they choose. Occasionally, more than just the solos are improvised, such as when the leader on a whim decides to "count in" a normally up-tempo tune very slowly and thus on the spur of the moment transforms it into a languid ballad. The entire group, caught up in the leader's playful idea, continues to follow the written chart with precision, but they now interpret it differently, giving what were once a succession of sizzling riffs a new, mellower feel. The plan is never ignored; it remains the foundation for all the music that is played and heard. But the players know they have the freedom to improvise with considerable scope within the plan's framework, and they are sometimes inspired to produce their most satisfying music precisely when a number of new, unexpected elements are brought into play. As the clarinetist solos, a passing police siren is heard from the street through the open nightclub door; the clarinetist incorporates the wow-wow-wow pitch of the siren into his solo and makes the notes sound as if they belonged there and have always been part of the tune. The audience applauds with delight.

The classical musician does not have it quite so easy. If in the middle of a Bach cello sonata the soloist has the misfortune to break a string, it won't be a matter of improvising a bunch of new notes on different strings; the recital has to be interrupted until the string is repaired. If there happens to be no replacement string on hand, the recital is probably over.

Ambassadors of change learn to think of the various parts of their written plan as more like jazz charts rather than classical scores. Within the highly structured framework of the written plan, there is room to improvise, and in so doing to create what remains a wholly satisfying result. When the unexpected arises, when what was supposed to happen doesn't, or what wasn't supposed to does, all is by no means necessarily lost. With some creative improvising, it may still be possible to achieve a perfectly satisfactory conclusion. The unexpected intrusion of a passing police siren distracts and annoys a classical music audience, and it may break the musicians' concentration; the jazz musician says, "Is this something I can put to good advantage in some way?" So it is with the unexpected when it arises in implementing a strategic plan: "This isn't what I hoped would happen, but is it something I can put to good advantage in some way?"

Through an unexpected error on the part of a parcel delivery service, let's say, the information package we sent out doesn't make it to our Indiana office, and we remain unaware of the fact that the package hasn't been received. Through the grapevine, the folks in Indiana hear about what's going on and feel very slighted that they have been left out of the information loop. Since one of the items in the package is the launch of our "Breakfast with the CEO" idea, which is scheduled to begin in Iowa next month, we're instead going to launch the program in Indiana month. While he's there, the CEO is also going to make a special presentation to cover the rest of the material in the information package.

Everyone else gets the info via the package; only Indiana is getting it directly from the CEO in person.

As for the monthly employee newsletter, it seems that the only printer in town cannot produce the actual copies as quickly as we need at a cost we can afford. So we're looking into changing it to a monthly news video patterned after news-and-current-affairs-type TV programs, a video we will distribute to each department so that sizable groups of employees can watch it together. All of the celebration elements that were to be part of the newsletter will be incorporated into the news video; in fact, we think that creating employee interviews, in which the workers appear on camera to tell their own stories in their own words, will have considerably more impact than merely being quoted in print.

And so on. Although the spirit of the plan is honored at all times, the actual content is subject to ongoing revision, fine-tuning, and evolution as situations and circumstances change. For those who take a looser, jazzier approach to things, none of these unanticipated modifications represent calamities; if anything, they more often provide an opportunity to improve the overall implementation in some unexpected way. It's all in how you look at it.

But what's to be done when the thing that's going wrong with the plan is, very simply, that those who are responsible for implementing it aren't?

WHEN THE IMPLEMENTATION STALLS

It crops up in every implementation, sooner or later. Department manager Marco L. is all set to hold his first-ever focus group meeting with customers on Thursday. All the scheduling has been done, all the invited customers have agreed to participate, and just two days before the event Marco himself is adding a couple of questions to the many that are going to be asked in the meeting. On Friday morning, the keeper of the plan pops around to find out how everything went, and Marco admits that unfortunately it had to be canceled at the last minute; seems some kind of foul-up in the big Morrison order was spotted just as it was going out the door, and that had to be straightened out immediately or it could have meant losing the whole contract, worth zillions.

Crises like these arise from time to time; not even the coolest jazz musician in the world can find a way to satisfy the nightclub audience if he never arrives onstage because he's lying on the pavement outside the club, pinned under the wheels of a bus. But what if this is the fourth item Marco was responsible for implementing, and the fourth that didn't get done? A string of bad luck? Resistance on Marco's part? A bit of both?

Marco may simply not recognize that his commitments to the plan are considered as important as his other responsibilities, if not more important. Perhaps he somehow did not appreciate the full significance of his action when he added his signature to the plan. In other words, there may be an educational issue at play. (In Marco's recent performance appraisal interview, for example, perhaps his boss itemized a series of key performance areas for Marco to focus on but neglected to make any mention of the strategic plan.) Or it may be a matter of Marco's testing the organization to see if all this "plan" mumbo-jumbo is really as important as they say. ("Does all that stuff on the plan really come before doing my 'real' job? Let's find out.")

It doesn't matter. Failure to meet commitments on the plan should be treated no differently than failure to meet any other important organizational objective. There is almost certainly an established procedure in place for dealing with managers who consistently fail to meet their performance targets or objectives, even if personally they are in no way to blame; this same procedure applies here.

In short, the way to deal with stalled implementation is to demonstrate zero tolerance for stalls, and to do so with speedy and decisive action.

What if the individuals who fail to honor commitments within the plan are not among the ranks of management, but instead are frontline employees who never actually signed their own names to the plan? Here are two thoughts on this question. To begin with, as before, the failure of an employee to meet an objective set out by his or her organization should be dealt with according to the standard procedure in place for such transgressions, regardless of whether the unmet objective happened to be in the plan or not. More important, why *not* have the entire employee population sign the plan? So what if it requires several pages to contain all the signatures? So what if a fairly intense educational effort is required to fully explain what they are signing, and why; wouldn't such an educational undertaking constitute a superb second-big-question implementation (spreading the word internally)? What better way to generate a strong sense of involvement and ownership?

I'm not suggesting that employees below the management level should become engaged in yet another review-and-revision cycle, but rather that they simply be given the opportunity to add their own names to their company's plan for success, in a show of personal support for the initiative. I'm aware of a number of organizations that have used this approach, and though it would be difficult to attribute any of their implementation successes directly to the presence of employee signatures in the plan, certainly none appear to have suffered any ill effects from this practice.

KEEPING THE KETTLE BOILING

If the plan's list of activities covers a time span of two years or more, the greatest likelihood is that over this period of time some of the initial enthusiasm will wane, some of the energy will dissipate, some of the attention being paid to the implementation in the early stages will eventually wander to other matters. For the ambassador of change, the challenge becomes how to maintain the focus, how to sustain the momentum. What's needed is some mechanism for reenergizing the initiative and reengaging the management workforce when involvement shows signs of flagging.

An effective way to inject new life into the implementation-in-progress of a corporate plan for change involves holding mini-academies to create local plans at the divisional, departmental, or functional level.

There are a number of significant benefits to be derived from these cascaded mini-academies. The most obvious is the development of smaller-scale action plans that support the corporate plan by introducing ideas or activities unique to the division, department, or function in question. But equally valuable is the educational component. To plan for ways to answer the first big question and become local ambassadors of change, for example, attending managers need to appreciate the full implications of the terms and learn about stump speeches, core values, and so on. For all of the 8 Big Questions, participants similarly need to fully understand the rationale behind each before they can begin to find answers. It is this heightened awareness of the philosophical foundation of the planning process that tends to refocus energies so effectively.

LOCAL MINI-ACADEMIES

Determining the Length of Mini-Academies

In most cases, mini-academies are two-day events. This is to ensure adequate time to cover the various educational exercises in sufficient depth.

If, for example, it seems advantageous to encourage local managers to develop the leadership elements of vision, mission, and values for their own areas, these exercises (combined with the stump-speech exercise) alone can take up the better part of a day. Day one might conclude with an educational overview of the 8 Big Questions themselves, with some discussion of why they are (or aren't) important for the organization as a whole, and for the division, department, or function participating in the mini-academy. As a rule, brainstorming and activity planning around the 8 Big Questions at the local level can be covered in a single day, albeit a longish one: four "big questions" before noon, four after.

If in your corporate plan under spreading the word internally there is already an effort to address some of these educational elements at the local level, then it may be possible to shorten your mini-academies to a day and a half, or even to a single (loaded) day.

When Should Mini-Academies Be Held?

The rule of thumb is to schedule mini-academies for about halfway through the life span of the corporate plan, or when energy and enthusiasm for the implementation are visibly beginning to wane, whichever comes first.

Assuming that there are to be a number of these mini-academies held in various divisions, departments, or functions, it is usually advantageous to schedule as many of them at the same time as possible, or nearly so. Because of their energizing nature, mini-academies tend to generate a certain amount of positive word-of-mouth; any groups that, for whatever reason, must wait to participate in their own session may feel somewhat dejected or resentful at being initially left out.

Who Should Participate?

The plan-building team at the local level should be made up of the head of the division, department, or function along with his or her direct reports. Even if this represents a team of no more than three or four people, all of the benefits associated with mini-academies still apply. If this produces quite a large assemblage (more than fifteen people), it means that during the brainstorming and activity-planning stages there is an option to break into two subgroups and have them work on the same big question concurrently, which may produce a richer output. Or, if time is tight, the subgroups can work on different big questions of their choice in parallel.

Who Should Facilitate?

The ideal facilitator for mini-academies is the corporate keeper of the plan. If this individual feels insecure about delivering some of the educational elements, however (which may require a more formal presentation-style delivery than was the case in the senior team's corporate academy), it may make sense to get the help of a cofacilitator with more polished platform skills, drawn from the training department, or from outside the organization if none are to be found within.

As part of the ongoing effort to spread the word internally (the second big question), the keeper of the plan considers how best to publicize highlights from the local plans to the rest of the organization once all the mini-academies are concluded. (Indeed, one of the key benefits associated with having the KOP as a facilitator at mini-academies is precisely that at least one person will have been present at every plan-building session throughout the organization. This individual is thus in a unique position to intelligently answer questions any one group may have about how any other group handled this or that aspect of their planning exercise.)

How Should Mini-Academies Be Facilitated?

The mini-academy typically has a greater educational component than the corporate academy, combined with a somewhat diminished planning component.

The educational elements can be as elaborate as the facilitators wish, with key points summarized on flipcharts or overheads and even in a participant's workbook if time and budget permit. But the basic format can be simplicity itself. The participants can first be put through any or all of these exercises, as appropriate: strategic priorities; mission, vision, and core values (recall the chapter "Learning to See the Future"), but applied to their own division, department, or function; and the stump speech exercise (outlined in the chapter "Asking Big Questions").

Then an overview of the 8 Big Questions can take the form of a simple learning exercise for each, in which the idea is not so much to tell members of the audience why it's important as to ask them the questions and allow them to discover the answers on their own—your basic Socratic method, which has held up very nicely for two and a half thousand years or so.

Here is an example of how the learning exercise for each of the 8 Big Questions might proceed:

- What do you think ["acquiring and using customer data," for example] actually means?

- Do you think this is something our organization as a whole should be concerned with? Why?

- Do you think this is something we in [our division, department, or function] should be concerned with? Why?

(Optional questions, time permitting):

- What sort of things, or behavior, might you see in a hypothetical organization that suggests to you that they are doing a good job of [acquiring and using customer data]?

- What sort of things, or behavior, might you see that would indicate they're not doing a good job of [acquiring and using customer data]?

Allow time for discussion and debate on each question, and for key elements of the collective responses to be understood by all.

This simple overview technique is usually sufficient to set the stage for applying the 8 Big Questions in a planning context. If the mini-academies are the forum in which the contents of the corporate plan are to be formally communicated, this is the best spot in the agenda to do so.

For the planning elements of the mini-academy, the object is for the team to follow the same approach the senior team used, as outlined in the chapter "Learning to See the Future," as well as in the plan-building exercises that conclude Chapters 1 through 8 (each of which addresses one of the 8 Big Questions in particular), but once again applied to their own division, department, or function. For some internal functions, some of the 8 Big Questions may seem less relevant than others; it therefore makes sense for the teams to spend less time in activity planning for some big questions than for others. The teams' objective is to identify a few key activities they can undertake (or perhaps stop doing) that support the corporate plan and help realize the vision.

What Do "Local" Plans Look Like?

The output of the mini-academies is not a new document, a smaller look-alike version of the corporate plan. Rather, it is a collection of (usually) two or three pages upon which are reproduced the answers to the activity-planning questions that the groups created in response to the 8 Big Questions, and not much more. It is then up to the corporate keeper of the plan to incorporate these local plans into, or otherwise affix them to, the corporate plan.

There is no formal review-and-ratification phase at the local level; that is, the teams participating in mini-academies are not encouraged to submit their activity plans to the rest of the division, department, or function for revision. As part of their own brainstorming on spreading the word internally, however, the teams should be encouraged to consider in particular how they might best communicate the contents of their own local plan after they return to the workplace.

Creating a Sense of Occasion

As with the original corporate academy, the mini-academy is taken seriously to the extent that it is perceived to be an important event. If it can therefore be held off site, away from telephones and fax machines, it certainly gains a great deal of credibility. As before, if it is not possible to hold the sessions off site, then a firm no-interruptions policy must be communicated to all secretaries, assistants, and colleagues, and it must be rigidly enforced. Lunches and refreshments should be brought in, and participants must be advised ahead of time that quick visits to their desks to see what's up are forbidden, as are cell phones in the meeting room.

Reaping the Benefits of the Mini-Academy

Mini-academies serve to expand the ambassadorship of change more widely throughout the organization, and to create a greater sense of ownership and involvement at the local level. Ultimately, of course, they also serve to keep the implementation moving forward and to bring the organization ever nearer to the vision of success that is the starting point for the entire planning process itself.

IN THE PREDAWN DARKNESS

"It is always darkest just before the day dawneth," suggested Thomas Fuller. As the list of successfully implemented activities grows longer, as the various celebrations begin to recede into the past, as the accumulation of unexpected problems and improvised solutions starts to fade into memory, and as the remaining-to-be-done inventory of planned activities dwindles ever smaller, an odd sort of quiet often settles upon the organization. Achievement of the mission and realization of the vision loom nearer now, a coming triumph that already lights up the horizon with a predawn glow. But then what? This vision, this plan, has fueled all of our thinking and all of our efforts for all of these months; now, with the plan almost implemented, and the vision almost a reality, where do we draw our inspiration from? What is there to fire our imaginations after this?

The ambassador of change knows the answer. While others are engaged in making plans for the biggest celebration of them all, to mark at last the successful realization of the vision, the visionary leader brings his or her leadership team together in closed chambers; together they set about defining what their current strategic priorities are, crafting a mission statement from this inquiry, and then fashioning from this a new vision of success for the organization.

The team also explores a number of related questions:

- Will it be useful to create a new written plan to guide the organization toward realizing the new vision?

- If so, will another senior-level academy be held to create the new plan?

- If so, when will the academy be held?

- Will it be useful to once again have an appointed keeper of the plan charged with overseeing the implementation of the plan?

- If so, should the present keeper of the plan be retained in that role, or is there any advantage to appointing a new person to the job?

■ If it is to be a new person, are there any obvious candidates? If not, does anyone care to make a nomination? If not, when should we meet again to make nominations and select a candidate?

Then, during or very soon after the triumphant celebration that brings the original plan to successful completion, the leaders unveil the new vision to the organization. For a moment, the taste of champagne is forgotten. The new mountain that is to be climbed appears to be so much bigger, and so much more intimidating, than the one that has just been successfully scaled.

"Ah yes," says the ambassador of change, "I recognize these concerns. They are the same ones that were expressed when the earlier vision was unveiled, the realization of which we are presently toasting with champagne."

And as the ambassador continues, the people within the organization, whose eyebrows initially shot upward, now find themselves grinning.

This is going to be fun.

Appendix:
Sample Agenda for a Three-Day Academy Workshop

What follows is necessarily a rough guideline in terms of content options and time frames for a three-day planning workshop. There are so many variables applying in such a variety of ways to each organization that it is impossible to design a single one-size-fits-all event to meet the needs of every leadership team equally well.

To design the academy format that works best for your organization, begin by determining how compelling the existing mission and vision statements are, and therefore how much time if any should be spent reworking them. This determines how much time remains to devote to actual planning exercises. (The times allotted to mission and vision in the following agenda assume they are being developed virtually from scratch.)

Also, whereas the sample agenda outlined below invests roughly 65 minutes of planning time in each of the 8 Big Questions, you may be able to anticipate that in your case some require more or less time than others; this too may affect the ultimate structure of your own final agenda.

If applicable, the content items listed below are followed by page references where more information relative to each can be found.

ACADEMY AGENDA: DAY ONE

9:00 a.m.:   Opening Remarks / 30 minutes

9:30 a.m.:   The Strategic-Priorities Exercise (pages 14–15)/ 60 minutes

10:30 a.m.:   Midmorning Break / 15 minutes

10:45 a.m.:   Creating a Compelling Mission State-ment (pages 16–18) / 75 minutes

12:00 p.m.:   Lunch Break / 60 minutes

1:00 p.m.:   Creating a Compelling Vision of Success (pages 19–21) / 60 minutes

2:00 p.m.:   The Core-Values Exercise (pages 22–24) / 75 minutes

3:15 p.m.:   Midafternoon Break / 15 minutes

3:30 p.m.:   The Stump Speech Exercise (pages 52–61, also optional supplementary exercise, pp. 140–143) / 90 minutes

5:00 p.m.:   Close

ACADEMY AGENDA: DAY TWO

9:00 a.m.:   Stump Speech Review Exercise / 60 minutes

10:00 a.m.:   Planning Exercise: Big Question 1 (pages 65–70) / 30 minutes

10:30 a.m.:   Midmorning Break / 15 minutes

10:45 a.m.:   Planning Exercise: Big Question 1 (continued) and Big Question 2 (pages 84–87) / 85 minutes

12:10 p.m.:   Lunch Break / 50 minutes

1:00 p.m.:   Plan-Building Exercise: Big Question 3 (pages 103–106) and Big Question 4 (pages 113–117) / 130 minutes

3:10 p.m.:   Midafternoon Break / 15 minutes

3:25 p.m.:   Plan-Building Exercise: Big Question 5 (pages 127–131) and Big Question 6 (pages 148–152) / 95 minutes

5:00 p.m.:   Close

ACADEMY AGENDA: DAY THREE

9:00 a.m.:   Stump Speech Review Exercise / 45 minutes

9:45 a.m.:   Planning Exercise: Big Question 6 (continued; pages 148–152) and Big Question 7 (pages 165–169) / 45 minutes

10:30 a.m.:   Midmorning Break / 15 minutes

10:45 a.m.:   Planning Exercise: Big Question 7 (continued) and Big Question 8 (pages 182–185) / 75 minutes

12:00 p.m.:   Lunch Break / 60 minutes

1:00 p.m.:   The Stop-Doing Exercise (pages 191–202) / 60 minutes

2:00 p.m.:   Storyboarding the Plan (pages 202–207) / 60 minutes

3:00 p.m.:   Midafternoon Break / 15 minutes

3:15 p.m.:   Storyboarding the Plan (continued) / 45 minutes

4:00 p.m.:   The Kick-Off Exercise (pages 208–209) / 30 minutes

4:30 p.m.:   Determining How the Plan Document Will Be Created (pages 216–217) / 30 minutes

5:00 p.m.:   Close

Index